Econometric Modelling of Agricultural Commodity Markets

ROUTLEDGE COMMODITY SERIES

Uranium: a Strategic Source of Energy
Marian Radetzki, Institute for International Economic Studies, Stockholm

Tin: its Production and Marketing
William Robertson, University of Liverpool

International Commodity Control:
A Contemporary History and Appraisal
Fiona Gordon-Ashworth, Bank of England

Commodity Models for Forecasting and Policy Analysis
Walter C. Labys and Peter K. Pollak

The Modern Plantation in the Third World
Edgar Graham with Ingrid Floering

The International Grain Trade: Problems and Prospects
Nick Butler

The Political Economy of Natural Gas
Ferdinand Banks

Commodity Policies: Problems and Prospects
A.I. MacBean and D.T. Nguyen

The Global Copper Industry: Problems and Prospects
Raymond F. Mikesell

Agricultural Commodity Markets
A Guide to Futures Trading
Michael Atkin, LHW Commodity Futures

The series is edited by Gordon Gemmill, Professor of Finance at the City University Business School, and Fiona Gordon-Ashworth, formerly of the University of Southampton, who now works at the Bank of England. (The views expressed in this book are not to be taken as those of the Bank of England.)

Econometric Modelling of Agricultural Commodity Markets

David Hallam

' - he's a Reading University man, isn't he?'
Daintry asked with what might have been a slight touch of disdain.

(Graham Greene, *The Human Factor*)

ROUTLEDGE

London and New York

First published 1990
by Routledge
11 New Fetter Lane, London EC4P 4EE

Simultaneously published in the USA and Canada
by Routledge
29 West 35th Street, New York, NY 10001

Reprinted 1993

Printed in Great Britain by
Antony Rowe Ltd., Chippenham, Wiltshire

British Library Cataloguing in Publication Data

Hallam, David
Econometric modelling of agricultural commodity markets. –
(Routledge commodity series)
1. Agricultural industries econometric models
I. Title
338.1011

ISBN 0-415-00405-5

Library of Congress Cataloging in Publication Data
has been applied for

Contents

Preface

Quantities traded and prices realised in agricultural commodity markets, whether national or international, reflect a complex of interrelationships between economic, technical, biological and institutional factors. Quantitative models of markets, which capture the key features of their workings, represent one approach to dealing with this complexity. The use of such models or information derived from them is now commonplace for many of those involved in analysing current market developments, predicting future developments, devising policy interventions, and actually buying and selling. World markets and, at least in the case of the industrialised countries, national markets, for almost every agricultural commodity have been modelled, some more than once.

A variety of methodologies - econometric, mathematical programming, systems dynamics, for example - have been employed in modelling agricultural commodity markets. These alternative methodologies are reviewed in another volume, *Commodity Models for Forecasting and Policy Analysis* by Walter Labys and Peter Pollak. This short book concentrates on the econometric approach. It is not an econometrics textbook, but rather a book about econometric modelling. Emphasis is given to a description of the nature, strengths and weaknesses of methodologies and methods commonly applied in the econometric modelling of agricultural commodity markets. The focus is on what is practised rather than theoretical issues. In Chapter 1 the nature and roles of econometric modelling are discussed. The process of econometric modelling is described and illustrated using a simple market model. Subsequent chapters consider particular aspects of modelling in more detail. In Chapter 2 issues of model specification are examined: the size and complexity of a model; the selection of variables; the nature of the causal relationships assumed to exist between them; the mathematical and statistical form of equations to describe these relationships. Chapter 3 is concerned with the problems of obtaining adequate data series for the variables of interest on the basis of which the relationships within a model can be quantified. Chapter 4 discusses the quantification or estimation of different statistical models and considerations in the choice of estimation technique. In Chapter 5 methods of solving a model for the values of the variables it purports to 'explain' are described. Appraisal of the adequacy of a model in relation to the purposes for which it was designed is discussed in Chapter 6 on validation procedures. The final chapter looks at the use of econometric models of agricultural commodity markets, and considers some issues in their management and administration. Since the uses of models is the focus of the Labys and Pollak volume, the treatment here is brief. This sequence of the chapters implies a rather stylised description of modelling as a progression from specification through estimation and validation stages and finally to actual use. In practice the process is iterative with models subject to revision and refinement as their shortcomings become apparent. The chapter headings do, however, provide a convenient if at times arbitrary division of the subject matter.

An attempt has been made to make the main text readable to the extent that is possible in any book dealing with econometrics. More technical points are dealt with in the notes appended to each chapter or references are provided to the more advanced literature. Some knowledge of mathematics and statistics will nevertheless be helpful in following the discussion. As far as mathematics is concerned, an acquaintance with the basic ideas of functions, algebra and calculus will be useful, while for statistics some knowledge of probability, hypothesis testing and regression is desirable. A rather more advanced knowledge of these subjects is necessary to follow the technical points in the notes. The attempt to provide a readable and approachable text favoured a relatively short volume which in turn implied a selective and, for some tastes a rather superficial, coverage. In relation to current practice, however, there are few signficant omissions.

This book is intended to help those with an interest in agricultural commodity markets, whether as analysts, forecasters, policy-makers or participants, towards a better appreciation of the possibilities and limitations of econometric modelling. It attempts to provide an overview of the subject from which perspective more advanced literature on econometric methods and applications might be approached. As such the book may also be of interest to students of agricultural economics following courses in econometric modelling. Suggestions for further reading are given at the end of each chapter. It is hoped that the book may stimulate readers to take a more active part in econometric modelling. There is no better way to understand what is involved.

1
Econometric Models and Econometric Modelling

You can't solve a problem? Well get down and investigate the present facts and its past history! When you have investigated the problem thoroughly, you will know how to solve it.

(Mao Tse-Tung, *Oppose Book Worship*)

Developments in agricultural commodity markets, whether national or international, continue to be the subject of much topical concern and discussion. Understanding, and particularly predicting, movements in prices and in the quantities demanded and supplied of agricultural commodities can be difficult, however.

The nature and functioning of agricultural commodity markets can be highly complex, more so than the markets for many industrial products. Production is influenced by biological and climatic factors, such as diseases and pests, droughts and frosts which can be controlled only imperfectly if at all. Production cycles can be long, particularly for perennial crops which may not come into production for several years after planting but then bear fruit for many years: oil palms, for example, bear their first crop only after three or four years, but then will go on producing for thirty-five. Production processes often have multiple outputs - wool and lamb, for example - and individual products, such as sugar, may have multiple uses as foods and as industrial raw materials. Developments in one agricultural market can be closely related to developments in others: prices of feedgrains, for example, can have a significant influence on supplies of livestock products. In international markets the countries involved in producing or consuming or both can be large in number and diverse in character. The same basic product, such as sugar, might be widely produced but production systems, and product characteristics can vary enormously. Within particular countries, national markets may involve complex marketing chains, with the product passing through many hands between producer and consumer, and with each marketing stage exerting its influence on prices received and paid throughout the chain. Finally, agricultural commodity markets, national or international, are subject to a wide range of official interventions aimed at modifying the free market solutions for prices and quantities. In national markets throughout the world governments intervene directly or indirectly producing distortions in agricultural prices such that they may differ substantially from those that would be realised in the free market. In the developing countries, such interventions have had the objectives of holding down retail food prices to urban consumers or to raise revenue for the government at the expense of returns to the farmer. The resulting depressed producer prices have been identified as one cause of Africa's poor agricultural performance, and recent policy shifts have been towards 'getting the prices right'. In the developed countries, the objectives of market interventions and the consequences for agricultural production have tended in the opposite direction. Prices have been raised above free market levels to support agricultural incomes against a secular decline as yields have increased but the demand for food has remained static. In some cases, the result has been chronic surplus production.

The prices and quantities realised on agricultural commodity markets, therefore, are the product of a series of complex dynamic interactions between prices and quantities traded and a wide range of exogenous factors. Those involved with agricultural commodity markets, in decision-making and policy-making, or analysis and advice, must contend with this complexity, taking into account and balancing all its disparate aspects. Formal quantitative models can assist them in understanding and explaining market developments, predicting future developments, and investigating the potential consequences of alternative decisions, policy options or the effects of possible external events. Though they may not realise it, all such individuals derive their opinions from models of the markets in which they are interested. These models are informal, however, carried in their heads rather than written down or programmed into a computer, and subjective, based on experience, casual observation and anecdote. As such they can be limited in the extent to which they can account for all relevant factors, their relative importance, and the complexity of the relationships between them in any consistent way. Their subjectivity means that their assumptions and logic are not explicit and open to examination and questioning. In many cases, it is only the kind of consistent, explicit, descriptive and analytical framework of a quantitative model which can provide a satisfactory basis for the study of complex markets.[1]

Approaches to Modelling

A range of modelling methodologies is available for the analysis of agricultural commodity markets, and have proved useful at one time or another. They differ in the mathematical and statistical techniques they employ, their data requirements, their computational needs and complexity, and in the tasks to which they can be put. Those most commonly applied include econometric modelling, mathematical programming, systems dynamics and Box-Jenkins statistical time series models. In practice, many modelling exercises combine elements of different methodologies - econometric and Box-Jenkins, for example. The focus of this book is the econometric approach which is perhaps the most widely used, and arguably the most flexible.[2]

The econometric approach attempts to produce a model composed of the quantified relationships between key market variables of interest: supplies and prices, or demand and income, for example. These are quantified using the techniques of mathematical statistics on the basis of historic data. Econometric modelling can, in fact, be the most demanding methodology in terms of the quantity and quality of the data required. It can also be highly demanding of skilled manpower and computing resources if the model concerned is large and complex. An econometric model can be made up of just one relationship or equation, or many. All the relationships within a model will have a causal interpretation, and describe how the market is assumed to have worked in the past. Econometric models can be used to improve understanding of how a market functions, to forecast future market developments, and as a vehicle for attempting to trace the likely effects of alternative possible courses of action. The latter *simulation* use of an econometric model is commonly employed in policy analysis. The flexibility of econometric models allows the incorporation of decision rules and other constraints not estimated statistically from past data. In agricultural market models, these might include purely technical or biological relationships describing the production process.

In contrast to the positive approach of econometric modelling, mathematical programming models of agricultural markets adopt a normative approach describing in their simplest form flows of a commodity between producing and consuming regions. Prices and demands are assumed to be given, and quantities transported between regions are determined as if these flows were such as to minimise transportation costs. This is the linear programming spatial equilibrium or transportation model which has been used to model various national and international agricultural commodity markets.[3] It can be used to examine the impact on quantities traded between regions of differing assumptions concerning, for example, prices or resource constraints. More complex formulations are also possible. With quadratic programming quantities and prices can be made endogenous rather than given and the objective of the market is asssumed to be maximisation of the economic welfare of producers and consumers. Multiple objectives can be handled by goal programming. While the simplest programming models are static, solutions over more than one time period can be obtained in dynamic and recursive programming models.

The systems dynamics approach developed by Jay Forrester[4] describes a market in terms of the interrelated flows of a commodity through it and the information feedback and consequent adaptation by market participants or by regulatory authorities which in turn feed back on to commodity flows and prices. Special attention is given to the delays inherent in these flows and responses to market developments. Economic responses are incorporated using 'table functions', showing, for example, the various levels of demand associated with particular prices. Description of the market normally begins with a flow chart showing commodity and information flows, feedback loops, and all relevant exogenous influences. This is then turned into a series of differential equations which can be solved on a computer to obtain a quantitative representation of the behaviour of the market through time. The model can be used to simulate the impact of market interventions and other exogenous factors. Special programs amd programming languages have been developed for these purposes.[5] Systems dynamics models have some similarities with econometric simulation models in terms of their operation, and the values contained in the various table functions can have an econometric origin. In general, however, the relationships included in a systems dynamics model are assumed rather than estimated statistically from historic data.

Box-Jenkins time series models[6] can provide a cheap method of forecasting commodity market variables. In their simplest form, a 'univariate' analysis, they abandon any attempt at defining any kind of causal descriptive model of the determination of market prices and quantities. Rather, an attempt is made to describe the time path of a variable of interest, say prices, solely in terms of the statistical characteristics of its own past behaviour. In particular, a model is identified which seeks to explain the current value of a variable in terms of its past values - the 'autoregressive' component - and random disturbances - the 'moving average' component. After tests of model adequacy, or 'diagnostic checking', the resulting model can be used for making short-term forecasts for the variable concerned. Obviously such simple models do not have any capability for economic analyses since no causal relationships are specified. More sophisticated forms can take into account cross correlations between data series in 'transfer function' analysis. The development of Box-Jenkins methods has had some influence on econometric analysis since it has drawn greater attention to the way in which data series are generated in the specification and evaluation of econometric models.[7] The obvious advantage of the Box-Jenkins approach, at least in the case of univariate models, lies in their limited requirements for data which means that they can be a relatively cheap tool for generating forecasts. Such models can be particularly useful for forecasting variables such as crop yields, where theoretical explanation of variations through time is problematic. Since detailed analysis of the characteristics of data is the whole basis for the method, however, accurate data are essential.

Although the focus of attention in this book is econometric modelling, this is not to be taken to imply that this approach is the most useful or best in all circumstances. The modelling methodology chosen should be that most appropriate to the particular circumstances of the problem to hand, although as noted above, econometric modelling is perhaps the most flexible, and most widely used. Econometric models of the vast majority of international and, at least in the developed countries, national markets for agricultural commodities have been constructed. Some markets have been modelled many times.[8]

Econometric models, whether of a complete market or perhaps more frequently particular aspects of it - the determination of market supply, for example - have proved a valuable aid to the understanding of how agricultural commodity markets function, and hence have provided a firmer basis for policy prescriptions and other decision-making. They have been used to forecast future market behaviour, allowing adverse developments to be avoided, or at least their worst effects mitigated. They have also been used to examine the likely consequences of alternative possible events or decisions - the effect on prices of alternative buffer stock purchase levels, for example. Econometric models and the results derived from them are now a common component of the decision-maker's information set.

Econometric modelling of agricultural markets, or at least aspects of them and particularly the demand for food, has a relatively long history. In fact, agricultural demand and supply studies were pioneering in the use of econometric techniques some seventy years ago.[9] This is partly due to the better than average availability of data relating to agricultural markets - a function of the administrative needs of widespread state interventions in the markets for food and other agricultural products. The use of econometric models has increased rapidly since the 'quantitative revolution' in economics of the 1960s when econometrics became, at least for a while, the centrepiece of macroeconomic policy-making, and economics' pretensions to parity with the natural sciences became widely entertained. The more widespread use of econometrics was encouraged by the increasing power and accessibility of computers and the necessary econometric software which removed the laboriousness of econometric calculations. A further significant impetus in more recent years has come with the ready availability of powerful microcomputers and the development of econometric software to go with them. Most of the econometrics and statistical packages developed for use on mainframes often at substantial and prohibitive cost have now been adapted for use on microcomputers. Unfortunately, the consequent painlessness of econometric calculation has led to some painful misuses, or at least ill-conceived uses, of econometric methods. While computers can replace the drudgery of calculation they cannot substitute for the creativity and mental discipline needed for effective model-building.

Paradoxically, there appears to be a certain amount of disillusionment with econometric modelling in general, a wave of scepticism having set in after the initial enthusiasm of the 'quantitative revolution'.[10] Scepticism was, and perhaps still is, particularly strong in relation to macroeconometric models, but there has been a tendency to generalise from the spectacular and well-publicised failures in this area, particularly in relation to forecasting, tarring all econometric applications, including agricultural market models, with the same brush. Expectations as to the contributions that econometric models could make were perhaps over-optimistic. Policy makers and other model-users failed to recognise the limitations of econometric models, and the difficulties of managing their construction and application. Model-builders, typically, were not at pains to point these out, and in some cases still neglect their educational role today. Any wider acceptance of econometric models is probably due as much to an increasing recognition of their limitations and hence a downward revision of expectations concerning their potential contributions as to any significant improvements in their performance. Nevertheless, most of those involved in the analysis of agricultural commodity markets would probably believe that econometric models have some contribution to make. While some may feel that they simply *ought* to have an econometric model, without any clear view as to what purposes it might serve, the fact that so many organisations are willing to invest so much time and money in econometric modelling speaks for itself.

The contribution which econometric models have made to our understanding of how agricultural commodity markets work is significant. Their value as a policy or business decision-support tool, other than in the general sense of improving the decision-maker's understanding of his or her environment, is perhaps less clearly established. There has not, for example, been any obviously greater rationality in agricultural policy-making since the 'quantitative revolution'.The question as to whether econometric models and their results have improved decision-making is not easily answered. Any definite answer would have to be based on a comparison of the outcomes of decisions made with and without the benefit of econometric advice. Without detailed quantitative information concerning the decision-maker's objectives and the probable consequences of alternative decisions, such a comparison can only be hypothetical. In any case, econometric results are only one element in the decision-maker's information set, and it is not clear how the proportion of any advantage attributable to their use might be ascertained. Where decisions, especially policy decisions, are largely determined by a bargaining process, the role of econometric models is relegated to providing support for the special pleading of particular interest groups, or more impartially, predicting the effects of decisions already made. Certainly, many interest groups participating in agricultural policy formation have recognised the potential value of econometric support to their causes. Even if econometric models are not central to decision-making, their influence, albeit indirect, can still be significant. Their role, therefore, merits some discussion. Unfortunately, to the extent that the use of econometric models is discussed at all, attention tends to be focused upon the purely technical aspects of model specification, estimation and solution.[11] Uncomfortable methodological issues and practical and administrative difficulties of model usage tend to be overlooked. The view taken or at least the impression given, is that the major obstacle to the realisation of the potential of econometric models is the need to make some technical improvements.[12] This raises the question of whether technical problems are the major stumbling block. Furthermore, it begs the question of just what is the 'potential' of econometric models in relation to the analysis and forecasting of agricultural commodity markets.

Econometrics and Econometric Models

An econometric model of an agricultural commodity market might be characterised, rather concisely, as being an attempt at the quantitative representation of algebraically expressed stochastic causal economic market relationships based upon sample data. A model will normally be a selective abstraction and simplification of the real market under study in terms of the variables considered and the relationships existing between them. This abstraction and simplification is guided by economic theory and other prior knowledge and information. The basic functions of a model are to improve our understanding of the market it represents and to predict its future development. A model should also be capable of manipulation so as to examine the consequences of alternative scenarios reflecting decision alternatives or assumptions concerning possible or actual exogenous events. The key constituents of an ecometric model are 'theory' and data, where 'theory' is broadly defined as any prior knowledge and beliefs concerning the market under study. These two constituents are central to the commonly used definitions of econometrics. The exact nature of the combination of theory and data can have important implications, however, for econometric methodology. One well-known definition, for example, defines econometrics as 'the application of mathematical statistics to economic data to lend empirical support to the models constructed by mathematical economics and to obtain numerical results.'[13] This might be taken to imply a methodology where the theory is imposed on the data, with the objective being simple measurement rather than *learning* from empirical data. Such a methodology might overemphasise estimation as the primary concern of econometric modelling. One of the earliest definitions of econometric modelling gave a more central role to data, stressing that the objective is to learn from empirical observation, and concluding that 'This mutual penetration of quantitative economic theory and statistical observation is the essence of econometrics.'[14] This definition and the implied methodology have been revived and reemphasised in recent years. One broad definition proposes that 'Econometrics is concerned with the systematic study of economic phenomena using observed data.'[15] The 'systematic study' is guided by and employs economic theory and statistical inference.

These definitions indicate the range of disciplines involved in econometric work: economic theory, mathematical economics, economic statistics, mathematical statistics. If any but the simplest of models with few variables and few observations are to be handled computing must be added to the list. As was emphasised in the editorial to the very first issue of *Econometrica*, however, econometrics is more than any one of these disciplines and more than simply the sum of these parts: it is their combination and interaction which is 'powerful' and which constitutes econometrics.[16]

The Process of Econometric Modelling

The process of econometric modelling can conveniently be seen as a sequence of stages: specification; estimation; validation; and finally application.[17] Obviously a definition of the objectives of the study and an assessment of the appropriateness of the econometric approach to the problem in hand are prior to these stages. The actual construction of an econometric model involves three basic tasks. First the specification of the model - selection of the variables to be considered, their definition in terms of available series of statistical observations, and of the mathematical and statistical form of the relationships hypothesised to exist between them. Secondly, the collection and manipulation of relevant data. Thirdly, the estimation of the parameters of the hypothesised relationships between variables. At the validation stage the estimated model is tested and evaluated. The validity of a model and of the information it can yield will be dependent upon the accuracy with which it reflects the real world. This in turn will be dependent upon its specification, the quality of the data from which its parameters are estimated, and the accuracy of the estimation method applied. That all three are adequate for the purpose at hand is an implicit assumption of all econometric analyses, but one which is frequently difficult to justify. The stages in the process of econometric modelling are illustrated in Figure 1.1.

Figure 1.1: The Process of Econometric Modelling

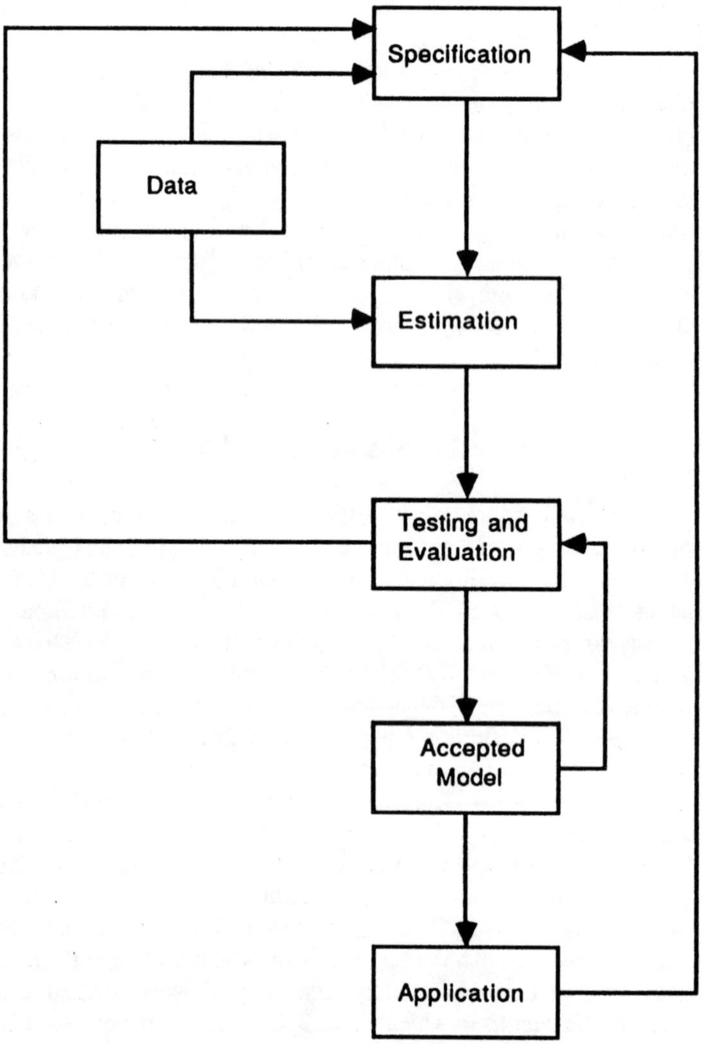

In practice the process is rather more complex than this brief summary suggests. As the feedback loops in Figure 1.1 indicate, the process is iterative rather than sequential. The model is reformulated until an acceptable version is achieved. This version of the model may itself be only temporarily accepted until it is superseded as the economic environment of the market changes or a new theoretical framework for analysis is developed. The rather stylised description of the modelling process also overlooks a number of important methodological steps or at least subsumes them under its broad headings. Specification, for example, involves the crucial and problematic steps of the identification of the broad relationships of interest in a market, and the mathematical and statistical formulation of these relationships expressed in terms of available data to provide a model which can be estimated.

Specification

The specification of an agricultural commodity market model should capture the salient economic, technical and institutional features of the market expressed in mathematical and statistical relationships between variables of interest. It should provide a description of the process by which the data on those variables are generated, embraced in a statistical model. As such it will represent a simplification and interpretation of reality guided by the model-builder's prior beliefs as to how the market works. The broad specification of agricultural commodity market models is rarely controversial. There are differences in matters of detail or emphasis, however, and these can have a significant influence upon the conclusions which can be drawn from the use of such models.[18] Specification may be constrained by the available data and is typically revised iteratively in the light of various formal hypothesis tests and assessments of its 'goodness of fit'. The most appropriate specification may remain uncertain, however, and correspondence of empirical results with prior beliefs can be an important criterion for model selection. Specifications finally adopted may, therefore, more frequently confirm rather than challenge prior beliefs.

It is convenient to consider the various dimensions of specification in turn, although in practice decisions in relation to each would be taken concurrently. The likely major determinants of variables of interest must be identified and summarised in one or more generalised expressions. Specification of this 'theory' model is conventionally derived from relevant economic theory or other prior beliefs, supported by institutional and technical knowledge. For agricultural commodity markets, relatively simple generalised 'theory' models have been found to have wide applicability. One typical example, applied to the world markets for cocoa, coffee, tea, wool, cotton, sugar, wheat and rice, involves only the four following basic relationships to describe the determination of quantities demanded and supplied, inventory levels and price.[19]

$$S_t = f(P_t, A_t, F_t, H_t, W_t)$$
$$D_t = g(P_t, X_t, Y_t, T)$$
$$I_t = I_{t-1} + S_t - D_t$$
$$P_t = h(I_t, D_t)$$

where

S_t is supply of the commodity in period t,
D_t is demand for the commodity in period t,
I_t is inventory of the commodity at the end of period t,
P_t is market price of the commodity in period t,
A_t is market price of alternative commodities in period t,
F_t is price of factors of production in period t,
H_t is production technology in period t,
W_t is weather in period t,
X_t is price of substitute (complementary) commodities in period t,
Y_t is income in period t,
T is tastes or technological factors affecting demand,
I_{t-1} is inventory of the commodity at the end of the previous period.

This basic structure of models proposed for the analysis of international and national agricultural commodity markets has remained largely unchanged for many years.[20] It is an equilibrium model and is derived on the assumption of perfect competition.[21] In many cases attention has focused on just one of the relationships: agricultural supply response to price, for example, has important implications for the design of agricultural price policy and consequently has been the object of much research.[22] In others, the USDA's SWOPSIM model, for example, multicommodity models have been developed.[23] In practice, the generalised relationships would be rendered more specific to allow for the economic, technical and institutional features of the commodity and market in question. These will be reflected in the way the variables are defined. The points in time at which the variables are measured, for example, must be specified to allow for biological delays in the production process. Additional variables will also normally be required. Further relationships might be added to describe the detail of production processes and end-uses. In modelling international markets the supply and demand equations might be specified for particular countries or regions. Simple though it is, however, the four equation market model here can be used to illustrate the features and discuss the problems of commodity market models in general.

The assumed mathematical form of the relationships must be specified. The simplest assumption is that they are linear:

$$S_t = \alpha_0 + \alpha_1 P_t + \alpha_2 A_t + \alpha_3 F_t + \alpha_4 H_t + \alpha_5 W_t$$

for example, where the α's are the as yet unknown parameters of the relationship measuring the effect of P, A, and so on on S.

All models are selective abstractions and simplifications of reality. There would obviously be far more influences on supply than are included explicitly in the above equation. The relationship must therefore be specified as a statistical model. This is accomplished by the addition of a *stochastic disturbance term, u* ,

$$S_t = \alpha_0 + \alpha_1 P_t + \alpha_2 A_t + \alpha_3 F_t + \alpha_4 H_t + \alpha_5 W_t + u_t$$

where u is assumed to account for all the omitted influences upon S. u is also assumed to account for errors in measurement of the left-hand side variable. The variables on the right-hand side are assumed to be measured without error. u is unobservable, but is assumed to have certain desirable properties, most commonly, at least initially, those which permit the estimation of the equation using ordinary least squares regression.[24]

A simple model of the world cocoa market illustrates the various refinements and reformulations of the generalised agricultural commodity market model described above.[25] The basic specification of the model is given below.

$$\ln S_t = \alpha_0 + \alpha_1 \ln (P/F)_{t-6} + \alpha_2 \ln (P/F)_{t-7} + \alpha_3 \ln (P/F)_{t-8} + \alpha_5 \ln T + \alpha_6 W_t + u_t$$

$$\ln D_t = \beta_0 + \beta_1 \ln (P/X)_t + \beta_2 \ln (P/X)_{t-1} + \beta_3 \ln (P/X)_{t-2} + \beta_4 (P/X)_{t-3} + \beta_5 Y_t + \upsilon_t$$

$$I_t = I_{t-1} + S_t - D_t$$

$$\ln P_t = \delta_0 + \delta_1 \ln (I/D)_t + \omega_t$$

The variables are as defined above, u, υ and ϖ are disturbances, and the α's, β's and δ's are the parameters to be estimated. Subscripts have been added to indicate the lags in the relationship between variables. The supply equation, for example, assumes that because of the biological delay before trees come to maturity it is prices six, seven and eight years previously which determine supply in any given year. The relationships between the variables are slightly more complicated than the simple linear example given above. Natural logarithms rather than absolute values of the variables are used and the price variables are combined into relative price terms in the supply and demand equations. Separate demand equations are in fact specified for developed, developing and centrally planned economies.

Data

Estimation of a model requires that its variables be defined in terms of observable, and in most cases available, data. The correspondence of the variables of a 'theory' model and observable counterparts is rarely perfect, although this is the implicit assumption. There may be available several different data series potentially relevant as observations on the theory variables with none corresponding exactly. Definitions of the variables are often vague: many models of international markets, for example, call for data on 'the world price'. In some cases, tastes for example, there may be no observable counterpart because the variable in question is inherently unmeasurable. In others, while a variable might be measureable in principle, for financial or administrative reasons it is not measured in practice. In such circumstances a proxy must be found. The data available, therefore, can be an important influence on the specification of the model to be estimated. That these data should be accurate, whatever, the series eventually selected, is self-evident. Sadly, equally self-evident are the deficiencies of economic data in this respect.[26] Besides the problems caused by data inaccuracy, constraints are imposed by the non-experimental origin of the data series with which the econometrician normally has to work. Such data are typically routinely collected for some possibly quite distinct purpose, and rarely, if ever, for econometric analysis. It is often necessary to contend with the discontinuities introduced by changes of definitions, base years, and collection methodologies of the data available with little scope for redress. Substantial 'massaging' of the data is often required, therefore, to assemble series of useable length.

The superimposition of the model of the world cocoa market outlined above on to available data results in some simplification and modification of the specification. The UN export price index for cocoa is taken to be the world price, and is assumed to be the relevant cocoa price variable in all the equations. Movements in the prices of factors of production are assumed to be reflected in movements in the OECD GDP deflator. The same deflator is assumed to reflect movements in the prices of substitute and complementary commodities, and is also employed in the demand equation. The effects of technical change and other secular influences are proxied in the supply equation by a trend which simply measures the passage of time. The effects of changing weather conditions are represented by 'dummy' variables for particularly favourable years.[27]

Estimation

Once reformulated in terms of available data, a model can be estimated to provide numerical values for its unknown parameters. The estimated supply equation of the cocoa model is

$$\ln S_t = \underset{(41.4)}{6.016} + \underset{(0.5)}{0.024} \ln (P/DEF)_{t-6} + \underset{(2.0)}{0.080} \ln (P/DEF)_{t-7}$$

$$+ \underset{(3.2)}{0.124} \ln (P/DEF)_{t-8} + \underset{(2.4)}{0.112} \ln (P/DEF)_{t-9}$$

$$+ \underset{(7.6)}{0.049}\ \text{TREND} + \text{weather dummy variables}$$

$$R^2 = 0.94$$

where P is the UN cocoa export price index and DEF is the OECD GDP deflator. The t-statistics in parentheses and R^2 are explained below. Separate demand equations are specified for developed, developing and centrally planned economies. The estimated demand equation for the centrally planned economies is

$$\ln D_t = -\underset{(37.2)}{7.66} - \underset{(2.9)}{0.122} \ln (P/DEF)_t - \underset{(3.1)}{0.138} \ln (P/DEF)_{t-1}$$

$$- \underset{(5.1)}{0.216} \ln (P/DEF)_{t-2} - \underset{(4.2)}{0.150} \ln (P/DEF)_{t-3} + \underset{(27.4)}{1.18}\, GDP_t$$

$$R^2 = 0.997$$

where GDP represents income. Similar equations are estimated for demand in the other types of economy. Inventories are determined according to the identity given above. The price equation is estimated as

$$\ln (P/DEF)_t = -\underset{(2.3)}{0.292} + \underset{(9.2)}{0.858} \ln (I/D)_t - \underset{(5.3)}{0.026}\, TREND$$

$$R^2 = 0.87$$

A wide variety of estimation methods are in fact available. The method applied should be appropriate to the nature of the statistical model. In practice this is often not the case. The divergence between what econometricians say, as evidenced by the technical literature, and what econometricians do, as evidenced by actual model building behaviour, is often noted. Although, paradoxically, econometricians have been criticised for overemphasising estimation to the detriment of other aspects of model building, it is with respect to estimation that this divergence is particularly pronounced.[28] In some cases, simplistic assumptions are made regarding the properties of the statistical model which justify the use of the simplest estimation technique - ordinary least squares regression - but which do not fully account for the differences between the original theory model, the model to be estimated, and the process which gives rise to the actual data used.[29] Ordinary least squares regression is then applied until tests of the assumptions concerning the statistical model indicate that this is inappropriate. In other cases, the nature of the statistical model and its relevance to the choice of estimation technique are disregarded in favour of practical considerations such as cheapness or simplicity, even when it is clear that the most appropriate technique is neither the cheapest nor the simplest.[30] Estimation of the cocoa model is by ordinary least squares, for example, which assumes a one-way causal relationship between the explanatory variables on the right-hand side of each equation and the dependent variable on the left-hand side. It appears, however, from the specification of the model that the causal relationships between demand, price and inventory levels are bi-directional, with the values of these variables being determined simultaneously. In these circumstances, ordinary least squares estimation yields biased estimates, or at least estimates which are more biased than might have been obtained with a more appropriate estimation method.

The estimation method employed can have a significant impact upon the parameter estimates obtained and model performance in forecasting and simulation. In modelling agricultural markets the choice of estimation technique often appears to be accorded relatively little importance. In particular, there appears to be a marked reluctance to abandon the ordinary least squares estimator in favour of more appropriate, albeit more complicated, estimators when the assumptions of ordinary least squares, especially that of a one-way causal relationship between the explanatory variables and the dependent variable, are clearly violated.[31] The argument that the theoretical gains from abandoning ordinary least squares are in practice negligible, at least relative to the additional cost and inconvenience of more appropriate estimation methods, is not always persuasive. The gains in terms of more reliable parameter estimates, and improved forecasting and simulation performance can be significant.

Validation

Validation involves the testing and evaluation of the estimated model to satisfy the model-builder of its adequacy to the purpose at hand prior to its actual use. Validation may be limited to a cursory check of the signs and magnitudes of estimated coefficients against prior expectations and the results of previous studies, and the appraisal of the goodness of fit of individual equations and the significance of their parameter estimates. R^2 is used to measure the proportion of the variation in the dependent variable 'explained' by the equation; t-statistics are used to assess whether the explanatory variables in the specification have any significant impact upon the dependent variable. The estimated cocoa supply equation, for example, explains 94 per cent of the variation in supply. The t-statistics show that all of the explanatory variables with the exception of price six periods previously have a significant effect upon supply. While 'validation' in this sense is important, particular attention focuses upon the ability of the model *as a whole* to generate time paths for its endogenous variables which approximate those actually recorded. Obviously, some reassurance that a model does correspond to reality to an acceptable degree is important if there is to be any trust in its prescriptions. This is typically sought in an examination of the correspondence of historical simulation results or *ex post* predictions generated by a model to actual data. Figure 1.2, for example, compares supply values generated by the cocoa market model with the corresponding actual values over a ten year period. The model appears to be quite successful in tracking broad trends, but is less successful in reproducing turning points.

Figure 1.2: Historical Simulation of World Cocoa Supply

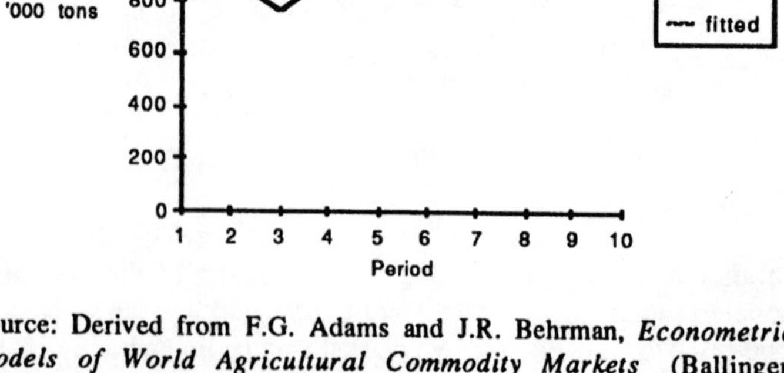

Source: Derived from F.G. Adams and J.R. Behrman, *Econometric Models of World Agricultural Commodity Markets* (Ballinger, Cambridge, Mass., 1976), Appendix B and Table 4.2.

The value of such comparisons rests on the assumption that if a model has behaved reasonably well in reproducing or predicting real system behaviour in the past it will continue to do so either in future time periods or under changed circumstances. The logic of this assumption is uncertain, however, and apparent past success in predicting real system behaviour may not be an unequivocal indicator of future success in actual applications. The exercise can, however, highlight deficiencies in a model and provide information of value in interpreting its results or guiding its reformulation.

The Uses of Econometric Modelling

The roles of econometric modelling are summarised in most econometrics textbooks as being quantitative measurement of economic relationships as part of a test of some economic hypothesis or simply to add quantitative precision to generalised economic knowledge, prediction of future values of economic variables, and policy analysis.[32] All of these applications can provide valuable information in support of decision-making, and econometric models and their results are a common element in the information set available to decision-makers, whether participating in agricultural commodity markets, or responsible for their regulation. In practice, the three somewhat arbitrarily defined roles overlap considerably. Equally, most econometric models are multipurpose, aimed at fulfilling more than one. The view that an econometric model should be constructed specially for a specific purpose[33] is unrealistic given the necessary time and resources involved. The need to generate results and forecasts rapidly in response to changing situations will usually imply usage of an existing model, whatever the use for which it was originally intended. Consequently, the construction of explicitly multipurpose models may be desirable.[34] Validation should involve wide-ranging tests of model adequacy accordingly.[35]

Measurement of economic relationships is, of course, synonymous with econometrics.[36] It is obviously the starting point for any econometric analysis, whatever its ultimate purpose. In itself it involves an opportunity to learn from the data, and add a quantitative dimension to a generalised knowledge of how markets work which is of potentially great value in policy-making and planning. The estimates of the cocoa market model, for example, show the quantitative relationships between prices and quantities.[37]

The long-run price elasticity of cocoa supply is estimated at 0.34. Estimated long-run elasticities of demand differ according to the nature of the economy: -0.33 in developed economies; -0.13 in developing economies; -0.63 in centrally planned economies. The objective of such measurement may be the testing of specific hypotheses concerning the nature of the relationships between economic variables: whether price has any effect upon supply, for example, or whether that effect is more or less than proportional. The reasoning underlying such tests is broadly as follows.[38] A relationship between variables should be revealed by an econometric analysis of series of observations on those variables. If the hypothesised relationship is not revealed then the hypothesis is disproved. If the hypothesised relationship is revealed then the hypothesis is not disproved. Unfortunately, the validity of this procedure rests on the assumptions that the specification and econometric methods used are entirely appropriate, and that the data on which the analysis is based are accurate measurements of the variables of interest. In practice these may be difficult to guarantee, leaving the test results unconvincing. More generally, econometric modelling can improve understanding of how a market works by providing a framework for the appraisal, compilation and collation of otherwise disparate subjective knowledge. The attempt to construct a model can itself be beneficial. The discipline imposed by the modelling process obliges the model-builder to think logically and consistently about the key market relationships. The need to collect observations on the variables in the model can expose lacunae in the data base and hence provide strategic guidance to future data collection.

Prediction and forecasting are sometimes seen as *the* role of econometrics and indeed of economics in general.[39] Econometric forecasts of the effects of expected exogenous changes can be prepared as these arise, or can be a routine element in the planning process, with predictions of market developments over the short or medium term regularly updated. Predictions are generated by incorporating future values - known, forecast or assumed - for the exogenous variables into an estimated model which is then solved for the corresponding values of the endogenous variables. The particular values assigned to the exogenous variables will clearly have an important influence upon the accuracy of the resulting forecasts. Several solutions may be generated for alternative assumptions concerning future values of the exogenous variables providing a series of scenarios. Action can then be taken to realise the most desirable scenario or avoid the worst. Forecast accuracy will also be dependent upon the accuracy of the estimates of the parameters of the model and their continuing relevance to the forecast period. Changing behaviour patterns, technology, policies and institutions may mean that the latter cannot be guaranteed.

In the context of policy analysis an econometric model might be solved for the values of various policy instruments necessary to achieve specified target values of certain variables, or might be employed as a vehicle for simulation experiments to investigate the implications of policy alternatives. The latter use is the most common policy application, adding to the policy-maker's information set and thus aiding decision-making. The United States Department of Agriculture's 'Food and Agricultural Policy Simulator' is typical of this type of application.[40] A policy simulation is simply a solution of an econometric model for the values of its endogenous variables on the basis of specified values for policy instruments and other exogenous variables. The specification of different sets of values for the policy variables allows the likely effects of policy alternatives to be assessed in relation to a yardstick 'control solution' established on the basis of existing policy or no policy. The solutions embodying the different policy options are sometimes referred to as 'shocked' solutions. The cocoa market model has been used to examine the effects on prices of restricting the quantity coming on to the world market. This is, of course, an issue of some importance for many international agricultural commodity markets. The simulation 'experiment' consists of administering a 'shock' in the form of a five per cent one period increase in world cocoa demand. Such a shock might represent the activities of a buffer stock programme. The resulting shocked values of real world prices are contrasted with those which would have ruled in the absence of intervention in Figure 1.3. The five per cent increase in demand has an immediate and significant impact upon prices - an increase of more than ten per cent in the first year. The higher price levels choke off demand to some extent, however, and by the fourth year after the intervention prices are back at their control levels. The response in supplies after seven or eight years eventually pushes prices slightly below their control levels.

Parallels are drawn between simulation experiments using econometric models and laboratory experiments in the physical sciences.[41] The extent to which simulation results concerning the consequences of a particular policy measure would be echoed in the real world, were the policy actually implemented, is uncertain.

Transferability of experimental results *mutatis mutandis* to the real world might be expected in the physical sciences. As noted above, changes in the economic environment constantly work toward rendering estimated model structures obsolete. It has been claimed that estimated structures will in any case be rendered obsolete since policy changes will be anticipated and behaviour patterns modified accordingly.[42]

Figure 1.3: Simulation of Five Per Cent Increase in World Cocoa Demand

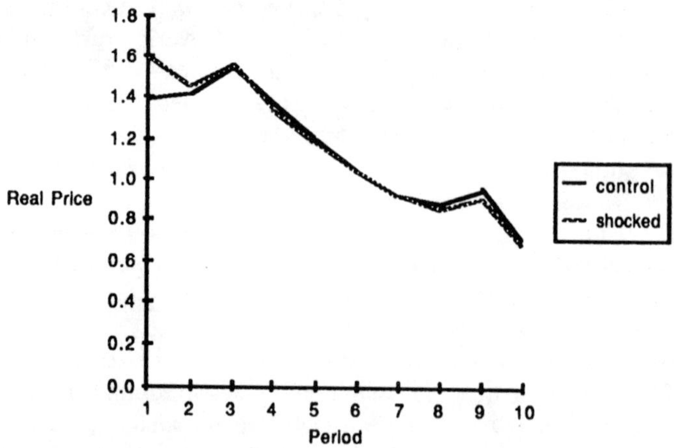

Source: Derived from Adams and Behrman, *Econometric Models of World Agricultural Commodity Markets*, Appendix B, Table 4.2 and Table 5.1.

In Conclusion - The Way Ahead

This brief overview of the nature of econometric modelling in relation to agricultural commodity markets has indicated some of the practical and methodological difficulties surrounding model construction and application. Subsequent chapters address these issues in greater detail, discussing aspects of the model-building process in particular. The practical and methodological difficulties involved have led econometrics to be compared to 'a search in a dark room for a black cat which has already left'. This short book is largely concerned with the procedures for obtaining an identikit picture of the cat and the organisation of the search on the assumption that the cat has not already left but may do so at any time.

Further Reading

A range of methodologies appropriate to modelling agricultural commodity markets is reviewed in W.C. Labys and P.K. Pollack, *Commodity Models for Forecasting and Policy Analysis* (Croom Helm, London, 1984).

There are many econometrics texts available. In general they are primarily concerned with methods rather than applications, and to the extent that applications are discussed there is a bias towards macroeconomics. M.D. Intriligator, *Econometric Models, Techniques and Applications* (North Holland, Amsterdam, 1978) provides a comprehensive but comprehensible coverage which includes a useful balance of theoretical and applied material. R.S. Pindyck and D.L. Rubinfeld, *Econometric Models and Economic Forecasts*, 2nd edn (McGraw Hill, New York, 1981), also has a good blend of theory and practice. A brief but thorough and up-to-date survey of econometrics is given in P. Kennedy, *A Guide to Econometrics*, 2nd edn (Blackwell, Oxford, 1985). For the more advanced reader *The Theory and Practice of Econometrics*, 2nd edn (Wiley, New York, 1985) by G.G. Judge, R.C. Hill, H. Lutkepohl, and T. Lee is an excellent reference book on econometric methods. In approaching most econometrics books some knowledge of mathematics and statistics is required, or at least desirable. M.J. Brennan and T.M. Carroll, *Preface to Quantitative Economics and Econometrics*, 4th edn (South-Western Publishing Company, Cincinnati, 1987) provides a good introduction.

The technical and academic journals provide perhaps the best source of examples of actual models. *American Journal of Agricultural Economics*, *Journal of Agricultural Economics*, *European Review of Agricultural Economics* and *Canadian Journal of Agricultural Economics* all publish econometric studies regularly. There are useful collections of international agricultural commodity market models in F.G. Adams and J.R. Behrman (eds.), *Econometric Models of World Agricultural Commodity Markets* (Ballinger, Cambridge, Mass., 1976) and World Bank, *World Bank Commodity Models*, World Bank Staff Working Paper No. 6 (World Bank, Washington, 1981). W.C. Labys, *Dynamic Commodity Models: Specification, Estimation, Simulation* (D.C. Heath, Lexington,

1973), remains probably the best detailed treatment of modelling agricultural commodity markets. For a brief overview of some of the issues see F.G. Adams, 'Implementation of Commodity Market Theory in Empirical Econometric Models' in F.G. Adams and J.R. Behrman (eds.) *Econometric Modelling of World Commodity Policy* (D.C. Heath, Lexington, 1978), pp. 47-70.

Notes

1. See, for example, J.R. Behrman, *Development, the International Economic Order, and Commodity Agreements* (Addison-Wesley Publishing Company, Reading, Mass., 1978).

2. A detailed review of mathematical programming, systems dynamics, and other methodologies is provided in a companion volume in this series, W.C. Labys and P.K. Pollak, *Commodity Models for Forecasting and Policy Analysis* (Croom Helm, London, 1984), Ch. 2.

3. See, for example, the applications collected in G.G. Judge and T. Takayama (eds.), *Studies in Economic Planning Over Space and Time* (North Holland, Amsterdam, 1973).

4. J.W. Forrester, *Industrial Dynamics* (MIT Press, Cambridge, Mass., 1965).

5. The most well known is probably DYNAMO. More recently STELLA has been developed for use on microcomputers.

6. G.E.P. Box and G.M. Jenkins, *Time Series Analysis* (Holden-Day, San Francisco, 1970).

7. See, for example, A. Spanos, *Statistical Foundations of Econometric Modelling* (Cambridge University Press, Cambridge, 1986), Chs. 1 and 26.

8. Labys and Pollak, *Commodity Models for Forecasting and Policy Analysis*, Ch. 7, provides a bibliography of commodity models which includes coverage of 45 agricultural commodity groups from apples to wool and runs to nearly 40 pages. Most of the models listed are econometric. This, however, understates the intensity of econometric modelling effort directed at agricultural markets since the bibliography is confined to models providing complete descriptions of markets rather than particular aspects of them.

9. See G.G. Judge, 'Estimation and Statistical Inference in Economics' in L.R. Martin (ed.), *A Survey of Agricultural Economics Literature* (3 vols., University of Minnesota Press for the American Agricultural Economics Association, Minneapolis, 1977), vol. 2, pp. 3-49, for a brief historical survey.

10. L.C. Thurow, *Dangerous Currents: the State of Economics* (Oxford University Press, Oxford, 1983).

11. See, for example, G.C. Rausser, 'New Conceptual Developments and Measurements for Modelling the US Agricultural Sector' in G.C. Rausser (ed.), *New Directions in Econometric Modelling and Forecasting in US Agriculture* (North Holland, Amsterdam, 1982), pp. 1-14, or K.J. Thomson and A.J. Rayner, 'Quantitative Policy Modelling in Agricultural Economics', *Journal of Agricultural Economics*, vol. 35, no. 2 (1984), pp.161-176.

12. See, for example, G.C. Rausser and R.E. Just, 'Principles of Policy Modelling in Agriculture' in Rausser, *New Directions in Econometric Modelling and Forecasting in US Agriculture*, pp. 763-800.

13. G. Tintner, *Methodology of Mathematical Economics and Econometrics* (University of Chicago Press, Chicago,1968), p.74.

14. R. Frisch, 'Editorial', *Econometrica*, vol. 1, no. 1 (1933), p.2.

15. Spanos, *Statistical Foundations of Econometric Modelling*, p.3.

16. Frisch, 'Editorial', p.2.

17. See, for example, W.C. Labys, *Dynamic Commodity Models: Specification, Estimation, and Simulation* (D.C. Heath, Lexington, 1973).

18. S.J. Turnovsky, 'The Distribution of Welfare Gains From Price Stabilisation: A Survey of Some Theoretical Issues' in F.G. Adams and S.A. Klein (eds.), *Stabilising World Commodity Markets* (D.C. Heath, Lexington, 1978), for example, shows that different assumptions as to how producers form price expectations can lead to quite different conclusions as to whether producers or consumers gain from price stabilisation.

19. F.G. Adams and J.R. Behrman, *Econometric Models of World Agricultural Commodity Markets* (Ballinger, Cambridge, Mass., 1976).

20. See, for example, G. Stojkovic, 'Market Models for Agricultural Products' in H.O.A. Wold (ed.), *Econometric Model Building: Essays on the Causal Chain Approach* (North Holland, Amsterdam, 1964), pp. 386-419.

21. For a discussion of the economic theory underlying econometric agricultural commodity market models see J.R. Behrman 'International Commodity Market Structures and the Theory Underlying International Commodity Market Models' in F.G. Adams and J.R. Behrman (eds.), *Econometric Modelling of World Commodity Policy* (D.C. Heath, Lexington, 1978), pp. 9-45.

22. See the review in H. Askari and J.T. Cummings, 'Estimating Agricultural Supply Response With the Nerlove Model: a Survey', *International Economic Review*, vol. 18, no. 2 (1977), pp. 257-292.

23. V.O. Roningen, *A Static World Policy Simulation (SWOPSIM) Modeling Framework*, ERS Staff Report AGES860625

(USDA, Washington, 1986).

24. These are that each *u* has an expected value of zero, a constant variance, a zero covariance with those associated with other observations on the dependent variable, and a zero covariance with the disturbances of other equations in the model. The assumption that *u* is normally distributed allows the use of statistical tests based on the normal distribution.

25. Adams and Behrman, *Econometric Models of Agricultural Commodity Markets.*

26. See O. Morgenstern *On the Accuracy of Economic Observations*, 2nd edn (Princeton University Press, Princeton, 1963) for an exhaustive discussion of sources of inaccuracy.

27. The nature and use of time trends and dummy variables are discussed in Chapter 3.

28. D.F. Hendry and K.F. Wallis, 'Editors' Introduction' in D.F. Hendry and K.F. Wallis (eds.), *Econometrics and Quantitative Economics* (Blackwell, Oxford, 1984), pp.1-12.

29. Spanos, *Statistical Foundations of Econometric Modelling*, pp. 15-21.

30. D. Hallam, 'The Neglect of Simultaneity in Agricultural Market Models', Discussion Paper 86/1, University of Reading Department of Agricultural Economics, 1986.

31. See, for example, S.R. Johnson, 'Discussion', *American Journal of Agricultural Economics*, vol. 59, no. 1 (1977), pp. 133-136.

32. See, for example, M.D. Intriligator, *Econometric Models, Techniques and Applications* (North Holland, Amsterdam, 1978), p.5.

33. See, for example, the 'first principle of policy modelling in agriculture' in G.C. Rausser and R.E. Just, 'Principles of Policy Modeling in Agriculture' in Rausser, *New Directions in Econometric Modeling and Forecasting in US Agriculture*, pp. 763-800.

34. L.R. Klein, 'Economic Policy Formation Through the Medium of Econometric Models' in M.D. Intriligator (ed.), *Frontiers of Quantitative Economics* (3 vols., North Holland, Amsterdam, 1977), vol. 3b, pp. 765-781.

35. See, for example, the range of criteria proposed by Hendry and Wallis in Hendry and Wallis, *Econometrics and Quantitative Economics*, pp. 4-7.

36. From the Greek words for economy and measure.

37. Adams and Behrman, *Econometric Models of World Agricultural Commodity Markets*, Ch. 6.

38. See I.M.T. Stewart, *Reasoning and Method in Economics* (McGraw-Hill, London, 1979), Ch. 9 for a detailed description.

39. See, for example, Hutchison, *Knowledge and Ignorance in Economics*, p. 8.

40. L.E. Salathe, J.M. Price and K.E. Gadson, 'The Food and

Agricultural Policy Simulator', *Agricultural Economics Research* , vol. 34, no. 1 (1982), pp. 1-15.

41. See, for example, T.H. Naylor, *Computer Simulation Experiments With Models of Economic Systems* (Wiley, New York, 1971), p. 5 or Rausser and Just, 'Principles of Policy Modeling in Agriculture', p. 763.

42. R.E.J. Lucas, 'Econometric Policy Evaluation: A Critique' in K. Brunner and A. Meltzer (eds.), *The Phillips Curve and Labour Markets* (North Holland, Amsterdam, 1976), pp. 19-46.

2
Specification

The form of the monster on whom I had bestowed existence was for ever before my eyes, and I raved incessantly concerning him.

(Mary Shelley, *Frankenstein*)

The specification of a model provides a stylised description of the salient features of the process by which the data on the variables of interest are believed to be generated. The description takes the form of a statistical model made up of a systematic and a stochastic component. The parameters of this statistical model, which measure the direction and magnitude of relationships between the variables involved and the variance of the stochastic disturbance term, can be estimated using an estimation technique appropriate to the particular statistical model to obtain the econometric model.

The systematic component reflects the model-builder's assumptions or hypotheses concerning the way in which the variables of interest are determined or interrelated, expressed mathematically. These beliefs are typically derived from relevant pieces of economic theory, and institutional and technical knowledge concerning the particular commodities in question. Such *a priori* information may identify the variables to be included in the model, the likely mathematical form of the relationships between them, and restrictions on the likely values of the parameters of these relationships. Where such prior information is limited or even non-existent the specification of a model must be rather more speculatively based with the attempt being made to identify relationships between variables from an *exploratory data analysis* involving a detailed visual consideration of the data.[1] A scrutiny of the observations on the variables of a model should be a preliminary stage in any econometric study whatever the quantity or nature of prior information available. Economic theory and other prior knowledge can be vague concerning the detail of a specification - lag lengths and the functional forms, for example. The broad specification suggested will usually be refined in the light of a consideration of the characteristics of the data. Of course, the data available will always be a constraint upon the specification which can be adopted.

Specification of a model represents a selective abstraction and interpretation, guided by economic theory and other relevant *a priori* considerations, of the apparent actual data generating process. The stochastic component reflects the fact that not all of the variables which determine the values of the variables of interest can be included in the model. Some will be quantitatively insignificant, others unmeasureable, others purely random effects. Their influence is expressed via a stochastic disturbance term whose statistical properties are specified by the statistical model selected.

Specification, therefore, involves a series of interrelated decisions: the selection and definition of variables to be included in the model; the mathematical and statistical form of the causal relationships assumed to exist between them; and their classification into ***endogenous*** variables whose values are determined within the model and ***exogenous*** variables whose values are determined outside the model and hence whose values can be regarded as given in obtaining the values of the endogenous variables. In practice these decisions have to be made in the face of uncertainty as to the nature of the 'true' model, and errors are therefore possible. As a result estimates of the parameters of the specified model will not necessarily be accurate or reliable estimates of the parameters of the 'true' model. Specification of a model is normally an iterative process with an initial specification being revised successively in the light of correspondence of empirical results with economic theory or other prior beliefs, statistical measures of goodness of fit, the outcome of various hypothesis tests concerning the selection of variables and the properties of the stochastic disturbance term, and forecasting and simulation performance.

This chapter discusses these issues in specification in the context of the basic agricultural commodity market model and its component relationships introduced in Chapter 1. It begins with a discussion of general issues in specification, and then considers various refinements of the basic model which allow the incorporation of additional economic, technical and institutional detail, and hence a more detailed description of the actual data generating process. It closes with a consideration of the problem of uncertainty regarding the appropriate specification, discussing the consequences of errors in specification and the procedures applied in the search for the 'correct' specification.

Specification of the Statistical Model

A basic general model of an international agricultural commodity market was presented in Chapter 1. This model is derived from the theory of perfectly competitive markets which has been considered to be relevant where agricultural commodities are concerned.[2]

$$S_t = f\,(P_t, A_t, F_t, H_t, W_t)$$
$$D_t = g\,(P_i, X_t, Y_t, T)$$
$$I_t = I_{t-1} + S_t - D_t$$
$$P_t = h\,(I_t, D_t)$$

Supply of the commodity, S, is taken to be determined by its price, P, the prices of other commodities which might be produced in its place, A, the price of factors of production, F, the state of technology, H, and the weather, W. Demand, D, is assumed to be dependent upon the price of the commodity, the prices of substitute or complementary commodities, X, income levels, Y, and tastes or technological factors, T. The balance between current supply and demand determines the addition to inventory levels, I. Inventory levels and the current state of demand are taken to determine the market price. The model is a closed equilibrium model, with all supplies being accounted for either by current demand or inventory adjustment. Models of national markets for a particular commodity would differ from the model described above in needing to allow for international trade. The inventory equation might be extended to include the addition of imports and the subtraction of exports, and additional relationships added to explain imports and exports in turn, in terms of, amongst other things, relative prices. In practice, the basic model would be refined according to the particular characteristics of the commodity and market in question. As the cocoa market model in Chapter 1 illustrated, such refinements will involve the selection and more precise definition of appropriate variables and the dynamics of the relationships likely to exist between them.

The model-builder's views concerning the likely gross relationships between the variables of interest are set in a statistical model intended to describe the data generating process and whose parameters can be estimated. The initial choice is usually of a simple statistical model whose underlying assumptions are then tested. The statistical model is then revised in accordance with the outcome of these tests if the initial model is apparently inadequate. Two basic classes of statistical model can be defined according to the nature of the causal relationships between variables of interest in the model. These relationships may be assumed to be unidirectional from right to left in each equation, where the independent or explanatory variables on the right-hand side condition the values of the dependent variables on the left, but not vice versa. A supply equation, for example, may relate current supply only to prices in previous periods because of delays inherent in the production process. Here the *general linear statistical model* may be appropriate. Alternatively, causal relationships between the 'dependent' and the 'independent' variables may be assumed to be bidirectional. Demand for a particular commodity, for example, might be influenced by its price, but at the same time demand may be an important determinant of price. In this case the *simultaneous linear statistical model* may be appropriate.

The General Linear Statistical Model

The most common assumption at least initially is to assume that the relationship, or relationships, of interest can be set against the *general linear statistical model*. The dependent variable of interest is taken to be a linear function of a series of explanatory variables and an additive stochastic disturbance term. The demand function in the basic market model above, for example, might take the simple form

$$D_t = \beta_0 + \beta_1 P_t + \beta_2 Y_t + \upsilon_t$$

where demand is assumed to be a linear function of the price of the commodity and income, the β's are unknown parameters and υ is a stochastic disturbance. The specification is assumed to be 'correct' in that the equation includes explicitly all important variables influencing demand. It is assumed that these explanatory variables are fixed - not stochastic, and in particular independent of the disturbance term - and are linearly independent of one another. The parameters of the relationship between the dependent variable and the explanatory variables are assumed to be constants. Although the model is described as linear, the variables might be expressed in some non-linear form - as logarithms or reciprocals, for example - provided that the equation is *linear in the parameters*. The unobservable disturbance, υ, should reflect random influences and all those minor influences upon the dependent variable not explicitly included in the model. The disturbance is taken to have certain statistical properties. In a hypothetical multiple sampling of sets of observations on the variables of interest, the value of the dependent variable associated with any particular set of values of the explanatory variables is assumed to differ from one sample to another because of different values taken by the disturbance. The disturbance associated with any one set of observations on the explanatory variables should have a mean or *expected value* of zero. Disturbances associated with different sets of values of the explanatory variables should have a constant variance - be *homoscedastic* - and a zero covariance - be free of *autocorrelation*. Given that all these assumptions hold the parameters of the model can be estimated using ordinary least squares regression.[3]

Provided all these assumptions held for each equation in the market model, then each equation could be considered independently in the context of a general linear statistical model. Most econometric studies concerning agricultural markets have in fact been single equation studies, concentrating on only one of the relationships of the model to obtain estimates of key parameters such as demand or supply elasticities.

In most cases, it is likely that the assumptions of the general linear statistical model will not all hold.[4] If not, an alternative statistical model must be specified. Possible alternatives cater for situations where disturbances cannot be assumed to have a constant variance or a zero covariance, for example, or where the explanatory variables cannot be regarded as fixed. A common example of the latter is where the equation of interest is in fact part of a system of simultaneous equations. A more detailed consideration of alternative statistical models and the appropriate estimation techniques is postponed until Chapter 4.

The Simultaneous Linear Statistical Model

The assumption that the causal relationship between variables of interest is unidirectional will in many cases be unrealistic. In the simple demand equation set in the context of the general linear statistical model above, for example, it is assumed that price influences demand but not vice versa. Yet, as basic economics textbooks point out, the chain of causation might more appropriately be specified as bidirectional with demand and price simultaneously determined. In such models the explanatory variable, price in this case, is not independent of the disturbance term. A positive disturbance in the demand equation with its consequent upward shift in demand produces an upward shift in price, and hence price is positively related to the disturbance. Supplementary equations explaining the determination of price must be added for completeness in the description of the determination of demand. In this case the rest of the simple market model must be taken into account and a simultaneous linear statistical model specified. A simple simultaneous model might be

$$S_t = \alpha_0 + \alpha_1 P_t + \alpha_2 S_{t-1} + \alpha_3 W_t + u_t$$
$$D_t = \beta_0 + \beta_1 P_t + \beta_2 Y_t + \upsilon_t$$
$$I_t = I_{t-1} + S_t - D_t$$
$$P_t = \delta_0 + \delta_1 I_t + \delta_2 D_t + \omega_t$$

where the variables are defined as above. Here three *behavioural equations* explain the determination of supply, demand and prices, with inventories being determined by an *identity*. Demand, supply, price and inventories are the *endogenous variables* whose values are determined within the model. For completeness there must be as many equations as there are endogenous variables, and at least one of the equations must contain more than one endogenous variable for the model to be simultaneous. The remaining variables in the model are *predetermined*. Their values are given in the determination of the values of the endogenous variables. The predetermined variables can be sub-divided into *exogenous variables* such as income or weather whose values are determined entirely outside the model, and *lagged endogenous* such as supply in the previous period whose values are obviously determined within the model but are taken as given in solving for the current values of the endogenous variables. The statistical properties of the model are those of the general linear statistical model described above but with the major exception that the explanatory variables in each equation can no longer be regarded as fixed. They include endogenous variables whose values are determined in other equations of the model and hence are stochastic and not independent of the disturbances in each equation. The disturbances in each equation are consequently not independent. Estimation of the parameters of the model by ordinary least squares regression will produce biased estimates and an alternative estimation method must be found.[5]

The equations above represent the *structural form* of the model which describes the *direct* relationships amongst the endogenous variables and between the endogenous and the predetermined variables. The *structural parameters* show the effect of a one unit change in each of the right-hand side variables - endogenous and predetermined - on the left-hand side endogenous variable in each equation. Because of the interrelationships between the endogenous variables in the model the ultimate effect of a change in a predetermined variable upon a particular endogenous variable will differ from that shown by the relevant structural parameter. A change in income, for example will influence demand directly measured by β_2 but will also have indirect effects since a change in demand will lead to a change in price measured by δ_2 in the price equation which in turn will lead to a further change in demand measured by β_1. Further effects on demand will result from the change in supply measured by α_1 induced by the change in price which via the inventory equation will have further repercussions on prices measured by δ_1 and and hence on demand again measured by β_1. The *reduced form* of a model showing all of these effects explicitly can be derived algebraically from the structural form. The reduced form shows the direct and indirect dependence of each endogenous variable upon all of the predetermined variables in the model and all of the structural disturbances.[6] The reduced form of the simple market model is shown below.

$$S_t = \frac{\alpha_0(1+\beta_1\delta_1-\beta_1\delta_2) - \alpha_1(\delta_0+\beta_0\delta_1+\beta_0\delta_2)}{1-\alpha_1\delta_1+\beta_1(\delta_1-\delta_2)} + \frac{\alpha_2(1+\beta_1(\delta_1-\delta_2))}{1-\alpha_1\delta_1+\beta_1(\delta_1-\delta_2)} S_{t-1}$$

$$+ \frac{\alpha_3(1+\beta_1(\delta_1-\delta_2))}{1-\alpha_1\delta_1+\beta_1(\delta_1-\delta_2)} W_t + \frac{\alpha_1\beta_2(\delta_2-\delta_1)}{1-\alpha_1\delta_1+\beta_1(\delta_1-\delta_2)} Y_t$$

$$+ \frac{\alpha_1\delta_1}{1-\alpha_1\delta_1+\beta_1(\delta_1-\delta_2)} I_{t-1} + \frac{(1+\beta_1(\delta_1-\delta_2))u_t}{1-\alpha_1\delta_1+\beta_1(\delta_1-\delta_2)}$$

$$+\frac{(\alpha_1\delta_2-\alpha_1\delta_1)\upsilon_t}{1-\alpha_1\delta_1+\beta_1(\delta_1-\delta_2)}+\frac{\alpha_2\varpi_t}{1-\alpha_1\delta_1+\beta_1(\delta_1-\delta_2)}$$

$$D_t=\frac{\beta_0(1+\alpha_1\delta_1)-\beta_1(\alpha_0\delta_1+\delta_0)}{1-\alpha_1\delta_1+\beta_1(\delta_1-\delta_2)}+\frac{\alpha_2\beta_1\delta_1}{1-\alpha_1\delta_1+\beta_1(\delta_1-\delta_2)}S_{t-1}$$

$$+\frac{\alpha_3\beta_1\delta_1}{1-\alpha_1\delta_1+\beta_1(\delta_1-\delta_2)}W_t+\frac{\beta_2(1+\alpha_1\delta_1)}{1-\alpha_1\delta_1+\beta_1(\delta_1-\delta_2)}Y_t$$

$$+\frac{\beta_1\delta_1}{1-\alpha_1\delta_1+\beta_1(\delta_1-\delta_2)}I_{t-1}+\frac{\beta_1\delta_1 u_t}{1-\alpha_1\delta_1+\beta_1(\delta_1-\delta_2)}$$

$$+\frac{(1+\alpha_1\delta_1)\upsilon_t}{1-\alpha_1\delta_1+\beta_1(\delta_1-\delta_2)}+\frac{\beta_1\varpi_t}{1-\alpha_1\delta_1+\beta_1(\delta_1-\delta_2)}$$

$$I_t=\frac{\alpha_0(1-\beta_1\delta_2)-\alpha_1(\beta_0\delta_2+\delta_0)+\beta_0+\beta_1\delta_0}{1-\alpha_1\delta_1+\beta_1(\delta_1-\delta_2)}+\frac{\alpha_2(1-\beta_1\delta_2)}{1-\alpha_1\delta_1+\beta_1(\delta_1-\delta_2)}S_{t-1}$$

$$+\frac{\alpha_3(1-\beta_1\delta_2)}{1-\alpha_1\delta_1+\beta_1(\delta_1-\delta_2)}W_t-\frac{\beta_2(1-\alpha_1\delta_2)}{1-\alpha_1\delta_1+\beta_1(\delta_1-\delta_2)}Y_t$$

$$+\frac{1+\beta_1\delta_2}{1-\alpha_1\delta_1+\beta_1(\delta_1-\delta_2)}I_{t-1}+\frac{(1-\beta_1\delta_2)u_t}{1-\alpha_1\delta_1+\beta_1(\delta_1-\delta_2)}$$

$$-\frac{(1+\alpha_1\delta_2)\upsilon_t}{1-\alpha_1\delta_1+\beta_1(\delta_1-\delta_2)}+\frac{(\alpha_1-\beta_1)\varpi_t}{1-\alpha_1\delta_1+\beta_1(\delta_1-\delta_2)}$$

$$P_t = \frac{\alpha_0\delta_1+\beta_0(\delta_1-\delta_2)-\delta_0}{1-\alpha_1\delta_1+\beta_1(\delta_1-\delta_2)} + \frac{\alpha_2\delta_1}{1-\alpha_1\delta_1+\beta_1(\delta_1-\delta_2)} S_{t-1}$$

$$+ \frac{\alpha_3\delta_1}{1-\alpha_1\delta_1+\beta_1(\delta_1-\delta_2)} W_t - \frac{\beta_1(\delta_1-\delta_2)}{1-\alpha_1\delta_1+\beta_1(\delta_1-\delta_2)} Y_t$$

$$+ \frac{\delta_1}{1-\alpha_1\delta_1+\beta_1(\delta_1-\delta_2)} I_{t-1} + \frac{\delta_1 u_t}{1-\alpha_1\delta_1+\beta_1(\delta_1-\delta_2)}$$

$$- \frac{(\delta_1-\delta_2)\upsilon_t}{1-\alpha_1\delta_1+\beta_1(\delta_1-\delta_2)} + \frac{\varpi_t}{1-\alpha_1\delta_1+\beta_1(\delta_1-\delta_2)}$$

The reduced form parameters are amalgams of the structural parameters. Estimates of the reduced form parameters can be derived from estimates of the structural parameters to obtain the *restricted reduced form*, although this procedure can be computationally burdensome. Alternatively, they can be estimated directly to obtain the *unrestricted reduced form*. The reduced form can provide a convenient vehicle for analysis since its parameters - also known as *impact multipliers* - measure the total effect of changes in predetermined variables. The full implications of changes in policy variables, for example, can be seen immediately. The reduced form can also be of value in forecasting. Since only predetermined variables appear on the right-hand side of each equation forecasts can be generated for endogenous variables individually. Use of the structural form requires forecasting of all endogenous variables simultaneously.

Recursive Models

Not all the equations of a model need be simultaneous. Models can be to varying extents *recursive*. In a recursive model the values of the endogenous variables are determined sequentially rather than simultaneously. A *causal chain* runs through the model and in each equation the causal relationships between variables are entirely unidirectional even though some of the explanatory variables appearing on the right-hand side of some of the equations may be endogenous.[7,8] A simple recursive model of quantity and price determination for an agricultural commodity might be

$$Q_t = \alpha_0 + \alpha_1 P_{t-1} + \alpha_2 W_t + u_t$$

$$P_t = \beta_0 - \beta_1 Q_t + \beta_2 Y_t + \varpi_t$$

where Q is quantity, P is price, and W and Y are exogenous variables. Here, quantity supplied is determined because of delays in the production process by price in the previous period. Quantity coming on to the market is therefore predetermined as far as the second equation is concerned so price simply adjusts to clear the market. The market clearing price then determines quantity in the next period.[9] Provided the endogenous variables are independent of the disturbances in the equations in which they appear on the right-hand side, each equation of a recursive model can be estimated in turn by ordinary least squares regression.

Biological, technological and decision-making delays lead to the time lags characteristic of the relationships of agricultural commodity market models. It might be argued that all economic models are fundamentally recursive. Variables must be defined in terms of the available data for estimation, however, and the temporal aggregation involved in most measurements may imply simultaneity in the estimable model. A recursive relationship between current price and quantity, for example, with the latter determined by price in the previous quarter would appear as a bidirectional simultaneous relationship between quantity and price if defined in terms of annual observations on the variables. A major advantage of short-period data is that the degree of simultaneity in a model can be reduced and a more detailed description of dynamic causal relationships provided.[10] In fact, agricultural commodity market models will often preserve a significant element of recursiveness even when defined in terms of the typically temporally aggregated data. Biological delays in production processes, will often imply relatively long lags in supply relationships, which together with the perishability of some produce, can mean that supply is largely predetermined as far as price determination is concerned.[11] In some cases, however, changes in stocks or international trade can provide scope for rapid, although perhaps limited, responses to short-run price variations. Some simultaneity may thereby be introduced into the estimable model, giving a *block-recursive* structure.[12]

Model Size and Level of Aggregation

Actual models of agricultural comodity markets may involve a rather more detailed description of the various causal relationships assumed to exist between variables and incorporate rather more economic, technical and biological detail concerning the production and use of the commodity in question. This is likely to involve a model which is larger in the sense of having an increased number of equations and variables, and less aggregated. An upper limit on model size and aggregation will be set by the data available.

The number of equations in a model depends upon the classification of its variables into endogenous and predetermined. Any variables which can properly be regarded as endogenous will have their values explained in a separate equation - supply demand, price and inventories in the simple market model. Failure to demarcate the boundaries of the model correctly may lead to bias in the eventual estimates of a model's parameters. Obviously, all variables, perhaps with the exception of time, are endogenous somewhere. The practical issue is whether in the equations of a model there is a bidirectional causal relationship between variables, in which case a model which fails to account for this through additional equations will only provide a partial explanation of the determination of variables of interest.[13] In modelling markets for some livestock products, for example, the primary concern may be to determine the supply of the product in question. A major determinant of the number of livestock will be the prices of feeds as a major input. But the price of feeds may be dependent upon the demand for feed which in turn obviously depends upon the number of livestock. There will therefore be a bidirectional causal relationship betweeen livestock numbers and feed prices. Accounting for this would involve modelling feed price determination in terms not only of demand but also supply factors such as cereal prices which may also be bidirectionally related to feed prices. Model size increases significantly.[14]Assuming that feed prices are predetermined may lead to biased estimates of the effects of feed price changes on livestock numbers and hence livestock product supply.[15] The practical policy relevance of single-equation supply models is limited to situations where supply from all sources is discrete and/or production lags long relative to the the data observation period, or where prices are determined exogenously by policy or market power. Similarly, modelling one national market in isolation may be inadequate where international trade is a possibility. Through trade demand and supply factors can be transmitted between markets and hence prices in different national markets can be interrelated. In some cases, supplementary equations might be included to explain variables which for all practical purposes can be regarded as exogenous. Such equations can be helpful in providing inputs into the central equations of a model where it is to be used for forecasting. The scope of a model may therefore often be rather wider than might at first have been expected - the 'law of increasing model size'.

Given that almost all variables might be regarded as endogenous in some sense, the boundaries of a model are in the limit arbitrary and set largely for convenience to limit the scope of the study in hand to manageable proportions in relation to its purposes. It should normally be possible to identify causal discontinuities of sufficient degree to provide practical limits on the scope of the model. For many agricultural market models the boundaries may be relatively closely defined by exogenous policy or institutional variables reflecting the widespread intervention in agricultural markets, or input prices set by oligopolistic supply industries, or climatic and biological variables.

Closely related to the issue of the appropriate size and boundaries for a model is that of the appropriate level of aggregation. A number of interrelated dimensions of aggregation are relevant. An increasing amount of descriptive detail concerning the production, marketing and consumption of a commodity might be incorporated in a model. Rather than considering *the* price and *the* quantity in *the* market for a commodity, for example, separate considerations might be given to price and quantity determination in different marketing channels or at different marketing stages.

Disaggregating the ultimate variable of concern into the actual decision-variables impingeing upon it can allow a more precise and detailed description of the actual workings of the market. It can yield a model whose parameters are more easily interpretable as the effect of one variable upon another. The parameters of aggregated models are 'black-boxes' - amalgams of the parameters of a series of relationships. As a consequence interpretation of a model's parameters and simulation of changes in the underlying structure can be problematic. A parameter linking say, crop supply to output price would measure the effects of price on both area planted and yield and it may be difficult to judge the relative strength of the two effects. Disaggregation in this way can also lead to a reduction in lag lengths interposed between variables, easing degrees of freedom constraints. In the case of perennials, for example, focusing on the determination of additions to or removals from the stock of trees rather than the supply of the commodity itself would lead to investment and disinvestment equations with relatively short lags on prices. In an equation attempting to explain supply directly lags on prices might have to allow for a long gestation period. There is some evidence from macroeconometric models that by allowing a more accurate description of actual decision-making processes disaggregation might also lead to improved prediction accuracy.[16]

The level of aggregation of a model is also manifested in the extent to which separate explicit treatment is accorded to individual producers or classes of producer, individual marketing channels, individual consumers or groups of consumers, individual commodities or varieties of a commodity. It is possible that there will be differences in economic behaviour on the part of or in relation to these subsets of economic agents, which should not be overlooked if a desciption of behaviour patterns is to be accurate and complete. The simple market model discussed above will normally be disaggregated with separate demand and supply equations specified for different countries or regions - less developed, developed and centrally planned country demand in the cocoa model in Chapter 1, for example. The possibility that the same commodity from one country may not be a perfect substitute for that from another and hence command a differential price might also be entertained.[17] Where the possibility of differing behaviour according to economic units considered is overlooked and an aggregated model specified the parameters of that model will be complex weighted averages of the corresponding parameters relating to individual behavioural units.[18] Aggregate parameters may not be particularly informative where behaviour between units is expected to differ in their responses to changes in the explanatory variables. National level supply analyses, for example, which aggregate smallholder production and plantation production of a particular crop, are likely to be of limited value for the design of agricultural price policy.[19]

The appropriate level of aggregation in a model depends upon the purposes of the model. There will be little obvious benefit in disaggregation if there is no requirement for the more detailed results. Models can be even more aggregated than the simple market model. Two-equation models have been proposed to explain quantity and price determination.[20] There is some presumption against size and complexity, reflected in an adherence to the 'principle of parsimony' or the 'application of Occam's razor'. All things being equal a parsimonious representation might be preferred.[21] Aggregated models may be less demanding in terms of data requirements and the computational burden involved in their estimation and manipulation. The latter is obviously of declining significance with the greater availability and power of microcomputers and software. 'Simple' models are also appreciated by model-users, who may have little econometric expertise, and who value their superficial transparency and ease of use, although paradoxically, as noted above, the 'black-box' parameters of such 'simple' models may make them awkward to use and interpret. They may also prove difficult to apply to purposes other than those for which they were specifically designed. Simplicity cannot necessarily be equated with a limited number of equations - single equation models might be extremely complex in their dynamic structure, for example.[22]

Nonlinear Models

The assumption that the dependent variable is a linear function of the explanatory variables is not necessarily restrictive. Models nonlinear *in variables* can be accommodated within the general linear model by simply defining a new variable equal to the nonlinear form. This new variable will be linearly related to the dependent variable. A wide variety of nonlinear functional forms have been handled in this way to describe the Engel curve relationship between food consumption and income, for example[23]: relating consumption to the reciprocal or the logarithm of income allows consumption to increase at a declining rate as income increases and eventually approach a ceiling level; relating the logarithm of consumption to the reciprocal of income allows consumption to increase first at an increasing and then at a decreasing rate as income increases before approaching a ceiling level. Similar functional forms have been employed to describe the relationship between crop yields and the application of inputs, and the growth of yields through time. Nonlinear forms involving more than one explanatory variable, price ratios, for example, can be dealt with in the same way. Such models are nonlinear in the variables. Models nonlinear in the parameters can be less tractable, although some can be transformed into a linear form. One very commonly used model nonlinear in the parameters is the multiplicative form such as the simple demand function relating demand, D, to price, P, and income, Y.

$$D = \alpha P^{\beta} Y^{\gamma} e^{\upsilon}$$

Taking logarithms gives the log-linear form

$$\ln D = \ln \alpha + \beta \ln P + \gamma \ln Y + \upsilon$$

which can be accommodated by the general linear model and which has the convenient property that the parameters measure constant *elasticities*, β being the price elasticity and γ being the income elasticity.[24] This functional form has been employed in demand analyses by the National Food Survey,[25] and was used throughout the cocoa market model discussed in Chapter 1. Had the disturbance entered the original multiplicative form additively, however, the transformation would not have been possible.

Nonlinear models which can be accommodated either directly or after an appropriate transformation by the general linear statistical model are known as *intrinsically linear*. Models not amenable to such treatment are *intrinsically nonlinear*.[26] Although intrinsically linear models need not present problems in the specification and estimation of the general linear model, they can present problems in the estimation and solution of a simultaneous equation system where an endogenous variable appears in different nonlinear functions in different equations of the model. These difficulties are discussed further in Chapters 4 and 5.

Dynamic Models

Time lags are inherent in many relationships between economic variables as a result of delayed or incomplete responses of economic agents to changes in economic or technical conditions. Such dynamic relationships are particularly important in relation to the modelling of supply in agricultural commodity markets where the response of supply to changes in price will typically be delayed. Permanent price changes may not be recognised immediately, and decisions to adjust supply take time to make and implement. Adjustment incurs costs which may deter immediate and complete response to changes in economic conditions. In any case, given the biological delays inherent in agricultural production processes, immediate adjustment will not always be feasible.

Distributed Lags

For the reasons outlined, the effect of one economic variable upon another can be *lagged*. The cobweb model of agricultural supply where current supply is dependent upon price in the previous period

$$S_t = \alpha + \beta P_{t-1} + u_t$$

provides a well-known example. The effect of one variable on another may endure through several time periods, giving a *distributed lag* relationship such as

$$S_t = \alpha + \beta_0 P_t + \beta_1 P_{t-1} + \beta_2 P_{t-2} + \ldots + \beta_k P_{t-k} + u_t$$

Providing data for the lagged variables results in a loss from the sample of as many observations as there are periods in the maximum lag. The resulting loss of observations can lead to less reliable parameter estimates, and in the limit may exhaust degrees of freedom and make estimation impossible. Lags can be long, particularly in supply equations, and particularly in the case of perennials. There can be an extensive delay before trees reach bearing age and a further delay before they reach peak production. Relationships between supply of a perennial crop and producer prices for that crop can therefore involve very long lags. These can be avoided to some extent by disaggregating the supply relationship, if the data will allow, focusing on new plantings and removals from the stock of trees or area planted and explaining potential supply on the basis of an identity cumulating these net investments. In any case this procedure is likely to give a more accurate representation of the dynamics of the relationship between supply and price.[27]

A further estimation problem in distributed lag models can arise from the possibility that successive lagged terms may be closely correlated - the problem of *multicollinearity* - making it difficult to obtain reliable estimates of the individual lag coefficients.

The consequences of the two problems of loss of observations and multicollinearity are discussed in Chapter 3. In the face of these problems the usual way of proceeding is to impose restrictions upon the values of the lag coefficients, assuming that they follow a known distribution, and hence reducing the number of independent parameters to be estimated. The two most common assumptions made are that the lag coefficients decline in an infinite geometric progression, or alternatively that a finite sequence of values of the coefficients can be approximated by a polynomial function in the length of each lag.

In the geometric case, the infinite lag relationship is written

$$S_t = \alpha + \beta_0 (P_t + w P_{t-1} + w^2 P_{t-2} + w^3 P_{t-3} + \ldots) + u_t$$

where the unknown w lies between zero and one, giving the geometrically declining lag weights of β_0, $\beta_0 w$, $\beta_0 w^2$, and so on. The model is put into an estimable form using a *Koyck transformation*.[28] Lagging by one period and multiplying through by w yields

$$w S_{t-1} = w \alpha + \beta_0 (w P_{t-1} + w^2 P_{t-2} + w^3 P_{t-3} + w^4 P_{t-4} + \ldots) + w u_{t-1}$$

Subtracting this from the original expression eliminates all the lagged price terms except P_t

$$S_t - w S_{t-1} = \alpha (1 - w) + \beta_0 P_t + u_t - w u_{t-1}$$

or

$$S_t = \alpha (1 - w) + w S_{t-1} + \beta_0 P_t + u_t - w u_{t-1}$$

Geometric lag equations can be justified in a variety of ways, notably by the partial adjustment and adaptive expectations models discussed below. This particular form can present estimation problems since successive disturbances will not have a zero covariance and the lagged dependent variable will be both stochastic and dependent upon the disturbance. The assumptions of the general linear statistical model are therefore violated and the ordinary least squares estimator will be biased and inefficient.

Polynomial or *Almon*[29] lags involve the assumption that the lag weights can be approximated by some function of the length of each lag and that function can be approximated by a polynomial.

$$\beta_i = f(i) = a_0 + a_1 i + a_2 i^2 + \ldots + a_r i^r \qquad \text{for } i = 1,2, \ldots k$$

The appropriate degree of polynomial, r, and the maximum length of the lag, k, are assumed known. In a simple model involving a five period lag

$$S_t = \alpha + \beta_0 P_t + \beta_1 P_{t-1} + \beta_2 P_{t-2} + \beta_3 P_{t-3} + \beta_4 P_{t-4} + u_t$$

and a second degree polynomial the individual β's are given by

$$\beta_0 = a_0$$
$$\beta_1 = a_0 + a_1 + a_2$$
$$\beta_2 = a_0 + 2a_1 + 4a_2$$
$$\beta_3 = a_0 + 3a_1 + 9a_2$$
$$\beta_4 = a_0 + 4a_1 + 16a_2$$

Substituting into the original expression gives

$$S_t = \alpha + a_0 P_t + (a_0 + a_1 + a_2)P_{t-1} + (a_0 + 2a_1 + 4a_2)P_{t-2} + (a_0 + 3a_1 + 9a_2)P_{t-3} + (a_0 + 4a_1 + 16a_2)P_{t-4} + u_t$$

or

$$S_t = \alpha + a_0(P_t + P_{t-1} + P_{t-2} + P_{t-3} + P_{t-4}) + a_1(P_{t-1} + 2P_{t-2} + 3P_{t-3} + 4P_{t-4}) + a_2(P_{t-1} + 4P_{t-2} + 9P_{t-3} + 16P_{t-4}) + u_t$$

Estimation of this equation involving weighted sums of the lagged explanatory variables yields estimates of the a's which can then be used to obtain estimates of the β's. Provided that the degree of polynomial is less than the number of periods in the lag then the number of parameters to be estimated will be less than in the unrestricted distributed lag relationship. Some multicollinearity may, however, remain in the weighted sums of the lagged explanatory variables. While it is assumed that the degree of polynomial and the length of the lag are known, in practice there may be some uncertainty as to the appropriate values. Specification of incorrect values will lead to bias if the lag length or degree of polynomial are set too small, or inefficiency if they are set too large. The appropriate degree of polynomial should be small if there is to be any appreciable advantage in implementing this procedure. The degree should be one more than the number of turning points expected in the lag distribution. Thus a second degree polynomial will be appropriate in the perhaps most common case of weights which first rise then fall. In supply equations for some crops, particularly perennials, and some livestock products, a third or fourth degree polynomial might be appropriate. The peak effect of price can be twofold - upon planting decisions with a long lag, and upon harvesting decisions with a short lag - producing a double-peaked distributed lag distribution.[30] Selection of the degree of polynomial and lag length frequently relies on trial and error, selecting those values giving the 'best' results according to some *ad hoc* criteria. such as R^2. The appropriate values can be determined more systematically using the various model selection procedures described later in this chapter.[31]

Figure 2.1: Effect of Hog Prices on US Hog Supply - Distributed Lag Coefficients

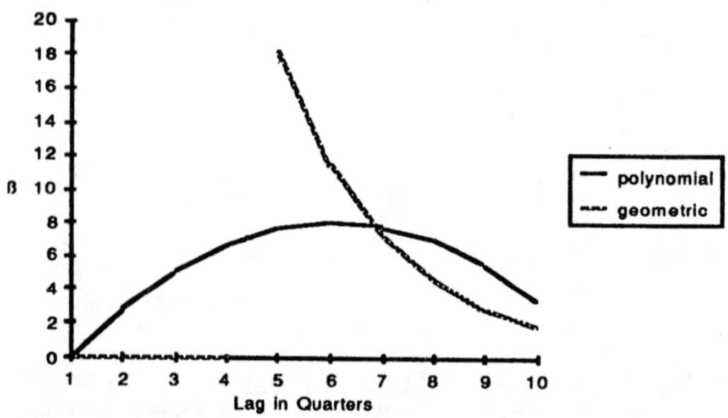

Source: K.D. Meilke, A.C. Zwart and L.J. Martin, 'North American Hog Supply: A Comparison of Geometric and Polynomial Distributed Lag Models', *Canadian Journal of Agricultural Economics*, vol. 22, no. 2 (1974), pp. 15-30.

The characteristics of the geometric and polynomial lags are compared in Figure 2.1. which shows the responses in US hog supply to changes in hog prices in previous quarters as reflected by each of the two lag structures. It can be seen that the geometric lag gives greatest weight to the first term in the lag, with the weights declining continuously thereafter back to infinity. Such a distribution may be unrealistic where the first term relates to the current quarter since the peak response to price changes may be delayed by adjustments costs or biological delays. The onset of the lag can be deferred to coincide with the peak response. This procedure implies no response to price changes in period prior to this, however, when in fact here may be some scope for short-run response albeit perhaps limited. Such responses might be captured by including additional price terms with lags shorter than the start of the lag, but this might lead to multicollinearity which the use of lag distributions was supposed to avoid. These difficulties are largely avoided by the more flexible polynomial lags which can be used to approximate any response pattern by suitable choice of degree of polynomial and lag length. In Figure 2.1 the degree is second and the lag length ten quarters. It indicates that the response to changes in prices less than five quarters previously is not zero as is implied by the geometric lag.

The Partial Adjustment Model

Because of technical delays, costs of adjustment or habit persistence movements from the current level of supply or demand to new equilibrium levels consequent upon changes in economic or technical conditions may not be instantaneous, but gradual, over a sequence of time periods. This process of gradual adjustment is of some interest and the *partial adjustment model* is commonly employed to represent it. The model describes the change in a variable, say supply, S, from one period to the next as some proportion, δ, of the difference between the current level and the desired level, S^*.

$$S_t - S_{t-1} = \delta (S^*_t - S_{t-1}) + u_t$$

or

$$S_t = (1 - \delta) S_{t-1} + \delta S^*_t + u_t$$

where δ lies between zero and one and the closer it approaches one the more complete the adjustment within the current period. Desired supply is unobservable and must be expressed as a function of variables which can be observed. Suppose that the desired level of supply can be taken to be a simple linear function of last period's price

$$S^*_t = \alpha + \beta P_{t-1}$$

Combining this with the partial adjustment model gives the equation

$$S_t = \delta\alpha + (1 - \delta)\, S_{t-1} + \delta\beta P_{t-1} + u_t$$

which can be estimated since it involves only observable variables. An estimate of the adjustment parameter, δ, can be obtained by taking one minus the estimated coefficient on the lagged dependent variable $1 - (1 - \delta)$. The short-run price effect is measured by the estimated coefficient on price which is equal to $\delta\beta$. Dividing this by the estimated adjustment coefficient gives an estimate of the long-run price effect, β, when supply has adjusted fully to its new equilibrium level. The partial adjustment model yields an estimating equation similar to that for the geometric distributed lag model discussed above, and does indeed imply a geometrically declining lag distribution of the effects of changes in past prices. Because the equation is not generated via a Koyck transformation, however, the disturbance term is not autocorrelated, although the lagged dependent variable on the right-hand side is obviously stochastic rather than fixed as the general linear statistical model assumes. The consequences of this are discussed in Chapter 4.

The Adaptive Expectations Model

Because of the delays inherent in the production processes, production and marketing decisions must be based upon *expectations* regarding the future values of relevant variables: planting decisions for example, may be made on the basis of prices expected for the crop at harvest. Since expectations will not normally be recorded, a model should include assumptions concerning the expectations formation process defined in terms of observable data. The cobweb model implies a naive expectations formation process where producers continue to expect the price in the next period to be the same as that in the previous period, in spite of being proved wrong each time.

A rather more sophisticated and widely used model of expectations formation is the *adaptive expectations model*. This model assumes that the variable of interest, say supply, S, is dependent upon expected prices, P^e.

$$S_t = \alpha + \beta P^e{}_t + u_t$$

Expectations are revised each period with the revision proportional to the error in the previous expectations.

$$P^e{}_t - P^e{}_{t-1} = \gamma (P_{t-1} - P^e{}_{t-1})$$

or

$$P^e{}_t = \gamma P_{t-1} + (1 - \gamma) P^e{}_{t-1}$$

The weight accorded to this error is measured by γ which will lie between zero and one. The closer it lies to one, the greater the weight given to the most recent observations in determining the current expectation. Expectations in previous periods could be written in a similar way, and the resulting expression substituted into that for current expectation. For period t-1

$$P^e{}_{t-1} = \gamma P_{t-2} + (1 - \gamma) P^e{}_{t-2}$$

from which

$$P^e{}_t = \gamma P_{t-1} + \gamma (1 - \gamma) P_{t-2} + (1 - \gamma)^2 P^e{}_{t-2}$$

Similarly, for period t-2

$$P^e{}_{t-2} = \gamma P_{t-3} + (1 - \gamma) P^e{}_{t-3}$$

from which

$$P^e_t = \gamma P_{t-1} + \gamma(1-\gamma)P_{t-2} + \gamma(1-\gamma)^2 P_{t-3} + (1-\gamma)^3 P^e_{t-3}$$

By continual substitution of this kind an expression for the expected price of the form

$$P^e_t = \gamma P_{t-1} + \gamma(1-\gamma)P_{t-2} + \gamma(1-\gamma)^2 P_{t-3} + \gamma(1-\gamma)^3 P_{t-4} + \ldots$$

or

$$P^e_t = \gamma\,[P_{t-1} + (1-\gamma)P_{t-2} + (1-\gamma)^2 P_{t-3} + (1-\gamma)^3 P_{t-4} + \ldots\,]$$

is obtained. Perhaps somewhat naively, therefore, producers are assumed to base their price expectations solely upon an extrapolation of past prices. Using this in the original supply equation gives

$$S_t = \alpha + \beta\gamma\,[P_{t-1} + (1-\gamma)P_{t-2} + (1-\gamma)^2 P_{t-3} + (1-\gamma)^3 P_{t-4} + \ldots\,] + u_t$$

which is the same form as the geometric distributed lag model discussed above. Applying the Koyck transformation yields an equation which can be estimated

$$S_t = \alpha\gamma + \beta\gamma P_{t-1} + (1-\gamma)S_{t-1} + u_t - (1-\gamma)u_{t-1}$$

Since it is derived in the same way, via a Koyck transformation, this equation presents the same estimation problems as the geometric distributed lag model discussed above. The lagged dependent variable on the right-hand side is stochastic rather than fixed, and the moving average disturbance means that successive values are not independent.

The Nerlove Supply Model

The partial adjustment and adaptive expectations models are

combined in the *Nerlove supply model* which has dominated econometric work on agricultural commodity supply for thirty years.[32] One survey lists applications to more than 500 commodities from artichokes to wool, including annual crops, perennial crops and livestock products, and relating to developed, less developed and centrally planned economies.[33]

In its simplest form the model assumes that there is some desired level of supply, S^*, dependent upon expected prices, P^e,

$$S^*_t = \alpha + \beta P^e_t$$

Actual supply adjusts towards the desired level according to the partial adjustment model

$$S_t - S_{t-1} = \delta (S^*_t - S_{t-1}) + u_t$$

Expectations are formed according to the adaptive expectations model

$$P^e_t - P^e_{t-1} = \gamma (P_{t-1} - P^e_{t-1})$$

Combining these elements results in the equation

$$S_t = \alpha\delta\gamma + [(1-\delta) + (1-\gamma)] S_{t-1} - (1-\delta)(1-\gamma) S_{t-2} + \beta\delta\gamma P_{t-1} + u_t - (1 - \gamma) u_{t-1}$$

which does not contain any unobservable variables and hence can be estimated. The estimating equation has the same problematic statistical properties as that in the case of the adaptive expectations model: namely, disturbances which are serially correlated and explanatory variables which include stochastic lagged dependent variables. Most applications of the Nerlove model have ignored these statistical problems, however, suppressing the disturbance in the partial adjustment model and simply adding a straightforward non-autoregressive disturbance to the final estimating equation. While this may reduce the statistical complexity of the model, the symmetry with which δ and γ enter means that estimates of these parameters and of α and β cannot be obtained from estimates of the compound coefficients of the resulting estimating equation. A common assumption in practice, therefore, has been that δ or γ are equal to one. This eliminates S_{t-2} and yields a simple coefficient on S_{t-1} from which δ or γ and hence α and β can be estimated, but implies either no delays in adjustment or a naive expectations formation process. Both may be difficult to justify. Proceeding in this way, however, the short-run price effect is measured by the compound coefficient on P_{t-1}, and the long-run effect by dividing that by one minus the coefficient on S_{t-1}. These difficulties in identifying the various individual parameters of the model from etimates of the compound coefficients of the estimating equation are avoided if the autocorrelated nature of the disturbance is acknowledged. The structure of the disturbance provides a value for γ which can be used to obtain an estimate of the value of δ and hence α and β.[34]

In most studies, movements in some measure of the scale of production such as area planted or number of livestock, rather than supply itself are the focus of attention. The scale of production, being the prime economic decision variable, is assumed to most closely represent 'planned supply'. Data concerning crop areas or livestock numbers are also typically more readily available from agricultural censuses and surveys. Focusing on area planted or numbers of livestock may however allow only a partial description of the determination of supply. Yield variations are assumed to be determined primarily by uncontrollable exogenous influences such as weather, but can also be a deliberate short-run response to changes in economic conditions. Measurements of supply response to price changes based upon an analysis of area or livestock numbers will underestimate the overall supply response by the extent of the yield response. A more complete analysis of supply might specify equations to explain both area planted or livestock numbers and yield per unit area or per animal. The area or herd equation will typically be of the Nerlove or partial adjustment type perhaps involving relatively long lags on the price variables while that for yield may be a relatively simple form involving climatic and price variables which are either contemporaneous or with short lags. In a World Bank study,[35] a simple model of tea supply was specified as

$$A_t = \alpha_0 + \alpha_1 P_{t-7} + \alpha_2 A_{t-1} + \alpha_3 T + u_t$$

$$YLD_t = \beta_0 + \beta_1 P_{t-1} + \beta_2 P_{t-2} + \beta_3 CLF_t + \beta_4 T + \upsilon_t$$

where: A is mature tea area in thousands of hectares; P is London price of tea in US cents/lb deflated by an index of input costs; T is a time trend; YLD is yield in tons per hectare; CLF is climatic factors such as the amount of rainfall; all lags are in years. Supply, S, is then given by the identity,

$$S_t = A_t.YLD_t$$

More precisely, area planted will determine *potential* supply for any given yield level. The quantity actually harvested may be less than potential supply. A downturn in prices close to harvest may induce producers to leave some proportion of the potential crop unharvested. Focusing attention purely on factors affecting the scale of production and hence potential supply may misjudge the nature of the dynamic response of actual supply to price. A supplementary equation must be specified to describe the harvesting decision in terms of potential supply and recent price developments.[36] A similar two-stage approach might also be employed to explain the determination of total supply and marketed surplus in peasant agriculture.

In the case of the supply of livestock products attention has again been focused upon scale of production reflected in overall livestock numbers or a particularly strategic subset such as breeding herd, and yield per animal. A more detailed disaggregated description of the dynamics of livestock populations can be attempted. Rather than the population itself, inflow into and outflow from the population might more properly be considered the decision variables to be explained by reference to economic conditions. The herd or flock in any one period is then derived as an identity

$$HERD_t = HERD_{t-1} + INFLOW_t - OUTFLOW_t$$

In the case of egg production, for example, the laying flock, LF, will change from one month to the next according to the balance between inflow in the form of newly mature layers which will reflect the number of chicks purchased, CP, around five months previously, and outflow in the form of culling of older birds, CULL.[37]

$$LF_t = LF_{t-1} + CP_{t-5} - CULL_t$$

The number of chicks purchased might depend upon expected egg prices, EP, and feed prices, FP,

$$CP_t = \alpha_0 + \alpha_1 EP^e_t - \alpha_2 FP^e_t + u_t$$

with expectations formed according to the adaptive expectations model

$$EP^e_t - EP^e_{t-1} = \gamma (EP_{t-1} - EP^e_{t-1})$$

for example, giving the estimating equation

$$CP_t = \alpha_0\gamma + \alpha_1\gamma EP_{t-1} - \alpha_2\gamma FP_{t-1} + (1 - \gamma)CP_{t-1} + u_t - (1 - \gamma) u_{t-1}$$

If birds are retained in the laying flock for a fixed period of time then the number of birds culled each month will be largely proportional to the size of the laying flock, but current profitability, reflected in egg and feed prices, may also influence the culling-retention decision

$$CULL_t = \beta_0 + \beta_1 LF_t - \beta_2 EP_t + \beta_3 FP_t + \upsilon_t .$$

These equations together provide a more detailed description of the actual decision-making processes involved and hence of the dynamics of the population than would an attempt to explain the stock of birds directly using the Nerlove model. The specification also has the practical advantage that the lags involved are thereby reduced.

The Rational Expectations Hypothesis

An alternative model of expectations formation is provided by the *rational expectations hypothesis*.[38] Expectations are assumed to be based upon a broader information set than the simple extrapolation of a variable's past behaviour assumed by the adaptive expectations model. More precisely, they are derived as if on the basis of a stochastic economic model of the determination of the variable concerned. Rational expectations of the endogenous variables of an econometric model are therefore consistent with that model's view of how the values of those endogenous variables are determined. On average, rational expectations of the value of a variable will be equal to the realised value, differing only as a result of purely random factors.[39] Rational expectations are self-fulfilling in that they must induce behaviour which ensures that this is the case.

The nature and implications of rational expectations can be illustrated using a simple market model, basically similar to a monthly model applied to the US broiler market.[40] Demand, D, is related to price, P, and income, Y.

$$D_t = \alpha_0 - \alpha_1 P_t + \alpha_2 Y_t + u_t$$

Supply in period t is determined by price expected in period t, P^e_t, where price expectations are formed in period t-1, and price of an important input, such as feed, I.

$$S_t = \beta_0 + \beta_1 P^e_t - \beta_2 I_t + v_t$$

In equilibrium

$$\alpha_0 - \alpha_1 P_t + \alpha_2 Y_t + u_t = \beta_0 + \beta_1 P^e_t - \beta_2 I_t + v_t$$

The relationship between the expected and the realised price is

$$P^e_t = \frac{\alpha_0 - \beta_0}{\beta_1} - \frac{\alpha_1}{\beta_1} P_t + \frac{\alpha_2}{\beta_1} Y_t + \frac{\beta_2}{\beta_1} I_t + \frac{u_t - v_t}{\beta_1}$$

Since rational expectations will produce a realised value for price on average equal to the rationally expected price

$$P^e_t = \frac{\alpha_0 - \beta_0}{\beta_1} - \frac{\alpha_1}{\beta_1} P^e_t + \frac{\alpha_2}{\beta_1} Y^e_t + \frac{\beta_2}{\beta_1} I^e_t + \frac{u^e_t - v^e_t}{\beta_1}$$

or

$$P^e_t = \frac{\alpha_0 - \beta_0}{\beta_1 + \alpha_1} + \frac{\alpha_2}{\beta_1 + \alpha_1} Y^e_t + \frac{\beta_2}{\beta_1 + \alpha_1} I^e_t + \frac{u^e_t - v^e_t}{\beta_1 + \alpha_1}$$

which shows how the rationally expected price is based upon the structural parameters of the model and expected values of its exogenous variables. Substituting this expression into the supply equation gives

$$S_t = \frac{\alpha_0\beta_1 + \alpha_1\beta_0}{\beta_1 + \alpha_1} + \frac{\beta_1\alpha_2}{\beta_1 + \alpha_1} Y_t^e + \frac{\beta_1\beta_2}{\beta_1 + \alpha_1} I_t^e$$

$$- \beta_2 I_\tau + \frac{\beta_1 (u_t^e - v_t^e)}{\beta_1 + \alpha_1} + v_t$$

Implementation of this rational expectations model requires that the expected values of the exogenous variables be defined in terms of observable data. Time series models can be fitted and used to define expected values of the exogenous variables.[41] Using simple autoregressive models, for example, such as

$$Y_t = \rho\, Y_{t-1} + w_t$$

would lead to the replacement of the expectational terms in the supply equation by expressions such as the right-hand side of this autoregressive model. The dynamic stochastic processes for the exogenous variables then determine the dynamic stochastic properties of the rational expectations model.

The rational expectations hypothesis is an improvement on the extrapolative expectations models in attempting to broaden the information set upon which expectations are assumed to be based. Rational expectations models of the US broiler market have provided evidence to support the applicability of the rational expectations hypothesis to agricultural markets.[42] It is however arguable whether large-scale US broiler producers with an active interest in economic and market analysis and forecasting can be regarded as representative of agricultural producers generally. Doubts have beeen raised as to whether the majority of producers would really have the type of information concerning the structure of the model and the determination of the exogenous variables presupposed by the rational expectations hypothesis, particularly where the structure was subject to change as a result of a changing economic environment.[43]

Varying Parameter Models

The assumption that the parameters of the statistical model are constants may be untenable in many cases. Secular change in the economic environment, with respect to technology and behaviour patterns, for example, will produce gradual shifts in the parameters of market relationships. Abrupt *structural shifts* may be produced by changes in policies or institutions. Regular shifts may result from seasonal variations in consumer behaviour patterns or livestock productivity. More subtle changes in parameters may result from variations in the weightings given to different economic units in deriving aggregated data. A variety of *varying parameter models* appropriate to each of these types of circumstances have been proposed. While many models might appropriately be specified as varying parameter models, the difficulty is to reconcile descriptive accuracy with useful abstraction.

A very general form is the *random coefficient model* which attaches a random additive disturbance, υ, to the coefficients

$$\beta_t = \beta^p + \upsilon_t$$

allowing them to vary from one period to the next around a central mean or permanent value, β^p.[44] Using this in a simple demand function yields an estimating equation

$$D_t = \alpha + (\beta^p + \upsilon_t)P_t$$

or

$$D_t = \alpha + \beta^p P_t + \upsilon_t P_t$$

whose disturbance will not have a constant variance but will be *heteroscedastic.*

The *adaptive regression model* allows parameters to vary randomly around a central value which 'drifts' in a random walk through time.[45] A recent study of the demand for oranges[46] assumed such parameter variation might result from changes in consumption behaviour patterns and trade policy over time, specifying a demand equation of the form

$$D_t = \beta_{0t} + \beta_{1t}P_t + \beta_{2t}Y_t$$

where each of the β's drifts according to

$$\beta_t = \beta^P{}_t + \upsilon_t$$

$$\beta^P{}_t = \beta^P{}_{t-1} + \varpi_t$$

Combining these elements into a model which can be estimated necessitates specifying reference values for the drifting β's. One possibility is the value immediately following the data period, which facilitates the use of the model in forecasting, with the values of the various β's derived from this by subtraction of the appropriate disturbances.[47] This results in an estimating equation whose disturbance is both heteroscedastic and autocorrelated.

Rather than simply acknowledging that parameters may vary over time and attempting to describe this variation, an attempt might be made to *explain* by reference to changes in specified variables. In the discussion of agricultural supply functions, the actual amount of a commodity coming on to a market was seen as the outcome of two decisions - a production decision which largely determined the potential supply, and a harvesting decision, perhaps based upon recent price movements, which determined what proportion of the potential supply would actually be harvested. A variable parameter model describing quantity harvested, H, might express this as some proportion, *k*, of potential supply, PS,

$$H_t = k\, PS_t + u_t$$

with *k* determined by recent prices, P,

$$k = \alpha + \beta P_t + \upsilon_t$$

giving the varying parameter model

$$H_t = \alpha PS_t + \beta P_t.PS_t + \upsilon_t.PS_t + u_t$$

Where, as in this case, the relationship determining the varying parameter is stochastic rather than deterministic, the disturbance of the final model will be heteroscedastic.

The varying parameter models discussed so far allow differing parameters for every time period. In *switching regression models* , parameters are assumed to remain constant for one sequence of time periods, but shift to new constant values for another sequence. Policy changes might give rise to structural shifts of this kind. The resulting discontinuity might be handled by fitting separate models for the different regimes.[48] Where the function should be continuous, albeit not smooth, the various segments can be constrained to join up to give a *spline function*.[49] Testing procedures, some of which are described below, are available to determine shift points where these are not known with certainty. Disequilibrium models might be considered as switching models. Quantity traded is determined by the short side of the market and hence quantity observations alternate between the demand and supply functions.[50] Models including parameters which vary seasonally also fall into the category of switching regression models. These are typically handled using *dummy variables* and are discussed in Chapter 3.

The possibility that the response of one variable to changes in another may differ depending upon whether the changes are positive or negative has led to the development of *asymmetric* or *irreversible* functions. These have been discussed particularly in relation to supply models where, it is argued, the response of supply to rising prices will be greater than that to falling prices. The justification for this is rather *ad hoc* relying upon the presence of fixed or durable assets such as trees, livestock, buildings or equipment in the production process. Such assets are considered to have an opportunity cost, usually assumed to be the salvage or scrap value, which is low relative to their cost of acquisition. Falling prices, therefore, do not lead to the disposal of these 'fixed assets' whose acquisition was justified when prices were high, and hence the reduction in supply is limited.[51] Asymmetric demand functions, resulting from factors such as habit persistence, have also been discussed.[52]

The incorporation of asymmetry into a supply function involves the segmentation of the price variable, or variables, and associated data series into rising and falling prices giving an equation such as

$$S_t = \alpha + \beta^r P^r{}_t + \beta^f P^f{}_t + u_t$$

where the superscripts r and f denote the rising and falling price variables. Different definitions of rising and falling prices and hence different methods of constructing the data sets for these variables have been proposed. One simple formulation defines the variables as follows:

$$P^r_t = P^r_{t-1} + \delta_1\{P_t - P_{t-1}\}$$

$$P^f_t = P^f_{t-1} + \delta_2\{P_t - P_{t-1}\}$$

where $\delta_1 = 1$ if $\{P_t - P_{t-1}\} > 0$, and 0 otherwise, and $\delta_2 = 1$ if $\{P_t - P_{t-1}\} < 0$, and 0 otherwise.[53] Thus, the data are generated, starting from the same base value, by adding positive changes to the rising price series, and negative changes to the falling price series. A study of coffee supply employing this formulation of irreversibility found responses to rising prices three times higher than responses to falling prices.[54] An implication of this formulation, however, is that at the end of any given period, output will be greater the greater the price variability during that period. In practice, greater price variability might be expected to be a disincentive to output expansion. A simple modification removes this implication and provides a basis for segmentation of the price series more consistent with the fixed asset theory which suggests that acquisition of fixed assets will be prompted by *historically* high prices rather than rising prices *per se*.[55] In this formulation, it is assumed that additional fixed assets are acquired only if prices rise above the previous maximum level which justified the current stock. Hence, it is only price rises above the previous maximum level, P^{max}, which are added to the 'rising price' series. Any changes, whether positive or negative, which leave price below its previous maximum are added to the 'falling price' series.

$$P^r_t = P^r_{t-1} + \delta_1\{P_t - P^{max}_t\}$$

$$P^f_t = P^f_{t-1} + \delta_2\{P_t - P_{t-1}\}$$

where $\delta_1 = 1$ if $P_t > P^{max}_t$, and 0 otherwise, and $\delta_2 = 1$ if $P_t < P^{max}_t$, and 0 otherwise. This segmentation will be highly sensitive to the data period chosen. If, for example, the first observation on price is the highest in the series then all subsequent price changes will represent 'falls'. There will be no variation in the 'rising price' series and it will not be possible to estimate the associated parameter. A possible solution to this difficulty is to take into account the depreciation of the fixed assets over time, thus allowing price maxima gradually to become obsolete.

Supply studies employing irreversible functions have encountered a number of conceptual and econometric difficulties. While some studies report evidence of asymmetry in the response of supply to price, few include tests of the asymmetric specification. Concern with the most appropriate means of segmenting the price series has led to a neglect of other aspects of the supply specification. Dynamic aspects, in particular, have been problematic. Difficulties in specifying over what period and with what weightings rising and falling prices should be defined have been avoided by the specification of simple lags on the price variables with the naive price expectation processes these imply. It has also proved difficult to integrate asymmetry with a partial adjustment mechanism. Asymmetry in short-run responses of supply to price would result if the adjustment coefficient differed depending on whether prices were rising or falling, and hence whether desired supply was greater or less than current supply.

Incorporating Prior Knowledge

It was noted in the introduction to this chapter that specification of a model reflects the model-builder's prior beliefs, perhaps derived from economic theory or technical and institutional knowledge, concerning the process by which the data on the variables of interest are determined.[56] These prior beliefs may be subject to revision after tests of their validity. Typically, prior 'knowledge' relates to the systematic component of the model - which variables should be included, the mathematical form of the relationships between them, the signs and magnitudes of their parameters. The stochastic component is typically defined at least initially by assumptions as to its properties.

Incorporation of prior knowledge may involve *restrictions* specifying particular values for parameters or relationships between them. Such restrictions may be exact or stochastic, linear or nonlinear, exact linear restrictions being the simplest to handle. The restriction that a parameter should be equal to a particular value might be imposed on the basis of evidence from earlier studies. Perhaps the most common form are *zero restrictions* setting particular parameters equal to zero and hence specifying the exclusion of the associated explanatory variables from the model. Relationships between parameters might be specified as in the distributed lag models discussed above. These might be based upon theoretical considerations. In demand analysis, for example, restrictions might be derived from the homogeneity condition to specify that the own-price, cross-price and income elasticities should sum to zero or that the own-price elasticity should exceed the income elasticity.[57]

The incorporation of prior information can allow more reliable parameter estimates, in the sense of having smaller variances, whether the restrictions are correct or not. If the information is incorrect, however, its incorporation will lead to biased estimates.[58]

Specification Error

The appropriate specification for an equation will not always be known with certainty in all its dimensions. In practice, there may be uncertainty concerning the appropriate statistical model, the selection of explanatory variables, and the nature of the mathematical and statistical relationships assumed to exist between them. This uncertainty admits the possibility of *specification error* in any one of these dimensions.

Specification error, broadly defined, refers to any error in connection with any aspect of the statistical model of the data generating process, whether this is the systematic component involving the selection of variables and the mathematical form of the relationships asssumed to exist between them, or the stochastic component involving the nature and properties of the stochastic disturbance term. The term is often used in a narrower sense, however, to refer to errors in specifying the selection of variables to be included in a model - either the omission of relevant variables, or the inclusion of irrelevant variables. Of these, the former, omitting a relevant variable, is the most serious since it will lead to biased estimates of the parameters of the included variables. The same consequences follow if the mathematical form of the equation is incorrectly specified - a linear function when a nonlinear one is approriate, for example - or if the nature of the variables changes over time - increasing productivity of an input, for example. The extent and direction of bias resulting from the omission of a relevant variable depend upon the relationships of the omitted variable to the dependent variable of the equation concerned and to the explanatory variables which are included. The bias will be zero only if the omitted variable is uncorrelated with the included varibles. Where an irrelevant variable is included in an equation the estimated parameters will be unbiased but may be less *efficient* in the sense of having larger variances than they otherwise would.[59]

There may be circumstances where the model-builder wittingly makes a specification error, omitting variables known to be relevant, in spite of the biases this introduces. In some cases, there may simply be no data available for a variable so it cannot be included in the equation. In other cases, the inclusion of the variable may cause more serious problems than the bias which would result from its omission. Where two variables are linearly related, for example, estimates of their effects on the dependent variable will be difficult to ascertain and be imprecise. The bias introduced by omitting one of the variables may be regarded as a reasonable price to pay for greater precision in the estimation of the effect of the remaining variable, particularly where the direction of bias can be predicted. Such cases are discussed further in Chapter 3.

Testing Specification

Arriving at the final specification for the equations of a model is frequently an iterative process with trial specifications revised in the light of their correspondence with economic and other *a priori* criteria, and their performance against various statistical criteria. This section is concerned with the statistical measurements and procedures used in evaluating the specification of individual equations. Evaluation of the performance of entire models is discussed in Chapter 6.

Statistical hypothesis tests are available to address a variety of issues in specification of equations, and can be employed to inform the process of determining the most appropriate specification.[60] A number of different testing situations can be distinguished. First, tests or evaluations of an equation as a whole in terms of the validity of the assumptions underlying the statistical model and its overall goodness of fit and explanatory power, sometimes referred to as *tests of misspecification*. Secondly, the selection of a model from competing alternative specifications in terms of the selection of variables included, sometimes referred to as *tests of specification*. The problem of selection takes two basic forms. One where the choice is between models which are special cases of one another and where one model can be produced by the imposition of restrictions upon the parameters of the other. Such *nested* models are usually envisaged as the focus of tests of specification. The second relates to a situation where choice is between two or more completely independent specifications which cannot be derived from one another through the imposition of suitable restrictions. Such *non-nested* models involve a slightly different testing situation the outcome of which may be the selection of one specification in preference to the other or the rejection or acceptance of both. Different tests appropriate to these different testing situations are available.[61] The approach to testing specification and misspecification has been typically *ad hoc* , however, with reliance being placed upon a limited number of criteria whatever the particular aspect of specification being tested. Most notable of these criteria applied in a blanket way is the coefficient of determination, R^2.

R^2, measuring the proportion of the variation around the mean in the dependent variable accounted for by the specification, is widely applied to judge the overall goodness of fit of an equation and as a basis for comparison between competing specifications whether these are nested or nonnested.[62] High values close to unity are taken to indicate a 'good' or preferred specification. Where R^2 is employed to choose between competing specifications it must be adjusted if these involve differing numbers of explanatory variables since R^2 can be increased simply by adding variables to an equation. *Corrected* R^2, $\bar{R}^2$, achieves this

$$\bar{R}^2 = 1 - (T / (T - k)) (1 - R^2)$$

R^2 associated with specifications involving differing functional forms are also not directly comparable. Fitted values from a log-linear specification, for example, would have to be reexpressed in their absolute values before an R^2 comparable with that from a linear specification could be derived.[63]

Tests of misspecification are concerned with the validity of the assumptions underlying the statistical model and hence an assessment of the overall adequacy of the specification and the identification of areas in which it may be deficient. In the context of the general linear statistical model this would involve testing for the omission of relevant variables, misspecification of functional forms, varying rather than constant parameters, and heteroscedasticity or autocorrelation in the disturbances. While there may not be a specific alternative to the current specification in mind, particular misspecification tests can obviously imply an alternative or be indicative of improvements. Attention focuses particularly upon an analysis of the estimated residuals from the estimated equation, a procedure known as *diagnostic checking* . Obviously, as estimates of the unknown disturbances, the estimated residuals can reveal departures from the assumptions concerning the disturbance term of the statistical model. Since the residuals represent that part of the variation in the dependent variable not accounted for by the systematic component of the estimated equation and are therefore supposedly random, any systematic variation in the residuals may also be indicative of other forms of specification error. An omitted variable, for example, expressing its influence upon the dependent variable via the disturbance term might produce a smooth wave-like pattern in the estimated residuals. Such systematic behaviour can be discerned from a plot of the estimated residuals against time of the kind which is included routinely in the output of most econometric estimation software. Where inspection of the residuals suggests that a relevant variable may have been omitted, plotting data on likely candidates against the residuals can help identify those which should have been included. Plotting the values of those variables included in the equation against the residuals can indicate functional misspecification.

The possibility of misspecification can also be examined using *recursive residuals.* Recursive residuals are one period ahead prediction errors generated from an equation estimated using observations for those periods up to that prior to that for which the prediction is made. If a function is misspecified as linear when in fact it is nonlinear, recursive residuals derived from the misspecified equation and ordered according to the values taken by the explanatory variables will indicate any nonlinear functions by a sequence of residuals with the same sign. Examination of recursive residuals can also be used to identify structural shifts and varying parameters. Significant divergences from zero in plots of the cumulative sums of the squares, CUSUMSQ, of recursive residuals against time are also indicative of structural shifts and varying parameters.[64]

A variety of test statistics are commonly applied in testing for nonfulfilment of the assumptions concerning the properties of the disturbance term. These can also be indicative of other forms of misspecification since as noted above these may also result in nonrandom disturbances. The most popular test for autocorrelation involves the *Durbin-Watson statistic* , d,

$$d = \frac{\sum_{t=2}^{T} (e_t - e_{t-1})^2}{\sum_{t=1}^{T} e_t^2}$$

used in testing for first-order autocorrelation.[65] Omitted variables or functional misspecification can have similar implications for estimated residuals as positive autocorrelation where successive disturbances are positively correlated. Values of d close to two suggests no autocorrelation and no misspecification. Values of d approaching zero suggest positive autocorrelation or misspecification.[66] Tests for heteroscedasticity are perhaps less commonly applied than those for autocorrelation, since heteroscedasticity is often regarded as primarily a problem associated with cross-section data. Tests can, however, be indicative of varying parameters as well as heteroscedasticity. The simplest involve testing the hypothesis that the variance of the disturbance is related in some way to one of the explanatory variables. Perhaps the best-known is the *Goldfeld-Quandt test*.[67] Here, the observations are ordered according to the magnitude of the explanatory variable assumed to influence the variance of the disturbance. The ordered sets of observations are then divided into two distinct subgroups and the parameters of the model estimated from each. An F-test is then made for significant differences between the residual variances associated with each set of observations.

A variety of other tests can be used to investigate particular types of misspecification. Adding *powers* of the explanatory variables to an equation and testing their significance provides the RESET test for functional misspecification.[68] A commonly used test for structural shifts is the *Chow test*, which tests for significant differences between parameters estimated under the assumed different regimes.[69]

Where tests of *specification* are concerned, there is a clear alternative in mind: the question is one of choice between nested models. Non-nested models involve a rather different testing situation and are discussed separately below. A common test of specification determines whether estimated coefficients on particular explanatory variables are significantly different from zero, implying that the explanatory variables in question have no effect upon the dependent variable. The results provide a basis for decisions relating to variable addition or deletion. With the supplementary assumption that the disturbance in the equation is normally distributed, such tests on individual coefficients are typically carried out using the familiar t-test.[70] Since tabled critical t-values for the most commonly employed 95 per cent significance level two-tailed test of whether a particular estimated parameter is significantly different from zero are close to two over a wide range of degrees of freedom the t-test is often approximated by the rule of thumb that an estimated parameter can be considered significantly different from zero if it as at least twice its standard error. Any variable failing to be shown to be significantly different from zero might be deleted from the model. The hypothesis that all or a subset of the parameters of an equation are collectively zero can be tested using an F-test comparing the amount of the variation in the dependent variable attributable to variation in the explanatory variables or a subset of them to that left unexplained, accounted for by the residual.[71] No significant difference would suggest that the variables concerned have no explanatory power in relation to movements in the dependent variable, and on that basis a decision might be made as to the most appropriate selection of explanatory variables for the equation in question. The validity of any linear restrictions imposed upon the estimated parameters of a model can also be tested using the F-test. Here, the restrictions are deemed appropriate if the amount of variation in the dependent variable explained by the restricted model is not significantly increased when the restrictions are removed.[72] More generally, the specification of linear and nonlinear models, and the validity of linear and nonlinear restrictions upon their parameters, can be tested using *likelihood ratio*, *Wald* or *Lagrange multiplier* tests. These tests are asymptotically equivalent, but may yield conflicting results in small samples.[73] The test statistics are all taken to be distributed as κ^2, but differ in the precise quantities which must be calculated for their implementation and hence in their computational convenience. All involve maximum likelihood estimation of the model in question.[74,75]

Tests of non-nested models are perhaps less frequently encountered in the context of agricultural commodity market modelling. The specification of such models is rarely so contentious as to generate completely distinct equations to test, although non-nested tests can be used to test alternative functional forms. Selection of one model from two non-nested alternatives might be made on the basis of R^2 or $\bar{R}^2$. Tests specifically designed for non-nested models admit of additional possibilities, however, namely the acceptance or rejection of both models. One approach proceeds by the creation of an artificial general model embracing both of the non-nested alternatives. From two non-nested models

$$D_t = \alpha P_t + \upsilon_{1t}$$

and

$$D_t = \beta Y_t + \upsilon_{2t}$$

for example, a third general model

$$D_t = \alpha P_t + \beta Y_t + \upsilon_t$$

is formed. F-tests or likelihood ratio tests of whether α and β are significantly different from zero can then be undertaken in turn. Failure to reject one or other of the hypotheses results in the rejection of that model.[76]

Concluding Comments

Specification is in some ways the linchpin of a modelling exercise, and the major determinant of a model's performance subject to the control of the econometrician. The estimates of a model's parameters, and the range and type of information it can provide depend crucially upon the specification adopted. This is typically the result of an iterative procedure with trial specifications revised in the light of the outcome of various statistical tests, econometric problems encountered, accuracy of predictions generated, and correspondence of empirical results with prior beliefs. The specification of an econometric model represents a simplification of reality, but also an interpretation of reality, not an unbiased objective description of it. The prescriptions of a model are therefore determined, at least in part, by the particular prior beliefs built into it by the model-builder. In agricultural commodity market modelling, the specification of models is far less contentious than in, say, macroeconomics, since all, or virtually all, originate in the same economic paradigm. There would certainly be differences of opinions concerning the more detailed aspects, however, such as the most appropriate functional forms, on which theory offers little guidance. Such matters of apparent detail can have significant implications. Different assumptions concerning the way in which price expectations are formed by agricultural producers, for example, can lead to radically different conclusions regarding the likely distribution between producers and consumers of welfare gains resulting from price stabilisation policy.[77] A recent comparison of simulation results from six international trade models revealed major differences in predictions of the effects of a five per cent reduction in US wheat production. Price increases predicted as a consequence ranged from 1.5 to 17.1 per cent for wheat, 2.3 to 12.9 per cent for coarse grains, and 4.4 to 20.8 per cent for soybeans.[78] Selection of the 'correct' model from among competing alternatives is not always straightforward. The various tests of specification and mis-specification may not always provide clear guidance.[79] Econometrics also faces methodological difficulties in the testing of the hypotheses implicit in trial specifications. In particular, the fulfilment of the auxiliary assumptions, such as accuracy of the data, in the formal testing procedures cannot be guaranteed.[80] Selection of a specification may therefore rely to a significant extent upon the degree of correspondence of parameter estimates with prior beliefs. In these circumstances, the conclusions to be reached are likely to be those expected.

Further Reading

Study of as wide a range of actual models as possible is perhaps the best way to gain an appreciation of the specification of agricultural commodity market models. As suggested at the end of Chapter 1, the academic agricultural economics journals can be a productive source of such material. The recommendations given here deal with general issues in specification. On the relevant basic economic theory and its translation into econometric model specifications, see F.G. Adams, 'Implementation of Commodity Market Theory in Empirical Econometric Models', in F.G. Adams and J.R. Behrman (eds.), *Econometric Modelling of World Commodity Policy* (D.C. Heath, Lexington, 1978), pp. 47-70. A review of the specification of particular types of equation - demand, supply and so on - is provided by Chapters 2 to 5 of W.C. Labys, *Dynamic Commodity Models: Specification, Estimation, Simulation* (D.C. Heath, Lexington, 1973). Chapter 6 discusses specification of complete models. Most econometrics textbooks review the various statistical models employed in econometric model-building. G.G. Judge, R.C. Hill, W.E. Griffiths, H. Lütkepohl and T. Lee, *Introduction to the Theory and Practice of Econometrics*, 2nd edn (Wiley, New York, 1982), Chs. 5,6,8 and 14 gives a good comprehensible survey of the nature, properties and estimation of those most frequently encountered. Dynamic models, distributed lags, adaptive expectations and partial adjustment models are described thoroughly in G.S. Maddala, *Econometrics* (McGraw-Hill, New York, 1977), Ch. 16. On the Nerlove supply model and its applications, see H. Askari, and J.T. Cummings, 'Estimating Agricultural Supply Response With the Nerlove Model: A Survey', *International Economic Review* , vol. 18, no. 2 (1977), pp. 257-292. Chapters 1 and 5 of S.M. Sheffrin, *Rational Expectations* (Cambridge University Press, Cambridge, 1983) discuss the concept of rational expectations and its application in market models. A wide range of varying parameter models are surveyed in Maddala, *Econometrics*, Ch. 17. For a detailed discussion of tests of specification and misspecification, nested and non-nested models, see A.C. Harvey, *Econometric Analysis of Time Series* (Philip Allan, Oxford, 1981), Ch. 5.

Notes

1. The techniques of exploratory data analysis are described by J.W. Tukey, *Exploratory Data Analysis* (Addison-Wesley, Reading, Mass., 1977).

2. The theoretical basis of this model and non-competitive market models are discussed in J.R. Behrman, 'International Commodity Market Structures and the Theory Underlying International Commodity Market Models', in F.G. Adams and J.R. Behrman (eds.), *Econometric Modelling of World Commodity Policy* (D.C. Heath, Lexington, 1978), pp. 9-45.

3. More formally the general linear statistical model can be expressed as follows. (i) $\mathbf{Y} = \mathbf{X}\beta + \varepsilon$, where $\mathbf{Y}$ is a nx1 vector of observations on the dependent variable Y, $\mathbf{X}$ is a nxk matrix each column of which is a vector of n observations on each of k independent or explanatory variables, β is a vector of k unknown parameters, and **e** is a vector of n unobservable random disturbances. (ii) $E(\varepsilon) = 0$. (iii) $E(\varepsilon\varepsilon') = \sigma^2\mathbf{I}$. (iv) $\mathbf{X}$ has rank $k < n$. (v) $\mathbf{X}$ is fixed.

4. See G.G. Judge, R.C. Hill, W.E. Griffiths, H. Lütkepohl and T. Lee, *Introduction to the Theory and Practice of Econometrics*, 2nd

edn (Wiley, New York, 1982), pp. 185-186 for a brief critique of the model.

5. The simultaneous linear statistical model is conventionally expressed as **YB** + **XA** = **E**. **Y** is a nxg matrix of n observations on each of g endogenous variables. **X** is a nxk matrix of n observations on each of k predetermined variables. **B** is a gxg matrix of coefficients on the current endogenous variables, with each column being the coefficients from one equation. Conventionally the diagonal elements of **B** are set equal to one, implying that, for example, the first endogenous variable is the dependent variable in the first equation and so on. Some elements will be zeros implying that the endogenous variable concerned does not appear in a certain equation. In the case of identities the elements will normally all be zeros or ones. **A** is a kxg matrix of coefficients on the predetermined variables, again with each column containing the coefficients from a particular equation. **E** is a nxg matrix of unobservable stochastic disturbances, with each column being a vector of the disturbances from one particular equation. For identities, of course, these will be zero. The disturbances are assumed to have the following properties: $E(\varepsilon_i) = 0$, for all i = 1,2, ... g; $E(\varepsilon_i \varepsilon_j') = \sigma_{ij}\mathbf{I}$ for all i,j = 1,2, .. g.

6. Multiplying through the structural form **YB** + **XA** = **E**, by the inverse of **B** gives $\mathbf{YBB}^{-1} + \mathbf{XAB}^{-1} = \mathbf{EB}^{-1}$, and rearranging gives $\mathbf{Y} = -\mathbf{XAB}^{-1} + \mathbf{EB}^{-1}$, or $\mathbf{Y} = \mathbf{X}\Pi + \mathbf{V}$, where $\Pi = -\mathbf{AB}^{-1}$, and $\mathbf{V} = \mathbf{EB}^{-1}$. Π is the kxg matrix of reduced form parameters, with π_{ij} showing the impact of a one unit change in the ith predetermined variable upon the jth endogenous variable, and **V** is the nxg matrix of reduced form disturbances.

7. See R. H. Strotz and H.O.A. Wold, 'Recursive v. Non-recursive Systems: An Attempt at Synthesis', *Econometrica*, vol. 28, no. 2 (1960), pp. 417-427, for a discussion of recursive models.

8. The matrix of structural parameters on the endogenous variables is therefore triangular in a recursive model.

9. For a slightly more elaborate recursive model see G. Stojkovic, 'Market Models for Agricultural Products' in H.O.A. Wold (ed.), *Econometric Model Building: Essays On the Causal Chain Approach* (North Holland, Amsterdam, 1964), pp. 386-419.

10. D.T. Chen, 'The Wharton Agricultural Model: Structure, Specification and Some Simulation Results', *American Journal of Agricultural Economics*, vol. 59, no. 1 (1977), pp. 107-116.

11. For a simple example of a recursive agricultural market model see D. Hallam, *Econometric Forecasting in the UK Egg Market* (Eggs Authority, Tunbridge Wells, 1981).

12. Thus, while the endogenous variables parameter matrix may no longer be triangular - it may be block-diagonal, in fact - the number of non-zero elements above the principal diagonal will be

small.

13. R.V. Bishop, 'The Construction and Use of Causality Tests', *Agricultural Economics Research*, vol. 31, no. 4 (1979), pp. 1-6 provides a simple review of causality testing.

14. See, for example, D.R. Colman and T. Young, *A Forecasting System for UK Grain and Oilseed Imports*, University of Manchester Department of Agricultural Economics Bulletin 179 (1981).

15. L.E. Salathe, J.M. Price and K.E. Gadson, 'The Food and Agricultural Policy Simulator: The Poultry and Egg Sector Submodel', *Agricultural Economics Research*, vol. 35, no. 1 (1983), pp. 23-34.

16. G. Fromm and G.R. Schink, 'Aggregation and Econometric Models', *International Economic Review*, vol. 14, no. 1 (1973), pp. 1-32. This would of course require the sum of the prediction error variances of the disaggregated variables to be less than the prediction error variance of the aggregate variable. See L.R. Klein and R.M. Young, *An Introduction to Econometric Forecasting and Forecasting Models* (D.C. Heath, Lexington, 1980), p. 54.

17. See, T. Grennes, P.R. Johnson and M. Thursby, *The Economics of World Grain Trade* (Praeger, New York, 1978), for example.

18. Where the equation has only one explanatory variable, the estimated 'macro-parameter' will be a weighted average of the corresponding 'micro-parameters' with weights equal to the slope coefficients of the auxiliary regressions of each micro-variable on the macro-variable. Where, as usual, there is more than one explanatory variable, the relationship between the estimated macro-parameters and the corresponding micro-parameters is more complex. The macro-parameters will be weighted averages of not only the corresponding micro-parameters, but also the 'non-corresponding' micro-parameters with weights equal to the slope coefficients of the auxiliary regressions of each micro-variable on *all* of the macro-variables in the equation. The situation becomes even more complex where the relationships involved are non-linear. See H. Theil, *Linear Aggregation of Economic Relations* (North Holland, Amsterdam, 1954).

19. Although this is the type of evidence quoted in most discussions of reform of agricultural price policy. M.E. Bond, 'Agricultural Responses to Prices in Sub-Saharan African Countries', *IMF Staff Papers*, vol. 30, no. 4 (1983), pp. 703-726, provides a survey.

20. See, for example, Behrman's 'mini models' described in F.G. Adams, 'Implementation of Commodity Market Theory in Empirical Econometric Models', in Adams and Behrman (eds.), *Econometric Modelling of World Commodity Policy*, pp.47-70.

21. D.F. Hendry and K.F.Wallis, 'Editors' Introduction' in D.F. Hendry and K.F.Wallis (eds.), *Econometrics and Quantitative*

Economics (Blackwell, Oxford, 1984), pp. 1-12.

22. A. Zellner, *Basic Issues in Econometrics* (University of Chicago Press, Chicago, 1984), p. 7.

23. See L.M. Goreux, 'Income and Food Consumption'', *FAO Monthly Bulletin of Economics and Statistics*, vol. 9, no. 10 (1960), pp. 1-12, for a survey.

24. The price elasticity, for example, is given by

$$\eta = \frac{\delta D}{\delta P} \cdot \frac{P}{D} = \frac{\beta(\alpha P^{\beta} Y^{\gamma} e^{u})}{P} \cdot \frac{P}{D} = \beta$$

25. Ministry of Agriculture, Fisheries and Food, *Household Food Consumption and Expenditure* (HMSO, London, annual).

26. For a discussion of the specification and estimation of intrinsically nonlinear models see Judge, Hill, Griffiths, Lütkepohl and Lee, *Introduction to the Theory and Practice of Econometrics*, Ch. 12.

27. See, for example, M.R. Wickens and J.N. Greenfield, 'The Econometrics of Agricultural Supply', *Review of Economics and Statistics*, vol. 55, no. 4 (1973), pp. 433-440.

28. L.M. Koyck, *Distributed Lags and Investment Analysis* (North Holland, Amsterdam, 1954).

29. S. Almon, 'The Distributed Lag Between Capital Appropriations and Expenditures', *Econometrica*, vol. 33, no. 1 (1965), pp. 178-196.

30. See, for example, Wickens and Greenfield, 'The Econometrics of Agricultural Supply'.

31. G.G. Judge, W.E. Griffiths, R.C. Hill, H. Lütkepohl and T. Lee, *The Theory and Practice of Econometrics*, 2nd edn (Wiley, New York, 1985) pp. 360-364, discusses procedures for determining the degree of polynomial and lag length where these are unknown.

32. M. Nerlove, *The Dynamics of Supply: Estimation of Farmers' Response to Price* (John Hopkins University Press, Baltimore, 1958).

33. H. Askari, and J.T. Cummings, 'Estimating Agricultural Supply Response With the Nerlove Model: A Survey', *International Economic Review*, vol. 18, no. 2 (1977), pp. 257-292.

34. H.E. Doran and W.E. Griffiths, 'Inconsistency of the OLS Estimator of the Partial Adjustment - Adaptive Expectations Model', *Journal of Econometrics*, vol. 7, no. 1 (1978), pp. 133-146.

35. C. Chung and G. Ukpong, 'The World Tea Economy: An Econometric Model of Its Structure, Performance and Prospects' in World Bank, *World Bank Commodity Models* (2 vols., World Bank, Washington, 1981), vol. 1, pp. V-1 - V-49.

36. See, for example, Wickens and Greenfield, 'Econometrics of Agricultural Supply'.

37. D. Hallam, 'Producers' Response to Supported and Free

Market Prices', *Journal of Agricultural Economics*, vol. 29, no. 2 (1978), pp. 119-131, and D. Hallam, 'An Econometric Model of the UK Egg Market', *Oxford Agrarian Studies*, vol. 14 (1985), pp. 170-191.

38. Originated by J.F. Muth, 'Rational Expectations and the Theory of Price Movements', *Econometrica*, vol. 29, no. 3 (1961), pp. 315-335. For a detailed discussion see S.M. Sheffrin, *Rational Expectations* (Cambridge University Press, Cambridge, 1983).

39. More precisely, an individual's subjective expectation of a variable are equal to the mathematical conditional expectation of that variable.

40. T.H. Goodwin and S.M. Sheffrin, 'Testing the Rational Expectations Hypothesis in an Agricultural Market', *Review of Economics and Statistics*, vol. 64, no. 4 (1982), pp. 658-667.

41. See, for example, Goodwin and Sheffrin, 'Testing the Rational Expectations Hypothesis in an Agricultural Market'. An alternative procedure is to make use of the property of rational expectations that they will be equal to realised values except for purely random errors. The realised values might therefore be used as proxies for their expectations, although because of the random errors they include this produces an *errors in variables* model as discussed in Chapter 3. Estimates of the parameters of the rational expectations model might, however, be obtained using instrumental variables estimation. This approach is followed by R.L. Huntzinger, 'Market Analysis With Rational Expectations', *Journal of Econometrics*, vol. 10, no. 1 (1979), pp. 127-145 in another study of the US broiler market. Instrumental variables estimation is discussed in Chapter 4.

42. Goodwin and Sheffrin, 'Testing the Rational Expectations Hypothesis in an Agricultural Market'; R.L. Huntzinger, 'Market Analysis With Rational Expectations'.

43. Sheffrin, *Rational Expectations*, pp. 11-17, reviews critiques of the rational expectations hypothesis.

44. C. Hildreth and J. Houck, 'Some Estimators for a Linear Model With Random Coefficients', *Journal of the American Statistical Association*, vol. 63, no. 322 (1968), pp. 584-595.

45. T. Cooley and E.C. Prescott, 'Varying Parameter Regression: A Theory and Some Applications', *Annals of Economic and Social Measurement*, vol. 2. no. 4 (1973), pp. 463-473.

46. R.W. Ward, 'Time Varying Demand for Oranges in the EEC', *Journal of Agricultural Economics*, vol. 33, no. 1 (1982), pp. 57-70.

47. Cooley and Prescott, 'Varying Parameter Regression: A Theory and Some Applications'.

48. Hallam, 'Producers Response to Supported and Free Market Prices' provides an example.

49. See J. Johnston, *Econometric Methods*, 3rd edn (McGraw-Hill, New York, 1984), pp. 393-396, for an introduction.

50. R.C. Fair and D.M. Jaffee, 'Methods of Estimation for Markets in Disequilibrium', *Econometrica*, vol. 40, no. 3 (1972), pp. 497-514.

51. The notion of an irreversible supply function as a result of asset fixity is usually attributed to G.L. Johnson, 'Supply Functions - Some Facts and Notions' in E.O. Heady, H.G. Dresslin, H.R. Jensen, and G.L. Johnson (eds.), *Agricultural Adjustment Problems in a Growing Economy* (Iowa State University Press, Ames, 1958), pp. 74-93. A more recent review of some theoretical aspects is provided by M.A. Johnson and E.C. Pasour Jnr., 'An Opportunity Cost View of Fixed Asset Theory and the Overproduction Trap', *American Journal of Agricultural Economics*, vol. 63, no. 1 (1981), pp. 1-7.

52. T. Young, 'Modelling Asymmetric Consumer Responses, With an Example', *Journal of Agricultural Economics*, vol. 31, no. 2 (1980), pp. 175-186, for example.

53. R. Wolffram, 'Positivistic Measures of Aggregate Supply Elasticities: Some New Approaches - Some Critical Notes', *American Journal of Agricultural Economics*, vol. 53, no. 2 (1971), pp. 356-359.

54. R.G. Saylor, 'Alternative Measures of Supply Elasticities: The Case of Sao Paulo Coffee', *American Journal of Agricultural Economics*, vol. 56, no. 1 (1974), pp. 98-106.

55. B. Traill, D.R. Colman and T. Young, 'Estimatimg Irreversible Supply Functions', *American Journal of Agricultural Economics*, vol. 60, no. 3 (1978), pp. 528-531.

56. Bayesian methods which incorporate and exploit prior information in a comprehensive and systematic fashion are not discussed here. See J.D. Hey, *Data in Doubt* (Martin Robertson, Oxford, 1983) for an introduction to Bayesian methods and their applications in econometrics.

57. Exact linear restrictions in the linear statistical model $\mathbf{Y} = \mathbf{X}\beta + \mathbf{e}$ can be summarised in the form $\mathbf{R}\beta = \mathbf{r}$, where $\mathbf{R}$ is a (qxk) matrix describing the nature of q restrictions concerning the k parameters of the model, the β's, and $\mathbf{r}$ is a known q element column vector. The restrictions that β_2 should be equal to the sum of β_3 and β_4, and that β_5 should be equal to some scalar n, for example, would be represented as

$$\begin{bmatrix} 0 & 1 & -1 & -1 & 0 \\ 0 & 0 & 0 & 0 & 1 \end{bmatrix} \begin{bmatrix} \beta_1 \\ \beta_2 \\ \beta_3 \\ \beta_4 \\ \beta_5 \end{bmatrix} = \begin{bmatrix} 0 \\ n \end{bmatrix}$$

Estimation of the restricted model using ordinary least squares involves finding those values for $\boldsymbol{\beta}$, $\boldsymbol{\beta}*$, which minimise $(\mathbf{Y} - \mathbf{X}\boldsymbol{\beta})'(\mathbf{Y} - \mathbf{X}\boldsymbol{\beta})$ subject to $\mathbf{R}\boldsymbol{\beta} = \mathbf{r}$, or $\mathbf{R}\boldsymbol{\beta} - \mathbf{r} = \mathbf{0}$. In the case of exact linear restrictions this can be accomplished using Lagrange multipliers giving the Lagrangian function $\mathbf{L} = (\mathbf{Y} - \mathbf{X}\boldsymbol{\beta}*)'(\mathbf{Y} - \mathbf{X}\boldsymbol{\beta}*) - 2\boldsymbol{\lambda}'(\mathbf{R}\boldsymbol{\beta}* - \mathbf{r})$, where $\boldsymbol{\lambda}$ is a column vector of q Lagrange multipliers. Minimising this and solving for $\boldsymbol{\beta}*$ yields the restricted least squares estimator $\boldsymbol{\beta}* = \boldsymbol{\beta} + (\mathbf{X}'\mathbf{X})^{-1}\mathbf{R}'[\mathbf{R}(\mathbf{X}'\mathbf{X})^{-1}\mathbf{R}']^{-1}(\mathbf{r} - \mathbf{R}\boldsymbol{\beta})$ where $\boldsymbol{\beta}$ is the unrestricted ordinary least squares estimator.

58. In the exact linear restrictions case, if the restrictions are incorrect, i.e. $\mathbf{R}\boldsymbol{\beta} - \mathbf{r} \neq \mathbf{0} = \boldsymbol{\delta}$, then $E(\boldsymbol{\beta}*) = \boldsymbol{\beta} + (\mathbf{X}'\mathbf{X})^{-1}\mathbf{R}'[\mathbf{R}(\mathbf{X}'\mathbf{X})^{-1}\mathbf{R}']^{-1}\boldsymbol{\delta}$ and $E[(\boldsymbol{\beta}* - E[\boldsymbol{\beta}*])(\boldsymbol{\beta}* - E[\boldsymbol{\beta}*])'] = \sigma^2(\mathbf{X}'\mathbf{X})^{-1} - \sigma^2(\mathbf{X}'\mathbf{X})^{-1}\mathbf{R}'[\mathbf{R}(\mathbf{X}'\mathbf{X})^{-1}\mathbf{R}']^{-1}\mathbf{R}(\mathbf{X}'\mathbf{X})^{-1}$.

59. Suppose the 'correct' model is $\mathbf{Y} = \mathbf{X}\boldsymbol{\beta} + \mathbf{u}$, where $\mathbf{X}$ is a nxk matrix of n observations on each of k explanatory variables, but the 'incorrect' model $\mathbf{Y} = \mathbf{Z}\boldsymbol{\alpha} + \mathbf{v}$ is specified, where $\mathbf{Z}$ is an nxj matrix of n observations on each of j explanatory variables. j is not equal to k but $\mathbf{Z}$ may have some columns in common with $\mathbf{X}$.

The ordinary least squares estimator for $\boldsymbol{\alpha}$, $\mathbf{a}$, is $\mathbf{a} = (\mathbf{Z}'\mathbf{Z})^{-1}\mathbf{Z}'\mathbf{Y} = (\mathbf{Z}'\mathbf{Z})^{-1}\mathbf{Z}'\mathbf{X}\boldsymbol{\beta} + (\mathbf{Z}'\mathbf{Z})^{-1}\mathbf{Z}'\mathbf{u}$. Taking expected values, $E(\mathbf{a}) = \mathbf{P}\boldsymbol{\beta}$, where $\mathbf{P} = (\mathbf{Z}'\mathbf{Z})^{-1}\mathbf{Z}'\mathbf{X}$. The columns of $\mathbf{P}$ are the vectors of regression coefficients obtained by regressing each column of $\mathbf{X}$ on $\mathbf{Z}$. If relevant variables are omitted, $\mathbf{Z}$ will have k-j fewer columns than $\mathbf{X}$, and $\mathbf{P}$ will be the jxk matrix

$$\begin{bmatrix} 1 & 0 & . & . & 0 & r_{1,j+1} & . & . & . & r_{1,k} \\ 0 & 1 & . & . & 0 & r_{2,j+1} & . & . & . & r_{2,k} \\ . & . & . & . & . & . & . & . & . & . \\ . & . & . & . & . & . & . & . & . & . \\ 0 & 0 & . & . & 1 & r_{j,j+1} & . & . & . & r_{j,k} \end{bmatrix}$$

[**I R**] where **I** is a jxj identity matrix and **R** is the jx(k-j) matrix of regression coefficients with each element r_{nm} the coefficient of the regression of the mth column of **X** on the nth column of **Z**. $E(a_i)$ will therefore be equal to $\beta_i + r_{i,j+1}\beta_{j+1} + \ldots + r_{i,k}\,\beta_k$. If irrelevant variables are included, **Z** will have j-k more columns than **X**, and **P** will be the jxk matrix [**I 0**]' where **I** is a kxk identity matrix and **0** is a (j-k)xk null matrix.

60. Where a specification is chosen on the basis of the outcome of a hypothesis test a *pre-test* estimator is involved which can be biased. See T.D. Wallace, 'Pretest Estimation in Regression: A Survey', *American Journal of Agricultural Economics*, vol. 59, no. 3 (1977), pp. 431-443.

61. For a review see A.C. Harvey, *Econometric Analysis of Time Series* (Philip Allan, Oxford, 1981), Ch. 5.

62. R^2 = SSR / SST or (1 - (SSE / SST)) where SSR is the *regression* or *explained sum of squares*, $\Sigma\,(\hat{y}_i - \bar{Y})^2$, SST is the *total sum of squares*, $\Sigma\,(y_i - \bar{Y})^2$, and SSE is the *error* or *residual sum of squares*, $\Sigma\, e_i^2$.

63. H. Theil, *Introduction to Econometrics* (Prentice-Hall, Englewood Cliffs, 1978), pp. 271-273.

64. J. Rouhiainen, 'The Problem of Changing Parameters in Demand Analysis and Forecasting', *European Review of Agricultural Economics*, vol. 5, no. 3/4 (1978), pp. 349-359, provides an example in the context of modelling European cereal demand.

65. $u_t = \rho u_{t-1} + \varepsilon_t$, where ε_τ is a random disturbance with zero mean, constant variance, and zero covariance.

66. Tables of critical values of the Durbin-Watson statistic for different levels of significance and different sample sizes and numbers of explanatory variables are available in most econometrics textbooks. In testing for positive autocorrelation the estimated value of d is compared with the tabled values for the appropriate number of

observations and explanatory variables. If the estimated value is lower than the tabled lower value then the hypothesis of no positive autocorrelation is rejected. If the estimated value exceeds the upper tabled values the hypothesis is not rejected. If the estimated value falls between the two tabled values the test is inconclusive. The test is only appropriate for large samples and d is biased towards two where a lagged dependent variable appears among the explanatory variables. Where a lagged value of the dependent variable does appear among the explanatory variables, an appropriate statistic is the Durbin *h* statistic introduced in J. Durbin, 'Testing for Serial Correlation in Least Squares Regression When Some of the Regressors Are Lagged Dependent Variables', *Econometrica*, vol. 38, no. 3 (1970), pp. 410-421.

67. S.M. Goldfeld and R.E. Quandt, 'Some Tests for Homoscedasticity', *Journal of the American Statistical Association*, vol. 60, no. 310 (1965), pp. 539-547. A less restrictive test in terms of the form of heteroscedasticity assumed is provided by T.S. Breusch and A.R. Pagan, 'A Simple Test for Heteroscedasticity and Random Coefficient Variation', *Econometrica*, vol. 47, no. 5 (1979), pp. 1287-1294. Judge, Griffiths, Hill, Lutkepohl and Lee, *The Theory and Practice of Econometrics*, pp. 445-454 provides a detailed review of tests for heteroscedasticity.

68. J.G. Thursby and P. Schmidt, 'Some Properties of Tests For Specification Error in a Linear Regression Model', *Journal of the American Statistical Association*, vol. 72, no. 359 (1977), pp. 635-641.

69. G.C. Chow, 'Tests of Equality Between Sets of Coefficients in Two Linear Regressions', *Econometrica*, vol. 28, no. 3 (1960), pp. 591-605. The test statistic is

$$\frac{(SSE_{1+2} - SSE_1 - SSE_2)/k}{(SSE_1 + SSE_2)/(n + m - 2k)}$$

where subscripts 1 and 2 refer to the two regimes, k is the number of explanatory variables, n and m are the numbers of observations under the two regimes. The statistic, distributed as F with k and (n+m-2k) degrees of freedom, is used to test the hypothesis of no change in the corresponding parameters between the two regimes. Hallam, 'Producers Response to Supported and Free Market Prices' provides an example of its application.

70. To test the hypothesis that some estimated parameter, β, is zero against the alternative hypothesis that it is significantly different from zero, the test statistic is $t = \beta / s.e.(\beta)$ where s.e. (β) is the estimated standard error of β. The hypothesis is rejected if the

estimated t-value exceeds the tabled critical value.

71. In the linear model $\mathbf{Y} = \mathbf{X}\beta + \varepsilon$, an F-test of the hypothesis that the parameters, with the exception of the intercept, are jointly zero uses the test statistic F = (SSR / (k - 1)) / (SSE / (T - k)) which is distributed as F with (k - 1) and (T - k) degrees of freedom. Where one specification, equation 1, differs from an alternative, equation 2, in including q - k additional variables, the hypothesis that the associated additional parameters are jointly zero can be tested using the test statistic F = $((SSR_1 - SSR_2) / (q - k)) / (SSE_1 / (T - q))$ which is distributed as F with (q - k) and (T - q) degrees of freedom.

72. To test the hypothesis that the k parameters of a model are indeed subject to a set of r restrictions, the appropriate test statistic is F = $((SSE_* - SSE) / r) / (SSE / (T - k))$, where the subscript $*$ refers to the restricted model, and which is distributed as F with r and (T - k) degrees of freedom.

73. E.R. Berndt and N.E. Savin, 'Conflict Among Criteria for Testing Hypotheses in the Multivariate Linear Regression Model', *Econometrica*, vol. 45, no. 5 (1977), pp. 1263-1277.

74. Maximum likelihood estimation is discussed in Chapter 4. Briefly, maximum likelihood estimators of β and σ^2 are those which maximise the likelihood of obtaining the values of the variables in the current data set. They are obtained by maximisation of the likelihood function, which expresses the probability of obtaining the sample observations, with respect to these unknown parameters.

75. The likelihood ratio test compares the maximum value of the likelihood function obtained under the restricted and unrestricted models. If the restrictions are valid then that for the restricted model should not be significantly less than that for the unrestricted model. The Wald test involves estimation of the unrestricted model only, and tests whether $\mathbf{R}(\beta) - \mathbf{r} = \mathbf{0}$, i.e. whether the restrictions are correct. The Lagrange multiplier test involves estimation of the restricted model only, and tests whether the derivative of the likelihood function with respect to β evaluated using the restrictions is significantly different from zero, i.e. significantly different from the value it would take in the absence of the restrictions. The three tests, their rationale, and the relationships between them are discussed in Judge, Griffiths, Hill, Lütkepohl and Lee, *The Theory and Practice of Econometrics*, pp. 182-187 and pp. 215-217.

76. In the more general case, the competing models may have some explanatory variables in common. These are obviously not included twice in the creation of the general model. An alternative procedure for creating the general model is followed by the J-test proposed by R. Davidson and J.G. Mackinnon, 'Several Tests for Model Specification in the Presence of Alternative Hypotheses',

Econometrica, vol. 49, no. 3 (1981), pp. 781-793. Here the general model is created by using fitted values of the dependent variable obtained from each nonnested model as an additional explanatory variable in the other. t-tests or likelihood ratio tests of whether the estimated coefficients upon these additional variables are significantly different from zero are undertaken.

77. S.J. Turnovsky, 'The Distribution of Welfare Gains from Price Stabilisation: A Survey of Some Theoretical Issues', in F.G. Adams and S.A. Klein (eds.), *Stabilising World Commodity Markets* (D.C. Heath, Lexington, 1978), pp. 119-148.

78. K.D. Meilke, 'A Comparison of the Simulation Results from Six International Trade Models', University of Guelph Department of Agricultural Economics and Business Working Paper WP87/3, 1987.

79. Berndt and Savin, 'Conflict Among Criteria for Testing Hypotheses in the Multivariate Linear Regression Model'.

80. I.M.T. Stewart, *Reasoning and Method in Economics* (McGraw-Hill, London, 1979).

3
Data Problems

Number 6. 'What do you want?'
Number 2. 'Information.'
Number 6. 'You won't get it.'

(*The Prisoner*)

Collection of appropriate data from which to estimate its parameters usually follows the initial specification of a theory model, although as noted in the preceding chapters, the nature and characteristics of the available data might be regarded as an important consideration in the specification of the statistical model. Relevant data series for the variables (perhaps with the exception of inventories) of the basic agricultural market model discussed in Chapters 1 and 2 can usually be obtained, although the quality and quantity of the data available will vary from country to country and from commodity to commodity. There will, however, inevitably be gaps.

In general, agricultural commodity data are more plentiful for the production level than for later stages in the marketing chain. While series can usually be obtained for areas planted, yields, producer prices and so on, there is often little or no information available suitable for econometric analysis for quantities and prices at wholesale level, in processing, for inventories, and sometimes even for retail or final consumption. What data there are may relate only to one particular marketing channel - usually the official one. This type of data is important in disaggregation of the basic market model since it is often useful to distinguish between different end uses and the passage of produce towards them. In some countries, for example, marketing can be through official and 'parallel' marketing channels - a division which can involve quite different returns to the producer, and which is of some significance in the design of marketing reforms.

A chapter on data inevitably focuses its attention upon the weaknesses rather than the strengths of the data. In spite of this, data availability and its quality are often superior for agricultural commodity markets than for those in other sectors. This is in part due to the long history of government intervention in agricultural and food markets and the administrative and information needs of that intervention. The position does, of course, vary from country to country. For some less developed countries, which can be important in the production of particular agricultural commodities, the data base can be poor. For most countries, however, agricultural economic statistics are readily available from ministries, central banks, marketing boards and commissions, and trade associations, and there are often far more data available than are actually published. Some countries produce helpful annual compendiums of agricultural statistics. Agricultural commodity market data are also collected and published by international organisations. The most notable of these is the United Nations Food and Agriculture Organisation with its annual *Production Yearbook* which presents statistics on a country by country basis, of areas cultivated, yields and production for a wide range of crops, livestock numbers, meat, milk and egg production, and associated producer price data. For some commodities, such as coffee, there are international organisations responsible for market regulation which publish detailed and often short-run price and quantity data.[1]

The Nature of Economic Data

The discussion of the nature of econometrics in Chapter 1 emphasised the central role of data in model-building. In fact, that role is multi-faceted. The data are not only the raw materials used in the attempt to model the real world, for example, they *are* the real world, or at least they are what is taken to reveal the real world in assessing the success or otherwise of that attempt. The characteristics and quality of the data input will obviously have an important influence upon the properties and validity of an econometric model and the conclusions which can be drawn from it - a position usually summarised in the maxim 'rubbish in - rubbish out'. Sadly, the presumption that published economic data are to varying extents 'rubbish' is common, and in some cases perhaps justified. It is essential when drawing conclusions from an econometric analysis that the nature of the data upon which it is based is taken into account whatever their quality .

A common assumption implicit in much econometric work is that there exist exact measured counterparts for the variables of the theory model. The model to be estimated defined in terms of the available data is therefore the same as the theory model except for the stochastic disturbance term.[2] In practice such an exact relationship will rarely exist. The reasons for this lie in the nature of the actual processes which generate economic data, the non-participation of the econometric model-builder in data collection, and possible biases in the data collection methodology.

Unlike the researcher in some of the natural sciences, the econometric model-builder does not collect observations on the variables of his or her model as the outcomes of experiments. Observations are generated non-experimentally by complex and dynamic real world economic processes over which the model-builder has no control. Third variables cannot be held constant making it difficult or impossible to identify and quantify relationships between one variable and another. The real world data generating processes are themselves changing as a result of, for example, policy interventions or technological change. The model-builder therefore is faced with a moving target. A period of stable behaviour may not be long enough to yield sufficient observations for model-building.[3] Where an adequate number of observations can be obtained they may display insufficient variability to allow reliable parameter estimation.[4] In short, the non-experimental origins of the data the econometric model-builder has to use can mean that observations on the variables of a model may not contain sufficient information to allow reliable estimates of the model's parameters.

Typically the model-builder has no direct involvement in the collection of data employed for model-building. Rather they will be collected by other individuals or organisations, usually for purposes quite other than econometric model-building. It is the needs of these other purposes, such as administration, policy-making or market intelligence, which will determine which data are collected, how and when. It is unlikely that these imperatives will be such as to produce data which are ideal from the model-building point of view. The length of the series of observations may be inadequate for model-building, and there may be gaps or inconsistencies in it due to changes in the data collection methodology over time. The available data may not correspond exactly with the variables of the theory model, in which case the variables in the model will be measured with error. Theory models for their part do not always suggest precise definitions for their variables, of course. There may in fact be no measured counterpart either because for administrative reasons information concerning the variable in question is not collected, or because the variable - expected price or consumer tastes, for example - is inherently unmeasureable in which case some proxy must be found. In other cases the model-builder might have to select a set of measurements from several potential candidates for the same variable. Where there is not sufficient quantity data to allow computation of a weighted average price, for example, it may be necessary to select and use the most representative of the prices for different grades or in different markets as the 'average'.

A further practical problem arises from the separation of the model-builder from the data collection process. Because of this separation the user of data is often in a position of some ignorance concerning the exact nature of the data with which he or she is working. The information provided with published data is not always entirely helpful. While precise definitions of what the measurements are supposed to represent may be given, albeit sometimes in some publication distinct from that which contains the actual figures, there is not always sufficient information provided for the user of data to judge how successful the figures are likely to be in representing what they are supposed to represent. Meat production statistics, for example, may only cover production in inspected abattoirs which in many countries can account for only a small proportion of the total. Trade statistics only include legal trade passing through customs, but smuggling to obtain higher producer prices or to avoid exchange controls might account for a significant proportion. Recourse to the actual suppliers of the data is not always informative, particularly where the data concerned are historic. Uncertainty as to the likely validity of the data is increased where the model-builder has only an imperfect knowledge of the phenomena being modelled: most model-builders have little if any direct experience or prior knowledge of the markets and production processes they are called upon to model.

Even where the measured data are in principle a reasonable approximation to the theory variables, economic data seem to be prone to various deficiencies. Published data series can be disrupted by missing observations, and inconsistencies due to changing definitions and methodologies. Measurements can be infrequent. Agricultural censuses, the most comprehensive and consistent data source for the agricultural sector, can be undertaken only every five or ten years, for example, and some countries have never had one. The number of observations available for analysis can be limited, therefore. Errors in the actual measurements may also be commonplace. Of the data series which are available, not all will represent direct measurements of the variables concerned but rather will be derived from other series. Output statistics, for example, may be derived from an estimate of land area or livestock numbers multiplied by estimated yield per unit area or per animal. The values of some variables may be determined as residuals after all else is accounted for from some total amount. Domestic consumption of a perishable product, for example, might be determined from measurements of domestic output after addition of imports and subtraction of exports. The relationship between some data series and the variables they are intended to represent may be even more tenuous. Livestock population statistics in some countries, for example, have been known to be derived by the simple application of a constant growth rate from some base year population measurement or estimate. Whatever the closeness of the relationship between what it is intended to measure and theory variables, in practice there can be significant divergencies. The combination of all these difficulties means that substantial 'massaging' of the data is often required before they can be used for model building.

The greater the disaggregation of the model the greater the data requirements in terms of detailed measurements. Data limitations may set the limit on the degree of disaggregation which is possible. Unfortunately many data series are for aggregated categories. Estimates of output, for example, may be national totals and not specified according to the nature of the production unit. Thus, they may not differentiate between, say, smallholder and plantation production, yet the division might be important for policy purposes and economic behaviour of the two sectors might be expected to differ. Separate treatment in modelling supply of the product concerned might, therefore, be required. Similarly, measurements of livestock numbers might again be only national totals, not broken down into the decision-making categories such as 'breeding herd' or 'young stock'. Modelling actual decision-making can therefore be problematic.

Assembly of useable data series for variables of interest is frequently one of the more challenging aspects of econometric modelling, and can be particularly so for those agricultural commodity markets where those less developed countries with weak data collection services can be the most important sources of supply. The quantity and quality of the data available can be a binding constraint upon the nature of econometric analysis which is possible. Econometric modelling is perhaps the most demanding of the modelling methodologies in this respect. In some cases the data available may not be adequate to support an econometric approach at all and some other methodology must be adopted. In other cases, perhaps more commonly, inadequate data may prevent the modelling of a complete set of commodity market relationships and will permit modelling of only certain aspects of the market. As with the drunk searching for his keys under a streetlamp because of the better illumination there despite knowing they were dropped elsewhere, the direction and nature of econometric research is inevitably dictated by the data available.

The Problem of Multicollinearity

Because the model-builder has no control over the design of the experiment which society conducts and which generates data for econometric analyses, it is not possible to hold variables constant allowing the specific impact of individual variables to be examined. In practice, all variables will be changing at once - often producing sample data series with similar patterns in time. Such similarities can arise in a variety of circumstances, but the typical variables of agricultural commodity market models are perhaps particularly prone. Product prices and input prices in supply equations can move together over time; in pig and poultry production, for example, feed costs can account for as much as 70 per cent of total costs so inevitably product and feed prices are closely related. In demand equations similar patterns might be observed in the time series of the price of the product of interest and the prices of substitute and complementary products, or incomes. Successive lagged terms in distributed lag models are also likely to be closely related as described in Chapter 2. Where such similarities can be described as an approximately linear relationship between variables there is a problem of multicollinearity.

In most equations, complete linear independence, or *orthogonality*, of the variables is unlikely given their nature, although this is the state of affairs which is typically assumed to prevail. Perfect multicollinearity, where one variable is an exact linear function of one or more other variables, is also unusual. Under these circumstances, estimation of individual coefficients becomes impossible. Multicollinearity is a question of degree rather than kind. Some degree of multicollinearity is perhaps the rule rather than the exception for economic data series. The difficulty lies in unequivocally detecting the presence of multicollinearity and in deciding when it becomes harmful.

The estimated parameters of an equation supposedly show the effects on the dependent variable of a one unit change in the explanatory variable on the assumption that the values of all other explanatory variables are held constant. If there is multicollinearity this assumption will be unjustified since movements in one explanatory variable will be matched by movements in one or more of the other explanatory variables. There will be insufficient independent variation in the explanatory variables to disentangle their separate effects. More precisely, estimates of a model's parameters might be obtained which are unbiased, that is equal to the true values of those parameters on average, but they will be unreliable in the sense of having variances larger than they otherwise would.[5, 6] As a result, confidence intervals for estimated parameters will be wider than they otherwise would have been and the results of statistical hypothesis tests concerning their values may be misleading. There may be a tendency to indicate that particular parameters are not significantly different from zero, for example, which could lead to the unjustified decision to drop a variable from the analysis. The paradoxical situation can arise where none of the estimated coefficients on the explanatory variables appear to be significantly different from zero, yet measures of the overall goodness of fit, such as R^2, suggest that the equation as a whole explains well. Where a high degree of multicollinearity is present parameter estimates can be highly unstable. Slight changes in the data set used or in the specification adopted can lead to large variations in the magnitudes of estimated parameters and even changes in their signs. Multicollinearity can therefore be seriously disruptive. Some limited comfort might be drawn from the fact that multicollinearity need not adversely affect the predictive powers of a model provided that the pattern and nature of multicollinearity remain unchanged through the prediction period.

While multicollinearity to some degree may be assumed to be commonly present amongst the explanatory variables of agricultural commodity market models, detecting when that degree becomes harmful with the adverse consequences outlined above, ascertaining its nature, and removing or mitigating its harmful effects are problematic.

Detection of harmful multicollinearity is normally based on a recognition of the symptoms, such as large variances or unstable parameter estimates, outlined above, although multicollinearity is not the only cause of such problems. Various *ad hoc* procedures have been suggested for detecting the presence of harmful multicollinearity although they do not constitute formal tests, and are unsatisfactory in not always being conclusive or suggestive of possible remedies.[7] Unstable parameter estimates and large estimated variances which lead to the apparent non-significance of relevant explanatory variables in combination with a high overall degree of explanation indicated by R^2 for the equation are usually taken to be indicative of multicollinearity. Large variances are not an unequivocal indicator of multicollinearity, however, since they might also be due to insufficient variation in the data sets for the variables concerned. There is also a tendency to blame multicollinearity for any failures of estimated parameters to correspond with prior expectations. A close linear relationship between two variables would be revealed by a simple correlation coefficient. Since this only considers one pair of variables it can be misleading: pairwise correlations among a set of variables might be low suggesting no multicollinearity even when there is a close linear relationship involving three or more explanatory variables. Linear relationships among explanatory variables might also be investigated by undertaking regressions of each variable in turn upon one or more of the others, and examining the explanatory power of the resulting equations. There will almost always be some relationship, however, and it is not easy to decide at what point this becomes indicative of harmful multicollinearity. In any case it may not be possible from such regressions to discern the exact nature of multicollinearity and hence identify possible solutions. Another possibility is to drop each variable from an equation in turn and examine the consequences for the overall goodness of fit of the equation. If a variable is part of a multicollinear relationship then its influence upon the dependent variable will be largely carried by the other variables in the equation. Dropping such a variable should not lead to any appreciable decline in the overall explanatory power of the model. Again, however, the amount of useful information this procedure reveals about the nature and the pattern of multicollinearity is limited.

As with the approaches to detection of multicollinearity, so the procedures applied in an attempt to remove it are in many cases *ad hoc*.[8] Furthermore, some of those 'corrections' most commonly applied only reduce multicollinearity at the expense of introducing a new and different problem.

Since multicollinearity is a problem of the sample data, an obvious, though rarely practicable, solution is to obtain more or different data which are free of multicollinearity. If possible, additional observations might extend the time series available, quarterly data might be used in place of annual observations, or an alternative relevant data set might be substituted. Scope for such adjustments is sometimes limited, however, because the model-builder is not always in a position to choose between different measurements of the same variable, or to leave any observations unused. Where more or different data are not available, the way in which the existing data are used in the model might be changed. An average of several collinear variables might be used, or perhaps one variable taken to be representative. Such a procedure might be applied where, for example, several price variables appear in one supply or demand equation. A more sophisticated variant of this is the use of *principal components* which are essentially weighted averages of the collinear variables reflecting their combined variation. Another possibility is to use *first differences* - the changes in rather than the levels of variables - in the hope that any close linear relationship between the levels would not be echoed in the changes. Unfortunately, while multicollinearity might be reduced, autocorrelation might be introduced since the disturbance term of the first differences equation would involve the current and preceding period's disturbances of the original equation. The ordinary least squares estimator would therefore no longer have the minimum variance and be less reliable. Collinear variables might also be combined in the form of ratios. In some cases the use of ratios might be theoretically more appropriate. In supply equations, for example, it may be the ratio of output prices to input prices which more closely reflects the considerations upon which supply decisions are made. Rather than rearranging the variables, relationships between the values which parameters can take, as in the *a priori* distributed lag schemes discussed in Chapter 2, can be specified where obtaining reliable independent estimates is problematic.

A collinear variable can also be removed from the equation to be estimated by making use of estimates of its coefficients obtained elsewhere and incorporating the restriction that the parameter has that value. The data on the dependent variable can then be corrected for the effect of the collinear variable and estimation proceeds as usual using this corrected form. In the demand function

$$\ln D_t = \beta \ln P_t + \delta \ln Y_t + \upsilon_t$$

(where D is quantity demanded, P is price, Y is income, β is price elasticity, δ is income elasticity, and υ is a disturbance term), for example, price and income may prove to be collinear. If an estimate of the income elasticity, δ^*, can be obtained from elsewhere, perhaps from a household budget survey, the restriction that $\delta = \delta^*$ can be incorporated and the equation rearranged to give

$$\ln D_t - \delta^* \ln Y_t = \beta \ln P_t + \upsilon_t$$

This equation can then be estimated.[9] The basic problem is to obtain an estimate of the income elasticity which is relevant to the whole of the time series on quantity demanded.

A common but rather drastic solution to the multicollinearity problem is simply to drop collinear variables from the model. The multicollinearity problem is removed but at the expense of specification error. As Chapter 2 explained, the omission of a relevant variable will produce biased estimates of the model's remaining parameters. The model-builder, therefore, has to trade-off the large variances resulting from multicollinearity against the bias resulting from specification error.[10]

Another common response to multicollinearity is in fact to do nothing. The apparent presence of serious multicollinearity is noted along with the presentation of estimation results, perhaps with some comments as to its possible implications for the reliability of the parameter estimates. Given the limitations of many of the suggested remedies, this may be a realistic response to a chronic and persistent problem. On the other hand, the temptation to blame multicollinearity for any infelicities, such as unexpected signs or magnitudes, in an estimated model should be resisted.

Inadequate Sample Size and Missing Observations

The greater the amount of data available for modelling, the more reliable - in the sense that estimated parameters will have smaller variances - will the results of that modelling be. Unfortunately there are many factors which militate against the availability of long data series, limiting the distance a useable series can extend into the past and the proximity with which it can approach the present.

Changes in policies, institutions, market structures and

technology all contribute to the constant modification of the behaviour patterns of market participants. The introduction of guaranteed producer prices, for example, by reducing price uncertainty can encourage greater levels of supply than would have been offered had the same prices been generated by the operation of market forces.[11] Supply at all prices might also be increased by improvements in the efficiency of agricultural marketing systems, as is envisaged in the various liberalisation programmes being mounted in Africa.[12] The value of historic data describing historic behaviour patterns in modelling current market behaviour, and particularly as a basis for predicting future behaviour can, therefore, be limited. The length of a useable time series of observations on variables of interest can be correspondingly curtailed as the relevance of observations diminishes the further into the past one goes. In some cases, of course, the distance one can go into the past with a time series will be limited to the starting point of that series. Collection and publication of data for some products may be a recent development. The availability of sufficient relevant data for analysis always lags behind developments in production, marketing and consumption since official statistics collection must first recognise the need for adaptation to changing circumstances, and then further time must elapse before an adequate number of observations builds up to permit econometric analysis. In Western Europe and North America increasing concentration in food retailing and the shortening of the agricultural marketing chain is not yet reflected in the available price data for many agricultural commodities. These data often still relate to prices realised in traditional marketing channels now by-passed by the greater proportion of produce. The trigger which leads to the inclusion of coverage of a product can be that it has recently grown in importance or is expected to do so. While there may be a certain amount of interest in analyses relating to that product, sufficient data to accomplish these may not yet have amassed. Many tropical countries are interested in the possibility of diversifying their exports into tropical fruits, for example, and the indications are that there is substantial scope for success in this policy. Because they receive only limited, if any, coverage in the trade and consumption statistics of the importing countries, it is difficult to analyse the current and predict the future demand for these horticultural exports.[13]

Delays in the publication of current or recent data can squeeze the length of time series of observations from the other end. Data collection, analysis, and eventual publication can be enormous and complex tasks, particularly in the case of agricultural census data, and involve a considerable amount of time and effort. This can mean that observations on crucial variables such as areas of crops planted or livestock numbers are simply not available for the most recent periods. It can be several years before all census data are processed and published. Provisional figures are sometimes released but these, and indeed sometimes 'final' figures, can be subject to substantial revisions.

Just as new data series can be added to the list of those collected and published so the collection and publication of existing series may be terminated. This might be because the variable measured has become unimportant, at least from the point of view of the data collection agency, or simply for financial or administrative reasons. The requirements of econometric model-building will rarely be a major consideration in official data collection exercises.

Where they are available, and where they are appropriate to the production and marketing cycle of the commodity in question, quarterly or monthly data can obviously provide certain advantages over annual data. They allow either an increased number of observations for any given data period, or a similar number of observations but for a shorter, perhaps more recent and relevant period. Quarterly or monthly data may also allow more effective modelling of short-run variations in quantities and prices. With short-period data greater detail in modelling the direction and strength of causal relationships between variables can be achieved, reducing simultaneity and even allowing the specification of a recursive model. At the same time, however, such data can involve greater risk of autocorrelation.[14]

Irrespective of the overall length of a time series, and even if market behaviour remains unchanged through time such that all observations are potentially relevant, data series can still prove inadequate because of the difficulty of obtaining sufficient *consistent* measurements of the variables concerned. There are many cases where this will not be so, once again largely arising from the fact that data are collected for administrative rather than econometric purposes. The whole basis of a data collection exercise can be revised either in terms of its coverage, timing, regularity, methodology, or definitions employed, producing discontinuities in the series of observations on the variables concerned. In 1970, for example, the coverage of the United Kingdom agricultural census was changed from 'agricultural holdings' to 'commercially significant' holdings, and in 1973 there was a further change when the definition of what constitutes a 'commercially significant' holding was revised. The particular time at which a variable is measured can have an important bearing on the value recorded, particularly where livestock are concerned. Morgenstern, in his book *On the Accuracy of Economic Observations*, notes a particularly subtle example of this. On 1st January 1910, there were 527,311 pigs in Bulgaria. Ten years later on 1st January 1920, there were 1,089,699. The explanation for these figures was not that the number of pigs had doubled, but rather that the calendar had changed. Between the two observations, Bulgaria switched from the Julian to the Gregorian calendar, although the religious festivals remained unchanged. In 1920, on the new calendar, Christmas day was on 9th January. Census day on 1st January was therefore eight days before Christmas with that half of the pig population destined for Christmas dinner still alive and unaware of the fate to befall them.[15]

Some discontinuities are relatively easily dealt with. Many economic data series, particularly price series, are presented in index number form. The base year for such indices tends to be changed every few years. Splicing index numbers on to a common base year is easily accomplished.[16,17] Problems can arise, however, where the index number is representative of a group of commodities - an index of cereal prices, for example. A perfect splice might not be obtained if the change in base year is accompanied by changes in the weighting given to the different commodities in the calculation of the overall index.

Obtaining data series of adequate length to support the modelling of variables of interest is a major practical problem in modelling of agricultural commodity markets. In extreme cases, the amount of data available may be too limited to support econometric analysis, since the number of observations must exceed the number of parameters to be estimated.[18] The narrower is the gap between the number of observations and the number of parameters to be estimated the less reliable will be the resulting parameter estimates.[19]

It is not uncommon to find observations missing from one or more of the data series needed for model-building. Such gaps can be random, the result of unpredictable events such as strikes, wars, or outbreaks of livestock diseases, which temporarily prevent the collection or publication of data. In other cases, the gaps can be more systematic. Some series may only be available on an annual basis when quarterly data are required. The starting or end points of the available data series for the different variables of a model may vary for some of the reasons mentioned above. Data series for some variables may therefore contain fewer observations than the rest. Faced with missing observations the model-builder has to decide whether to limit the data period used for estimation to the extent of the longest unbroken series of observations common to all of the data series involved, or to attempt to fill in the gaps left by the missing observations with estimated values. If the former course of action is decided upon then it is possible that the number of observations which remain may be limited, with the adverse consequences outlined above. If the latter course of action is decided upon, then there is the possibility that the estimated values may not be particularly accurate. The consequences of this are discussed later in this chapter.

There are several ways in which gaps in a data series might arise and might be filled.[20] Where one or more observations are missing from within a series the gaps can be filled by *interpolation*. If only one observation is missing then the simplest form of interpolation is to take the average of the two adjoining observations. The same kind of *straight-line interpolation* might also be used where more than one observation is missing. An attempt might be made to take into account the trend in the data in determining the interpolated values. Interpolated values for the missing observations might be read off from a trend line fitted through the observations of the incomplete data series. More sophisticated Box-Jenkins type autoregressive models might also be used. Interpolations might be based upon movements in a related series for which complete sets of observations are available, rather than the incomplete series itself. The same percentage changes from one period to the next, or similar trends might be assumed to apply. Gaps in a series of cattle numbers, for example, might be interpolated using a series on meat output. Similar techniques might be used to *extrapolate* a data series which is shorter than those available for the other variables in the model. The appropriate means for conversion of temporally aggregated data to a less aggregated basis - annual to quarterly values, for example - depends upon the nature of the aggregated data. Where the observations are measurements at a particular point in time then interpolation methods of the kind described above might be used. Where the observations are totals cumulated over some relatively long time period - a year, for example, when quarterly values are required - then the values for the shorter time periods must be estimated by *distribution* of the cumulated total between them. The simplest procedure is to divide the total equally between the periods. Alternatively the distribution might attempt to take into account the overall trend in the series and possible seasonal variations. Again, movements in a related series might provide some guidance.

Unobservable and Unmeasurable Variables

Not all of the variables which might be included in an agricultural commodity market model are in fact observable or measurable. Expectations regarding future prices, for example, play a key role in determining agricultural supply decisions. Chapter 2 discussed some of the ways of defining the expectations formation process in terms of observed data. The level of agricultural supply might also be influenced by technical progress. The demand for agricultural products might be influenced by subjective factors like tastes.

In some cases where a variable is unobserved or unobservable a *proxy variable* might be proposed in its stead. A proxy variable, as the name suggests, should exhibit similar variation to, and might be related in some way to the unobserved or unobservable variable. The price of an agricultural commodity on a particular market might be taken as a proxy for the 'world price', for example. Since the proxy will not be an accurate measurement of the variable it is standing in for, estimates of the parameters of a model which includes proxy variables will be biased as discussed below. On the other hand, omitting the variable would constitute a specification error and would also lead to biased estimates. In most cases, however, using even a poor proxy will provide better results than omitting the variable.[21]

Where the unobserved variables are assumed to produce smooth secular movements in the dependent variable of a model a common means of representing such factors is a *time trend* . Time trends might be used in demand equations to represent the effects of changes in tastes, or in the distribution of income. In supply equations they might be used to represent the effects of technical progress on yields. In the simple generalised commodity market model discussed in Chapter 1, time trends are included in the demand equation to pick up both these effects of tastes and technological factors. The simplest form of time trend is the linear trend. Here, the trend variable is introduced into the model with the values 1, 2, 3, and so on, increasing by one with each time period. Various types of non-linear trend are also possible. One commonly used form is the exponential trend where the estimated coefficient on the trend variable can provide an estimate of the growth rate in the variable to be explained. In the cocoa supply equation in Chapter 1, for example, the estimated annual upward trend in supply is nearly five per cent. In many cases, particularly where a model is to be used for prediction, non-linear trends may be the most appropriate form to use. Time trends are often used to represent the influence of technical progress in modelling yields of crops or livestock products. In many lines of agricultural production there may be a biological ceiling on yield growth.[22] The use of a linear trend, which may provide a reasonable description of past growth would suggest that the same trend would continue indefinitely. Obviously, the further into the future yields were to be predicted the less likely would it be that linear trend growth would be sustained.

The inclusion of a time trend in an equation can be legitimately rationalised in various ways including those suggested above. At worst, however, the ubiquitous time trend is used as a catch-all for all those variables about whose nature the model-builder is ignorant or unwilling to explore. Because many economic time series will by their very nature have strong trends through time the inclusion of a time trend in an equation will almost invariably improve its fit as measured by R^2.

While most of the variables entering into an econometric model might be amenable to cardinal measurement, some may be qualitative and not measurable in any conventional sense. Such variables might indicate the presence or absence of some qualitative attribute at a particular point in time, or categorise time periods according to whether some particular state of affairs rules or not - whether the period is one of wartime or peacetime, or whether the period is one in which a particular policy is in operation or not, for example. They might also indicate a spatial categorisation - whether the country concerned is developed or developing, for example. Other variables, though quantitative in nature and hence amenable to cardinal measurement, might be expressed in a qualitative way. Weather, for example, might be measured in terms of temperature or rainfall, but it might also be categorised as 'good' or 'bad'.[23] Variables of this kind or expressed in this way can be represented in a model by *dummy* or *binary* variables. As the latter name suggests they can take on only two values, conventionally one or zero: one if the chosen attribute is present - a particular policy in operation, for example - and zero if it is not. Note that although there may be two possible states of affairs - policy-on or policy-off, for example -

there is only one dummy variable. Obviously this adequately describes both possibilities. If two dummy variables had been employed - one for each possibility - it would always be the case that when one dummy variable was equal to one the other would be equal to zero. If a constant term with its implicit value of one was also included in the equation then there would be a problem of perfect multicollinearity since the constant minus the sum of the values of the two dummy variables would always be equal to zero. This difficulty is known as the *dummy variable trap*. To avoid it there must always be one less dummy variable than the number of states of affairs to be described. Thus, in the very common use of dummy variables in agricultural market models to represent seasonal variation, in a quarterly model there would only be three seasonal dummy variables. Each dummy would be equal to one for the quarter to which it refers and zero otherwise, and their estimated coefficients would measure shifts relative to that quarter for which all the dummy variables were zero. It is quite permissible to include several dummy variables representing several different factors, provided the dummy variable trap is avoided in each case. Thus, an equation might contain three seasonal dummies to allow for seasonal variation and a further quite independent dummy variable for those periods in which say, a particular policy was in operation.

Dummy variables can affect an equation in one or both of two ways. They can either change its intercept or its slope coefficients, depending upon how the dummy variable is included. The possibilities can be illustrated with a simple supply model. Suppose the introduction of a price support policy leads to a greater supply, S, at all possible prices, P. This can be described by including an intercept-shifting dummy variable, D, equal to one in those periods for which the policy is in operation and zero when it is not.

$$S_t = \beta_0 + \beta_1 P_t + \delta D_t + \upsilon_t$$

Thus, in periods when the policy is not in operation, the intercept of the function is given by the estimate of β_0. For those periods when the policy is in operation the intercept would be given by the estimate of $(\beta_0 + \delta)$. The effectiveness or otherwise of the policy can be appraised by testing the significance of δ. If on the other hand the policy was assumed to change the slope of the function - reducing price uncertainty and hence encouraging a greater responsiveness to price changes, for example - then the dummy variable might be introduced multiplicatively.

$$S_t = \beta_0 + \beta_1 P_t + \delta D_t . P_t + \upsilon_t$$

Here the price effect in periods where the policy is not in operation is given by the estimate of β_1. In periods when the policy is in operation the price effect is given by the estimate of $(\beta_1 + \delta)$.

'On the Accuracy of Economic Observations'

The previous section, discussed instances where the data actually used in estimating a model do not represent actual measurements of the theory variables, the theory variables being unmeasured or unmeasurable. Even where the variables concerned are observable and measurable, however, there is a common suspicion that economic data may be inaccurate. The many sources of potential and actual inaccuracy in the measurement of economic variables were highlighted and catalogued by Oskar Morgenstern in his book *On the Accuracy of Economic Observations* first published nearly thirty years ago.[24] A recent review of economic data issues felt that much of Morgenstern's concern was still valid.[25] While econometricians rarely complain that they have too much data they frequently complain about the quality of those data they have.

Many economic data are derived from sample surveys rather than complete enumerations or censuses, due to the high cost and delays inherent in the latter. They are therefore prone to straightforward sampling error. The key source of data on food demand in the United Kingdom, for example, is based on a sample of only some six hundred households at any one time.[26] But they are also prone to the various biases arising from poor sample design resulting from imperfect knowledge of the characteristics of the population being sampled or from biased sample selection procedures. Many economic statistics are reported rather than measured, and inaccuracy in the resulting data can arise from poor questionnaire design, and inaccurate responses. Much of the responsibility for the accuracy or otherwise of the measurements falls on the respondent. Whether through ignorance, imperfect information, a wish to mislead, or simple indolence, respondents may provide less than accurate information. Farmers in many countries may not keep accurate records of their production, harvests, purchases and sales, and are suspicious of strangers asking questions, for example. Errors introduced into the data in this way may be unpredictable and unsystematic.[27]

While there may be grounds for assuming that there may be errors in the measurement of economic data, ascertaining the extent and nature of inaccuracy is problematic since there will not always be standards for direct comparison or cross-check. Where two measurements of the same variable are available one can only confirm the other. It cannot always demonstrate that the other is wrong, only different. It may be that both are inaccurate, although one might have greater faith in one figure if it was derived using a clearly superior methodology. Normally, there will not be alternative measurements of the same variable available for comparison. Cross-checks using related series are sometimes possible, however. Livestock population statistics are sometimes suspect, for example, although statistics on meat production or hide production which reflect officially inspected channels might be accurate provided there is not widespread unofficial slaughtering. A broad estimate of the implied offtake rate from the estimated livestock population might be derived on the basis of meat production or hide production, and used to judge the validity of the population estimate. A high estimated offtake rate may be incompatible with the reproduction of the population.

In some circumstances, it may not matter from the point of view of model-building if a variable is measured inaccurately if it is the *measurement* rather than the true value of the variable which determines the behaviour of economic agents. Production plans, for example, might be based upon published official estimates of average prices, or sales planned on the basis of published market intelligence, whatever the accuracy or otherwise of these statistics. Central market prices for horticultural products may be influential in determining production and sales even though most produce by-passes central markets and the prices realised may therefore be a poor indicator of the actual average price producers and traders might obtain. In most cases market participants who cannot influence market developments or do not account for a significant share of the market will have little alternative but to rely on published data, whether accurate or not, rather than their own records for indicators of market developments in making their production and marketing decisions.

In general, however, inaccuracy in the data entering into our models - the problem of *errors in variables* - is cause for concern since it will obviously affect the reliability of the estimates of a model's parameters which can be obtained. More precisely, it is errors in the measurement of the explanatory variables which give cause for concern. Errors in the measurement of the dependent variable are absorbed by the equation's disturbance term. Similar difficulties arise where proxy variables are employed. Measurement errors in an explanatory variable render that variable stochastic rather than fixed, and because the errors are also included in the disturbance term of the estimating equation the inaccurately measured explanatory variable will not be independent of the disturbance. As a result, the ordinary least squares estimator, which requires that the explanatory variables be fixed and independent of the disturbance, will be biased and, because that bias will persist whatever the number of observations, inconsistent.[28] Some other estimation method should therefore be applied. One possibility is to use *instrumental variables* estimation, where instrumental variables, which must be correlated with the variable they replace but independent of the disturbance, replace those variables measured with error.[29] In practice, a common response to errors in variables, in spite of the widespread acknowledgement of the frequently poor quality of economic data, is to assume that they do not exist.

Conclusions

The discussion in this chapter suggests that the data with which the econometric model-builder works are far from perfect. For some, the limitations of the data available render remote the possibility of ever obtaining econometric results of any value. More constructive responses to data difficulties are possible.[30] There is little alternative but to use the data available in spite of misgivings the model-builder might have. At the same time, however, the limitations of the data must be investigated and acknowledged, and an attempt made where possible to mitigate their worst effects. The likely reliability of the data must always be borne in mind when using econometric results. As Nerlove, in his classic study of agricultural supply response advises

> '...an investigation of the nature of the data used in any statistical investigation is essential to the interpretation of

the results. More than that, it gives one an impression of the difficulties and complexities of empirical research in economics, an impression that it is wise to keep in mind when using statistical results to support arguments for any particular economic policies'. [31]

Further Reading

In spite of the widespread acknowledgement of the serious limitations on the data with which econometric model-builders have to work, data issues tend to be given little explicit attention in econometrics textbooks. An exception to this is provided by M.D. Intriligator, *Econometric Models, Techniques and Applications* (North Holland, Amsterdam, 1978), Ch. 3. A comprehensive review of the subject is given by Z. Griliches, 'Economic Data Issues' in Z. Griliches and M.D. Intriligator (eds.), *Handbook of Econometrics* (3 vols., North Holland, Amsterdam, 1986), vol. III, pp. 1465-1513.

Any econometrics textbook will deal with multicollinearity. G.G. Judge, W.E. Griffiths, R.C. Hill, H. Lütkepohl and T. Lee, *The Theory and Practice of Econometrics*, 2nd. edn (Wiley, New York, 1985), Ch. 22, provides a detailed treatment of the rather unsatisfactory state of affairs with respect to its detection and alleviation.

On missing observations and the various techniques, such as interpolation, extrapolation, the use of related series and so on, for filling gaps in data series, see G.S. Maddala, *Econometrics* (McGraw-Hill, New York, 1977), pp. 201-207. A good discussion of the different types of index numbers, shifting base years and splicing index number series is provided in W.C. Merrill and K.A. Fox, *Introduction to Economic Statistics* (Wiley, New York, 1970), Ch. 3.

Any econometrics textbook will also deal with dummy variables and time trends. On dummy variables in particular, J. Kmenta, *Elements of Econometrics* (Macmillan, New York, 1971) pp. 409-425 is good.

The classic book on data inaccuracy is Oskar Morgenstern, *On the Accuracy of Economic Observations*, 2nd. edn (Princeton University Press, Princeton, 1963) which discusses many interesting and at times alarming examples. I.M.T. Stewart, *Reasoning and Method in Economics* (McGraw-Hill, London, 1979), Ch. 8 provides a shorter treatment of the nature and sources of data inaccuracy and explores its epistemological consequences. On the formal consequences of errors in variables and appropriate estimation techniques, again most econometrics textbooks will have some discussion, but J. Johnston, *Econometric Methods*, 3rd edn (McGraw-Hill, New York, 1984), pp. 428-435, provides a concise treatment.

Notes

1. Data collection is not discussed here. For a review of methods of collection of basic agricultural statistics see I.D. Idaikkadar *Agricultural Statistics* (Pergamon, Oxford, 1979).

2. See A. Spanos, *Statistical Foundations of Econometric Modelling* (Cambridge University Press, Cambridge, 1986), pp. 15-21 and pp. 661-672 for a detailed development of this point and its implications.

3. For estimation to be possible the number of observations must exceed the number of parameters to be estimated. The greater the number of observations the smaller will be the variances of the estimated parameters.

4. The greater the variation in the observations the smaller will be the variances of the parameter estimates.

5. Properties of estimators are discussed in Chapter 4.

6. In the general linear model, $\mathbf{Y} = \mathbf{X}\beta + \varepsilon$ (where $\mathbf{Y}$ is a vector of n observations on the dependent variable Y, $\mathbf{X}$ is an nxk matrix of n observations on each of k explanatory variables, β is a vector of k coefficients to be estimated, and ε is a vector of n disturbances), for example, the ordinary least squares estimator of the variances and covariance of the estimated β's is given by $((\mathbf{e}'\mathbf{e})/(n - k))(\mathbf{X}'\mathbf{X})^{-1}$, where $\mathbf{e}$ is the vector of estimated residuals. In the presence of multicollinearity the determinant of $(\mathbf{X}'\mathbf{X})$ will be small - zero in the case of perfect multicollinearity - hence the inverse and the variances will be large. Some indication of the presence or otherwise of a high degree of multicollinearity can be derived from a consideration of the value of the determinant of a standardised $\mathbf{X}'\mathbf{X}$ whose elements are the simple correlation coefficients for each pair of explanatory variables.

7. See D.A. Belsley, E. Kuh and R.E. Welsch, *Regression Diagnostics: Identifying Influential Data and Sources of Collinearity* (Wiley, New York, 1980) for a detailed survey.

8. More complex procedures than those few discussed here are available. These are reviewed in G.G. Judge, W.E. Griffiths, R.C. Hill, H. Lütkepohl and T. Lee, *The Theory and Practice of Econometrics*, 2nd. edn (Wiley, New York, 1985), Ch. 22.

9. See J. Tobin, 'A Statistical Demand Function for Food in the USA', *Journal of the Royal Statistical Society,* Series. A, vol. 113, no. 2 (1950), pp. 113-141.

10. A decision might be made on the basis of a consideration of mean square error, MSE, which is equal to the variance plus the square of the bias.

11. D. Hallam, 'Producers' Response to Supported and Free Market Prices', *Journal of Agricultural Economics*, vol. 29, no. 2 (1978), pp. 119-131.

12. For a general discussion of liberalisation and its likely effects, see E. Reusse, 'Liberalisation and Agricultural Marketing', *Food Policy*, vol. 12, no. 4 (1987), pp. 299-317.

13. D. Hallam, *The United Kingdom Market for Fresh Exotic Fruit* (Overseas Development Natural Resources Institute, London, 1988).

14. D.T. Chen, 'The Wharton Agricultural Model Structure, Specification and Some Simulation Results', *American Journal of Agricultural Economics*, vol. 59, no. 1 (1977), pp.107-116; T.C. Liu and E.C. Hwa, 'A Monthly Econometric Model of the US Economy', *International Economic Review*, vol. 15, no. 3 (1974), pp. 328-365.

15. O. Morgenstern, *On the Accuracy of Economic Observations*, 2nd. edn (Princeton University Press, Princeton, 1963), pp. 46-47.

16. Suppose we have two index number series, one on a 1970 base (i.e. 1970 value =100) and one on a 1980 base. Provided there is some overlap in the two series, the 1980 based series can be shifted on to the 1970 base by multiplying its values by the 1970 based value for one of the overlapping years divided by the corresponding year's 1980 based value.

17. For a detailed discussion of index numbers see W.C. Merrill and K.A. Fox, *Introduction to Economic Statistics* (Wiley, New York, 1970), Ch.3.

18. This can arise particularly in the case of the application of simultaneous equations estimation methods. Estimation of an equation from a simultaneous equations model using two-stage least squares, for example, requires the regression of each endogenous variable on *all* the predetermined variables in the model as a whole. The difficulty is compounded where allowances must also be made for non-linearities or autoregressive disturbances. These issues are discussed further in Chapter 4.

19. More precisely, the greater will be the variances associated with parameter estimates. As shown in note 6 above, in the general linear model, $\mathbf{Y} = \mathbf{X}\beta + \varepsilon$, the ordinary least squares estimates of the variances and covariances of the β's are given by $((\mathbf{e}'\mathbf{e})/(n-k))(\mathbf{X}'\mathbf{X})^{-1}$. The greater is the number of observations, n, the smaller will be the resulting variances.

20. See G.S. Maddala, *Econometrics* (McGraw-Hill, New York, 1977), pp. 205-207 for a brief review.

21. M.R. Wickens, 'A Note on the Use of Proxy Variables', *Econometrica*, vol. 40, no. 4 (1972), pp. 759-761; D.J. Aigner, 'MSE Dominance of Least Squares with Errors of Observation', *Journal of Econometrics*, vol. 2, no. 3 (1974), pp. 365-372.

22. See, for example, K.L. Blaxter, 'The Use of Resources", *Animal Production*, vol. 23, part 2 (1976), pp. 267-279.

23. As in the cocoa supply equation presented in Chapter 1.

24. O. Morgenstern, *On the Accuracy of Economic Observations*, 2nd edn (Princeton University Press, Princeton, 1963).

25. Z. Griliches, 'Economic Data Issues', in Z. Griliches and M.D. Intriligator (eds.), *Handbook of Econometrics* (3 vols., North Holland, Amsterdam, 1986), vol. III, pp. 1465-1514.

26. National Food Survey, *Household Food Consumption and Expenditure* (HMSO, London, annual).

27. See I.M.T. Stewart, *Reasoning and Method in Economics* (McGraw-Hill, London, 1979), Ch. 8 for a brief survey.

28. Suppose that the matrix of observations on the explanatory variables is $\mathbf{X}$, but that some or all of these variables are measured with error, such that $\mathbf{X} = \mathbf{X}^* + \mathbf{V}$ where $\mathbf{X}^*$ is the matrix of the true values of the explanatory variables and $\mathbf{V}$ is a matrix of measurement errors. The theoretical model is $\mathbf{Y} = \mathbf{X}^*\beta + \mathbf{u}$, or $\mathbf{Y}=\mathbf{X}\beta+(\mathbf{u}-\mathbf{V}\beta)$. The ordinary least squares estimator of β is $(\mathbf{X}'\mathbf{X})^{-1}\mathbf{X}'\mathbf{Y}$, or $(\mathbf{X}'\mathbf{X})^{-1}\mathbf{X}'\mathbf{X}\beta + (\mathbf{X}'\mathbf{X})^{-1}\mathbf{X}'(\mathbf{u} - \mathbf{V}\beta)$ or $\beta+(\mathbf{X}'\mathbf{X})^{-1}\mathbf{X}'(\mathbf{u} - \mathbf{V}\beta)$. For the ordinary least squares estimator to be consistent, plim $[{}^1/_n\, \mathbf{X}'(\mathbf{u} - \mathbf{V}\beta)]$ must be zero. While plim$[{}^1/_n\mathbf{X}'\mathbf{u}]$ will be zero provided that $\mathbf{X}^*$ and $\mathbf{V}$ are uncorrelated with $\mathbf{u}$, plim $[{}^1/_n\, \mathbf{X}'\mathbf{V}]\beta$ will not be zero. plim $[{}^1/_n\, \mathbf{X}'\mathbf{V}]$ = plim $[{}^1/_n\mathbf{X}^{*\prime}\mathbf{V}]$ + plim $[{}^1/_n\mathbf{V}'\mathbf{V}]$, and while plim $[{}^1/_n\mathbf{X}^{*\prime}\mathbf{V}]$ will be zero provided the measurement errors and the true values of the explanatory variables are uncorrelated, plim $[{}^1/_n\mathbf{V}'\mathbf{V}]$, the matrix of the variances and covariances of the measurement errors, will not be zero.

29. Instrumental variables estimation is discussed in Chapter 4.

30. Z. Griliches, 'Economic Data Issues', p. 1507.

31. M. Nerlove, *Dynamics of Supply* (John Hopkins, Baltimore, 1958), p. 87.

4
Estimators and Estimation

The golden rule is that
there are no golden rules.

(George Bernard Shaw, *Maxims for Revolutionists*)

Estimation, the assignment of numerical values to the various unknown parameters of interest in a specified statistical model, has played a central, perhaps dominant, role in the conventional econometric methodology concerned with 'measurement of economic theory'.[1] A variety of *estimators* or rules for using samples of observations on the variables involved have been appropriated or developed to this end. The properties of these estimators vary according to the characteristics of the assumed statistical model to be estimated. A common starting point for estimation is the assumption that the data generation process can be adequately described by the general linear statistical model whose parameters can legitimately be estimated using a relatively simple estimator such as ordinary least squares regression. Apparent violations of one or more of the assumptions underlying the general linear statistical model lead to the specification of alternative statistical models demanding alternative, more complex, estimators. In practice, a number of other, purely practical, criteria, such as computational cost, may also be relevant to the choice of estimator. With the increasingly widespread availability of powerful computer software, particularly for microcomputers, however, such considerations should be of declining importance.

Properties of Estimators

The different properties which different estimators may have when employed to estimate the unknown parameters of a particular statistical model can provide a basis for estimator choice in the context of that model. These properties of estimators are established on the basis of a hypothetical repeated sampling procedure. In the simplest case of a two variable linear relationship this is envisaged as the repeated drawing of samples of values of the dependent variable conditional on particular fixed values for the independent variable. The observations on the dependent variable will vary from sample to sample as a result of random factors, and hence estimates of the parameters of the relationship will vary from sample to sample. Repetition of the sampling and estimation procedure allows a probability density function, or *sampling distribution*, for the estimator to be built up. It is the characteristics of this distribution, notably its mean and variance, which are of interest.

Desirable small sample properties for an estimator are *unbiasedness* and *efficiency*. An estimator is unbiased if the mean of its sampling distribution is equal to the true value of the parameter concerned, with *bias* being measured by the difference between the two.[2] An estimator is efficient, or *best unbiased*, if it is unbiased and has a smaller variance than any alternative unbiased estimator.[3] *Mean square error*, equal to the square of the bias plus the variance, allows comparisons where, for example, one estimator may be biased but have a smaller variance than an unbiased alternative.[4] The small sample properties of all estimators cannot be established conclusively. In these circumstances the *asymptotic*, or large sample properties, where sample size tends to infinity, are of interest, although they are not necessarily relevant to the more realistic context of limited sample size. An estimator is *asymptotically unbiased* if the mean of its sampling distribution is equal to the true value of the parameter concerned as sample size tends to infinity.[5] If, as sample size tends to infinity, its variance as well as any bias tend to zero, an estimator is *consistent*.[6] A consistent estimator whose variance tends to zero more rapidly than that of any other consistent estimator is *asymptotically efficient*.

Where they cannot be determined formally, some indication of the small sample properties of an estimator can be gleaned via *Monte Carlo studies*. These attempt to replicate the hypothetical repeated sampling procedure described above by generating artificial samples of observations. In the simplest case of a linear model, randomly generated additive disturbances are used with specified values for its parameters and for the fixed independent variables to generate 'observations' on the dependent variable. Estimates of the parameters can then be made from the resulting data set. With repetition of this procedure, a picture of the estimator sampling distribution emerges, and the properties of this distribution can be assessed against the known 'true' parameter values.[7] The use of different estimators with each data set allows comparisons of their properties to be made. Various econometric problems, such as specification error or multicollinearity, can be introduced to investigate their impact upon estimator performance. The simplicity of the models typically employed in Monte Carlo studies, however, can mean that their results are of restricted generality.

Methods of Estimation

Estimators appropriate to a variety of estimating situations can be derived from a limited number of basic estimation methods, the two most common being *least squares* and *maximum likelihood.*[8]

The familiar least squares estimation method is perhaps the most widely used. In the context of a simple two-variable linear model such as

$$y_i = \alpha + \beta x_i + e_i$$

values selected of the unknown parameters, α and β, are those which minimise the sum of the squared residuals, the e_i. The estimator is derived by formulating an expression for the sum of squared residuals

$$\sum_i e_i^2 = \sum_i (y_i - \alpha - \beta x_i)^2$$

Setting the partial derivatives of this with respect to α and β equal to zero for a minimum leads to the *normal equations* which can be solved for the values of the unknown parameters. These, together with the sample observations, allow estimation of other parameters of interest, such as residual variance. Other estimation methods using sample residuals are possible. Because of the squaring of the residuals, extreme observations, or *outliers*, can have an excessive influence upon the parameter estimates obtained using the least squares method. MAD - mean absolute deviation - reduces this risk by minimising the sum of absolute rather than squared residuals.[9]

The maximum likelihood method determines those values of the unknown parameters most likely to have given rise to the observed data. Implementation of the method requires the assumption of a particular statistical distribution, usually normal, for the disturbances. The assumption of a normal distribution with zero mean and variance σ^2 gives the probability of observing one particular disturbance as

$$f(e_i) = \frac{1}{\sqrt{2\pi\sigma}} \exp\left(-\frac{1}{2}\frac{(y_i - \alpha - \beta x_i)^2}{\sigma^2}\right)$$

and, if the disturbances are independent, by the multiplication rule the joint probability of obtaining all n sample disturbances is given by the joint probability density function

$$\prod_{i=1}^{n} f(e_i) = (2\pi)^{-n/2} \sigma^{-n} \exp\left(-\frac{1}{2\sigma^2}\sum_{i=1}^{n}(y_i - \alpha - \beta x_i)^2\right)$$

The joint probability density function interpreted as a function of the unknown parameters, α, β, and σ^2, constitutes the likelihood function, **L**

$$L(\alpha,\beta,\sigma^2) = (2\pi)^{-n/2} \sigma^{-n} \exp\left(-\frac{1}{2\sigma^2}\sum_{i=1}^{n}(y_i - \alpha - \beta x_i)^2\right)$$

The maximum likelihood estimates of the parameters are those values which maximise this likelihood function. The partial derivatives with respect to α, β, and σ^2 are set equal to zero for a maximum and the resulting equations solved. Since all others are constants, maximising **L** involves minimising the final term on the right-hand side, the sum of squared residuals. In practice it is convenient to work with the log of the likelihood function, which being a monotonic transformation, is maximised at the same values of the parameters as the original likelihood function. The value of the maximised likelihood function plays an important role in specification testing, as outlined in the notes to Chapter 2. While obtaining the maximum likelihood estimates is straightforward in the simple case discussed here, the partial derivatives of the likelihood function can be highly complex and non-linear in practice, requiring numerical optimisation methods for their solution.[10] The computational burden this imposes has, at least in the past, constrained the more widespread use of maximum likelihood methods, although this difficulty is reduced with the greater availability of appropriate computer software. Nevertheless, the greater familiarity and transparency of least squares methods remain attractive to many model-builders.

Estimation of the General Linear Statistical Model

The most common assumptions, at least in the first instance, as to the nature of the process generating the data from which the parameters of a model are to be estimated are those of the general linear statistical model. These assumptions in turn justify the use of the most familiar and popular estimator, ordinary least squares, OLS, which, besides being computationally convenient, possesses certain desirable properties in this context.

The characteristics of the general linear statistical model were discussed in Chapter 2. The dependent variable is specified to be a function of a *known* set of explanatory or independent variables and a stochastic disturbance term which captures measurement errors in the dependent variable, the influence of excluded, unknown or unmeasurable variables, and purely random effects. The function is assumed to be linear, at least in the parameters, and these parameters are assumed to be constant over the data period. The independent variables are assumed to be non-stochastic, fixed in repeated sampling, and to be linearly independent of one another. The stochastic disturbances are assumed drawn from a distribution with zero mean and constant variance - that is, they are *homoscedastic* rather than *heteroscedastic* - and are independent of one another - that is, they are free from *autocorrelation*. Where disturbances are homoscedastic and free from autocorrelation they are said to be *spherical*.[11]

The ordinary least squares estimator selects those values for the unknown parameters which minimise the sum of squared sample residuals. The residuals measure the deviations between the actual values of the dependent variable and the values which would be predicted by the estimated equation - the sample counterparts, in some ways, of the unknown stochastic disturbances. The estimator is derived as described in the previous section, and estimation of the general linear model is a straightforward application of the least squares principle.[12] In the context of this model the ordinary least squares estimator is unbiased and is *best*, in having a smaller variance than any other linear unbiased estimator, and hence efficient - properties summarised by the *Gauss-Markov theorem.*[13] Ordinary least squares is, however, also widely applied outside the context of the general linear statistical model, and in such circumstances it may have none of these desirable properties.

The additional assumption of normally distributed stochastic disturbances produces the normal general linear statistical model.[14] Normality is usually simply assumed on the basis of the central limit theorem, although various tests exist which can be applied to test the validity of the assumption, and data transformations are available to provide normality where it is apparently absent.[15] While not necessary for ordinary least squares estimation, normally distributed disturbances are required for the various hypothesis tests of the type discussed in relation to specification and model selection in Chapter 2. More significantly from the point of view of this chapter, the addition of the normality assumption provides the possibility of estimation using the maximum likelihood method as an alternative to ordinary least squares. In the context of the general linear model, maximum likelihood estimation amounts to a straightforward application of the principle outlined in the previous section.[16] In this particular case, the maximum likelihood estimator of the coefficients on the explanatory variables is the same as the ordinary least squares estimator, and therefore has the same desirable properties of unbiasedness and efficiency. The maximum likelihood estimator for the residual variance is slightly different from the ordinary least squares estimator, however, and is in fact biased. Where the disturbances are not normally distributed, the desirable properties of the maximum likelihood estimator are lost.

Estimation With Non-Spherical Disturbances

The assumption of spherical disturbances is clearly violated where they are autocorrelated or heteroscedastic. Some of the variety of circumstances which can give rise to these properties have already been noted. Where the disturbances are non-spherical, respecification of the statistical model to take account of this produces the *generalised linear statistical model.*[17] In this context the desirable properties of the ordinary least squares estimator are lost and a more appropriate estimator should be found.

The most common assumption concerning the nature of autocorrelation is that it is *first order*, with the disturbance in one period being related to that in the previous period according to

$$\varepsilon_t = \rho\varepsilon_{t-1} + \upsilon_t$$

where ρ is the *autocorrelation coefficient*, and υ is a random disturbance with mean zero, constant variance and zero covariance.[18] Autocorrelation may stem from the spreading over more than one time period of the effects of purely random influences on the dependent variable, a feature which can arise as a result of data massaging of the kind discussed in Chapter 3. In the frequently used adaptive expectations and Nerlove supply models, autocorrelation arises from the Koyck transformation used in their derivation. Perhaps the most common source of autocorrelation is specification error in the selection of variables or functional form. The influence of relevant variables omitted from a specification is captured by the disturbance, and where such variables follow a particular trend the disturbance will inevitably reflect it. Autocorrelation may also indicate misspecification of the dynamics of a relationship between variables, although specification of autocorrelated disturbances may offer a simple alternative to the specification and estimation of a more complex dynamic model.[19] In general, however, where autocorrelation is a manifestation of specification error attention should be given to the correction of that error.

Heteroscedasticity is accorded relatively little attention in modelling agricultural commodity markets since it is widely regarded as a problem associated primarily with cross-section analyses. Heteroscedastic disturbances may arise in the context of varying parameter models, where it takes the most commonly assumed multiplicative form with the variance of the disturbances being dependent upon the values taken by one or more of the explanatory variables.

Where non-spherical disturbances are not expected *a priori*, specification of an alternative statistical model and search for an appropriate estimator are usually instigated after tests of misspecification based on the sample residuals suggest that the assumptions of the general linear statistical model are violated. The most commonly employed tests for autocorrelation and heteroscedasticity were mentioned in Chapter 2.

The Durbin-Watson statistic, d,

$$d = \frac{\sum_{t=2}^{T} (e_t - e_{t-1})^2}{\sum_{t=1}^{T} e_t^2}$$

is by far the most popular test statistic in testing the hypothesis of no autocorrelation against the alternatives of either positive or negative autocorrelation. It can be shown to be approximately equal to 2 (1 - ρ), from which the logic of the reference values of d is more easily seen. In the case of no autocorrelation ρ is equal to zero and d will be equal to two. Perfect positive autocorrelation gives ρ equal to one and d equal to zero. Perfect negative autocorrelation gives ρ equal to minus one and d equal to four. Estimated values close to one or other of these reference values are taken to indicate the presence or absence of autocorrelation. Critical values for different degrees of freedom are tabulated in the form of upper and lower bounds since the precise values appropriate in any one situation depend upon the data set involved. Where the estimated value falls between the upper and lower bounds the test is inconclusive. The Durbin-Watson test is applied in a wide range of circumstances although it is a test for first order autocorrelation only, and the statistic is biased towards two where a lagged dependent variable appears among the explanatory variables. Where a lagged dependent variable does appear as an explanatory variable, the Durbin *h* statistic is appropriate.[20] The detection of higher order autocorrelation usually relies on consideration of the significance of autocorrelation coefficients calculated, using the least squares formula, for different lags between sample residuals.[21]

Tests for heteroscedasticity investigate the possibility that the variance of the disturbances is related to one or more of the explanatory variables. The Goldfeld-Quandt test discussed in Chapter 2, for example, tests whether the variances associated with different ranges of values of an explanatory variable are significantly different. The Glejser test actually estimates and tests for significance a variety of functional relationships between the absolute values of the sample residuals and particular explanatory variables, providing information of value in implementing the estimated generalised least squares estimator discussed below.[22] The Breusch-Pagan test allows investigation of heteroscedasticity where this involves more than one explanatory variable.[23]

Estimators appropriate to the general linear statistical model are inefficient, both in small samples and asymptotically, in the context of the new statistical model, although they may remain unbiased and consistent. The ordinary least squares estimator of the variance of the disturbances is biased and consequently so are the estimators for the variances and covariances of the regression coefficients.[24] Positive autocorrelation, for example, may lead to underestimates of the true variances. Bias in estimates of the variances and covariances of the regression coefficients implies potentially misleading results in hypothesis tests concerning those coefficients.

Alternative estimators which take into account information or assumptions concerning the varances and covariances of the disturbances and which consequently have smaller variances can be identified. Ordinary least squares estimators can be adapted to embrace a range of assumptions concerning the variances and covariances of the disturbances to produce the efficient *generalised least squares*, GLS, estimator.[25] This relies on knowledge of the particular form of disturbance variances and covariances. Such knowledge will rarely be available, but estimates may be used, yielding the *estimated generalised least squares* , EGLS, estimator. Poor estimates may result in a less efficient estimator than ordinary least squares, however, and this may also result where samples are small and autocorrelation is not strong.[26] In any case, since this procedure may be rather cumbersome, transformations of the data are commonly relied upon to secure the same effect. In the case of autocorrelation there are several possibilities which make use of *generalised differences* rather than the absolute values of the variables of interest and then apply ordinary least squares. These can be illustrated with the simple model

$$y_t = \alpha + \beta x_t + \varepsilon_t$$

where ε_t follows the first order autoregressive scheme

$$\varepsilon_t = \rho\varepsilon_{t-1} + \upsilon_t$$

The generalised difference form of the model, obtained by lagging one period, multiplying through by ρ, and subtracting the result from the original,

$$y_t - \rho y_{t-1} = \alpha(1 - \rho) + \beta(x_t - \rho x_{t-1}) + \varepsilon_t - \rho\varepsilon_{\tau-1}$$

has a transformed disturbance equal to υ_t, and hence free from autocorrelation. Several means of assigning values to the unknown ρ are available. Rearranging the approximation to the Durbin-Watson statistic given above, an estimate of ρ can be derived as (1-1/2d). The *Hildreth-Lu procedure* searches over a grid of possible values, estimating the generalised difference equation in each case and selecting those values of ρ, α and β which minimise the sum of squared residuals. Perhaps the most commonly used is the iterative *Cochrane-Orcutt procedure* which estimates ρ from the sample residuals and α and β from the generalised difference equation in turn until the estimates converge on particular values. The *two-step Cochrane-Orcutt procedure* stops this process after the first iteration. Formation of the generalised differences loses the first observation on each of the variables involved. The *Prais-Winsten method* provides a means of retaining these observations, multiplying them by $\sqrt{(1 - \rho^2)}$.

Non-spherical disturbances can also be accommodated by maximum likelihood methods, with the form of autocorrelation or heteroscedasticity present appearing in the likelihood function.[27] Maximising this may yield equations nonlinear in the parameters for which they must be solved.

Estimation With Stochastic Explanatory Variables

The assumption made in applying the general linear statistical model that explanatory variables can be regarded as fixed rather than stochastic in repeated sampling is untenable in a variety of common circumstances. The stochastic nature of variables subject to measurement error was considered in Chapter 3. Lagged dependent variables appearing among the explanatory variables, in the dynamic models discussed in Chapter 2, for example, will clearly be stochastic. Variables appearing as explanatory in a particular equation but determined simultaneously through mutual interaction with the dependent variable and hence endogenous to the system as a whole, will also be stochastic. All these circumstances give rise to the *stochastic regressor model*.

The precise consequences of stochastic regressors depend upon the nature of their relationship to the disturbance term.[28] Where the explanatory variable is stochastic but independently distributed of the disturbance then the parameters of the equation can be estimated using the ordinary least squares or maximum likelihood estimators appropriate to the general linear model discussed earlier, and these will provide unbiased, efficient and consistent estimates.[29] A lagged dependent variable among the explanatory variables will not be independent of the disturbance, although there may be no contemporaneous correlation. Where they are contemporaneously uncorrelated, as in the case of the partial adjustment model, for example, the ordinary least squares estimator will be biased, but consistent, and so it remains the most common choice.[30] The presence of a lagged dependent variable is, however, frequently accompanied by autocorrelation in the disturbance. This difficulty arises in the adaptive expectations model and the Nerlove supply model, and indeed in any dynamic model derived using a Koyck transformation. Because of autocorrelation, a lagged dependent variable will be contemporaneously correlated, via the lagged disturbance, with the current disturbance. The ordinary least squares estimator will be biased and inconsistent. The same contemporaneous relationship arises, and the same consequences follow, in the case of errors in variables and simultaneous equations models. A positive relationship between the stochastic explanatory variable and the disturbance will lead to an overestimate of the associated parameter, a negative relationship an underestimate.[31]

The *instrumental variables estimator* is often recommended for the stochastic regressor model, although the gains from using it in preference to ordinary least squares can be uncertain. The qualifications demanded of an *instrumental variable* are that it should be correlated with the stochastic regressor but not correlated with the disturbance of the equation to be estimated. The estimator is derived using the chosen instrumental variable together with the stochastic regressor to break the link between the latter and the disturbance, and is consistent though not efficient.[32] Typically, several candidates, often including the lagged values of the stochastic variables, meet the requirements of an instrumental variable, and a choice must be made between them. This choice can be arbitrary, although the closer the correlation between the instrumental variable and the stochastic regressor the smaller will be the variance of the resulting estimator.

Where, as in the case of the adaptive expectations and Nerlove models, stochastic regressors are accompanied by an autocorrelated disturbance, estimators are available which can account for both. The precise nature of the relevant estimator depends upon the precise nature of the model, whether the disturbance is autoregressive or moving average, for example.[33] Maximum likelihood methods are efficient but may involve complex search procedures. Iterative combinations of instrumental variables and estimated generalised least squares or generalised difference transformations can also be used, with the autocorrelation coefficent estimated from the instrumental variables estimated residuals. Estimation is slightly more straightforward in the case of the adaptive expectations or Nerlove models. The lagged term in the moving average disturbance has the same coefficient as the lagged dependent variable in the former, and is one half of the symmetrical coefficients on the lagged dependent variables in the latter, as was shown in Chapter 2.[34]

In spite of the inconsistency of ordinary least squares it remains nonetheless a popular choice for the estimation of the Nerlove model and other dynamic models, the implicit assumption being that the disturbances are most appropriately attached to the final estimating equation rather than its component models. One consequence of this, again as explained in Chapter 2, is that separate estimates of the expectations and adjustment coefficents cannot be obtained. Ordinary least squares also remains a popular choice even in the context of the simultaneous equations models. This is discussed further below.

Estimation of Simultaneous Equations Models

The discussion so far has been of estimation of single equation models. The information such models can provide, however, will often be limited and incomplete. Consideration of their wider setting within a system of equations describing a complete set of market relationships, with a separate equation for each endogenous variable, may be more useful. Such systems may be characterised by simultaneous determination of several variables of interest and described by the simultaneous equations statistical model introduced in Chapter 2.[35] Where this is so, the estimation methods appropriate to single equation models may not be appropriate, and estimators specifically designed for simultaneous equation models are needed. Endogenous variables appearing on the right-hand side of an equation clearly constitute stochastic regressors, contemporaneously correlated with all the disturbances in the system as the reduced form shows. Consequently the ordinary least squares estimator is subject to *simultaneity bias* and is inconsistent. Of course, systems of equations need not be simultaneous. As noted in Chapter 2, the biological delays inherent in agricultural production processes can lead to a fundamental recursiveness in many agricultural commodity market models, with their equations showing unidirectional chains of causation from one variable to another. Each equation can be regarded, for the purposes of estimation, as an independent general linear model and estimated accordingly by, for example, ordinary least squares. On the other hand, some systems of equations, while not simultaneous, may nonetheless be interrelated. The *seemingly unrelated regression equations*, SURE, model, in which equations are related via their disturbances, is a case in point. In a recent study of the demand for fresh US citrus in several export markets, for example, the same changes in shipping and marketing conditions, climatic variations, and other random factors were expected to affect export demand in all markets. The disturbances of the demand equations for each market were therefore likely to be related.[36] Taking such additional information into account can provide an improvement on the efficiency of ordinary least squares applied to each equation in turn, although ordinary least squares will be unbiased and consistent. Estimation of the seemingly unrelated regressions model uses information concerning the covariances of the disturbances of different equations in a generalised least squares framework. Where these covariances are not known *a priori* , they first have to be estimated using ordinary least squares residuals, giving the *Zellner two-stage Aitken estimator*.[37,38]

While the structural form of a simultaneous equation model may not appropriately be estimated using ordinary least squares, the reduced form, which incorporates all the information concerning the data generating process available from the sample observations, may be, since it involves only predetermined variables on the right-hand sides of its equations.[39] For some purposes, such as policy analysis using the *impact multipliers* which are the reduced form coefficients, or forecasting, estimation of the reduced form may be all that is required.[40] Ordinary least squares will provide unbiased estimates provided that the predetermined variables do not include any stochastic regressors such as lagged endogenous variables. Under certain conditions, the estimated reduced form coefficients can be manipulated to obtain estimates of the structural coefficients of which they are functions. The resulting *indirect least squares* estimator is biased for small samples but consistent. In practice, however, it is seldom used.

The possibility that the reduced form coefficients cannot be manipulated to yield estimates of the structural coefficients constitutes the *identification problem.* An equation is *underidentified* if this cannot be achieved, and indeed no estimator will provide estimates of the structural coefficients in this case. At least as many reduced form coefficients are required if estimates of the structural coefficients are to be derived and hence an equation is to be *identified.* Since the reduced form involves all the predetermined variables in a model, this requirement translates into the *order condition* for identification that the number of explanatory variables, both endogenous and predetermined, in the structural equation under consideration should be equal to or greater than the total number of predetermined variables in the model as a whole. An alternative, more convenient, form of the order condition states that for an equation to be identified, the number of predetermined variables excluded from it must be equal to or greater than the number of endogenous variables included less one - the 'less one' arising since the structural coefficient on the endogenous variable regarded as dependent will be known to be equal to one. Under certain conditions, non-linear functions involving endogenous variables can be treated as predetermined variables for the purposes of the order condition.[41] The order condition is a necessary but not sufficient condition for identification, and should be supplemented by the *rank condition* which requires that the equations linking the estimated reduced form coefficients and the unknown structural coefficients should be independent. In practice the fulfilment of this condition is rarely verified.[42] An equation is *exactly identified* if the number of predetermined variables excluded from it is equal to the number of endogenous variables included less one. In this case, unique estimates of the structural coefficients can be derived and indirect least squares is an appropriate estimator. Where the number of predetermined variables excluded exceeds the number of endogenous variables included less one an equation is *overidentified*, and indirect least squares estimates of the structural coefficients will not be unique.

By the order condition, identification of an equation clearly depends upon the number of variables, particularly predetermined variables, it excludes and accordingly is most commonly secured by means of *zero restrictions* upon its structural coefficients.[43] In practice, it is widely considered that commodity models tend to be overidentified, since the majority contain many predetermined variables relative to the typically small number of endogenous variables.[44] On the other hand, it has been argued that apparent overidentification is a result of the adoption of oversimplified specifications, and the inclusion of all relevant variables would result in underidentification.[45]

Since simultaneity leads to stochastic regressors, the instrumental variables estimator might be applied to estimate the parameters of a simultaneous equations model. A supply of instrumental variables is offered by the predetermined variables of the model which by definition possess the required properties. The instrumental variables estimator is consistent, but not asymptotically efficient. Except where an equation is exactly identified, in which case there will be just as many predetermined variables available as instruments as are needed, instrumental variables estimates will not be unique. In the overidentified case, there will be more than the necessary number of instruments from which a largely arbitrary choice must be made.

The *two-stage least squares* estimator achieves greater efficiency by taking all predetermined variables into account, and is appropriate for overidentified equations.[46] The first stage consists of the estimation of the reduced form equations for each endogenous variable appearing on the right-hand side of the equation of interest. Fitted values for the endogenous variables are estimated from the estimated reduced form equations, and since these fitted values are functions only of predetermined variables, they represent the endogenous variables 'purged' of the stochastic element which correlates them with the model's disturbances. Non-linear functions involving endogenous variables - price ratios, perhaps - will be non-linear functions of the disturbances. These can be accommodated by first-stage regressions which include powers of the predetermined variables.[47] The second stage uses the fitted values of the endogenous variables from the first as instrumental variables for the estimation of the original equation.

Two-stage least squares is perhaps the most popular of the simultaneous equations estimators since it offers a consistent estimator which is asymptotically efficient compared to instrumental variables or indirect least squares, but which is relatively transparent and easily implemented. Difficulty may be encountered in undertaking the first-stage reduced form regressions, since where the number of predetermined variables in the model is large, or the number of observations is small, available degrees of freedom may be insufficient. The problem is obviously exacerbated where allowance for non-linearity is also necessary. The use of principal components, or selection of a subset of predetermined variables, based, for example, on rankings according to the proximity of their causal connections with endogenous variables, have been suggested as means of contending with this.[48] Where the additional problems of autoregression and autocorrelation commonly encountered in agricultural commodity market models are present in a simultaneous equations model, two-stage least squares will no longer be consistent. Iterative adaptations to cope with such cases have been proposed.[49] Lagged endogenous variables appearing among the predetermined variables will clearly be correlated with autocorrelated disturbances and implementation of two-stage least squares requires fitted values as instruments for lagged endogenous variables in these circumstances. The first stage must therefore involve regression of all current and lagged endogenous variables upon all current and lagged predetermined variables if the stochastic element is to be purged completely. The autocorrelation coefficient can be estimated using the residuals obtained from this application of two-stage least squares, and a generalised difference equation formed. Iterative application of two-stage least squares to the generalised difference equation and estimation of the autocorrelation coefficient will lead to convergence on estimates of the parameters of the equation and the autocorrelation coefficient which are consistent. Any degrees of freedom problems with the first stage of two-stage least squares are again clearly exacerbated by this procedure since the need to include lagged as well as current values of the predetermined variables in the very first step doubles the number of reduced form coefficients to be estimated. Where the number of observations available is limited, the possibility of dealing with both simultaneity and autocorrelation may be precluded. The choice of estimation strategy in such circumstances is discussed below.

The two-stage least squares estimator is a single-equation or *limited information* estimator. Greater efficiency might be achieved by using more information, such as zero restrictions in other equations or covariances of disturbances across equations, concerning the model as a whole rather than simply the list of its predetermined variables. Systems or *full information* estimators achieve asymptotic efficiency by taking such information into account, estimating all equations in a model simultaneously.

The *three-stage least squares* estimator combines two-stage least squares with the seemingly unrelated regressions model.[50] The first two stages are in fact a straightforward application of two-stage least squares to each equation of the model. The resulting parameter estimates are discarded, but the reduced form fitted values for the endogenous variables are retained as instrumental variables for the variables concerned where they appear as explanatory variables, and the residuals are used to estimate the covariances of the disturbances across different equations for use in the third stage. This involves estimation of the entire model using the seemingly unrelated regressions approach and hence accounts for both restrictions on each equation and covariances of disturbances across them. The *full information maximum likelihood* estimator embraces the same information, and has the same properties as three-stage least squares. Maximisation of the likelihood function leads to highly non-linear equations which must be solved for the unknown parameters, however, imposing what may be a prohibitive computational burden.[51]

Computers and Econometric Modelling

Developments in computer hardware and software, particularly in relation to microcomputers, have permitted the specification and estimation of larger and more complex models using increasingly sophisticated techniques, and have been instrumental in popularising the use of econometric modelling. Laborious calculations and expertise in programming econometric methods have been made largely redundant by modern 'user-friendly' software packages. Computational costs, which were once a major constraint upon the choice of estimation technique and often effectively ruled out the use of maximum likelihood methods, have been reduced enormously, although they can still be high for estimators necessitating iterative solutions of highly non-linear equations. Perhaps the major breakthrough on the cost and accessibility of econometric methods has been the result of the specific development of software, or the translation of mainframe packages, for use on microcomputers, although as yet there is relatively little available for other than PC-compatible machines.

Some econometric methods, including some of the more straightforward estimators, are available in the common general statistical packages such as Minitab.[52] All offer ordinary least squares estimation, and provided that fitted values and residuals can be estimated and saved for reuse, some other estimators such as Cochrane-Orcutt, instrumental variables and two-stage least squares can be derived, albeit a rather clumsy procedure. An increasingly wide and powerful range of specialist econometrics software provides for almost every eventuality, although it would not be unfair to say that estimation methods rather than model-testing procedures are emphasised and Bayesian methods are little represented. Packages such as TSP include least squares and maximum likelihood estimators for all the commonly encountered statistical models discussed in this chapter, and a range of supplementary statistics and information of value in misspecification and specification testing.[53] Microcomputer versions of some packages, such as MicroTSP, are available, although these may offer a restricted set of the mainframe version's features.[54]

There is a school of thought which, while welcoming the advances in software capabilities and efficiency, regrets the concomitant possibility of what might be called 'push-button econometrics'. The ease with which parameter estimates are obtained can encourage a research methodology which relies less on the guidance of economic theory and other *a priori* considerations than on heuristics, and efficient software packages can form a barrier between the model-builder and familiarity with his or her data. Sophisticated estimation techniques can be implemented with little appreciation of their uses and limitations beyond what is needed to call up the appropriate routine on the computer. It seems unlikely, however, that such an uncritical approach would make effective use of econometric techniques or produce results of any real value.

Choice of Estimation Technique

It is evident from the discussion thus far that in the typical agricultural commodity market model departures from one or more of the assumptions of the general linear statistical model might be expected. Where such departures occur, the familiar ordinary least squares estimator will be unsuitable. The 'correct' specification in terms of the variables to be included, their classification into endogenous and exogenous, the functional form of the relationships assumed to exist between them, and the nature of the stochastic disturbance terms, will be uncertain. Since tests of misspecification and specification are rarely thorough, some specification error may remain. Partly as a result of such specification error, but also arising out of the dynamic nature of some of the models widely used - the adaptive expectations model, for example - autocorrelation is common. Again arising from the dynamic structure of frequently employed models, lagged endogenous variables often appear as explanatory variables. Non-linearities arise from the use of ratios or products of variables - deflated prices or output defined as area multiplied by yield, for example - although provided, as in these examples, non-linearity is confined to variables rather than parameters, the problem is one for model solution rather than estimation.[55] In spite of the relatively long production cycles for many agricultural commodities, fully recursive models are unlikely to be appropriate since there will normally be scope for short-run adjustments to many variables within one time period: current supply levels might be influenced by stock or trade variations with short lags, for example. Elements of simultaneity are therefore likely in most comprehensively specified models. Assembly of consistent and accurate data series of usable length for the variables of interest is usually problematic. The nature of these variables is such that series of observations within the sample can display similar trends, making it difficult to disentangle their individual effects.

Given such violations of the assumptions of the general linear statistical model, alternative, rather more complex, statistical models will be appropriate, and hence alternatives to the ordinary least squares estimator, which may prove biased, inefficient or inconsistent, are required. The response of the agricultural market model-builder to these difficulties is frequently partial, however. In some cases, notably data deficiencies, there may be little that can be done anyway. Measures to combat autocorrelation are applied, but problems arising from simultaneity are frequently accorded little consideration in determining the choice of estimator. In Chapter 2 it was noted that the core of most agricultural commodity market models often preserves a fundamental recursiveness. Simultaneity is typically introduced when a model is made richer in detail, and hence more disaggregated in terms of its variables: international trade or stock variables may introduce a bi-directional relationship between total supplies and product price; prices and quantities at several successive marketing stages may be simultaneously determined with the product price at one stage being the input price at the next. The neglect of simultaneity is manifested in two basic related ways. First, the endogeneity of certain explanatory variables may not be recognised, and consequently specifications may be incomplete, ignoring the system in which the relationship of interest should be embedded. Secondly, inappropriate estimators, notably ordinary least squares, are often applied to simultaneous relationships. Leaving aside ignorance - a failure to recognise simultaneity where it exists - a number of justifications for the neglect of simultaneity and the tendency to employ familiar estimators whatever the nature of the statistical model might be identified and have been proposed.

Firstly, even with additional detail of the kinds suggested above, the degree of simultaneity in most agricultural market models remains limited.[56] The more limited the extent of simultaneity the less the likely bias resulting from application of ordinary least squares.

Secondly, for small samples, the consistent methods are themselves biased anyway.

Thirdly, and following on from the first two, compared to those of other econometric problems such as specification error, the consequences of neglecting simultaneity are slight.[57] In certain circumstances this may be so, but there seems to be little justification for adding a further source of bias - inappropriate estimation methods - which can be avoided to all those others which cannot. In any case, selection of variables and functional forms cannot be divorced from specification of the statistical model with its implications for suitable estimators. The presence of such additional problems does, however, appear to reduce the divergence between ordinary least squares and other estimators in terms of desirable properties.

Fourthly, although the extent of the bias resulting from neglect of simultaneity may be uncertain, its direction may be predictable. Knowledge that a parameter estimate may be an upper or lower limit on the true value may be sufficient for some purposes. The greater the number of endogenous variables, however, the more difficult it becomes to predict even the direction of bias.

Fifthly, most consistent methods are demanding in terms of degrees of freedom. These may be in short supply, due not only to the difficulties of obtaining consistent data series of serviceable length, but also to the need to allow for lags reflecting the delays in agricultural production processes. The latter may be particularly important in the case of perennials. The degrees of freedom needs of some consistent methods can sometimes be reduced. Various modifications to the two-stage least squares estimator proposed to this end were indicated above. The problems are compounded, again as indicated above, in the common situation where autocorrelation or non-linear functions of endogenous variables are also present. Where autocorrelation is present the first-stage regressions should include all the predetermined variables and their lags and the lags of the endogenous variables to ensure consistency.[58] Where the model-builder is faced with the twin problems of autocorrelation and simultaneity, further complicated by the dynamic structure of the model and shortage of degrees of freedom, a situation may arise in which a choice must be made between ignoring the problems, attempting to deal with both, or, perhaps most commonly dealing with one or the other depending upon which is perceived as the most significant.

Sixthly, the typical *modus operandi* of the agricultural market model-builder is piecemeal in its approach, developing a model equation by equation, and finally asembling the acceptable individual equations into the final complete model. This procedure is facilitated by the use of single equation least squares estimation methods.[59] Agricultural market models are rarely so large and complex that they cannot be conceived, specified and developed as systems, however, and the adoption of a systems approach from the beginning may reduce the risk of misspecification of the causal structure of the model.

Finally, it has been argued that a practical constraint on choice of estimation technique is the lack of computer software to implement the more sophisticated estimators, or where this is available the computational cost involved. In fact, as the previous section described, powerful and cheap software is now available for mainframes and increasingly for microcomputers.

The gist of these not always convincing arguments is that there is a trade-off between increased complexity and cost of appropriate estimators and the gains to be derived from their application. In the face of data deficiencies, uncertainty concerning specification and other difficulties, these gains are regarded as uncertain. Simplicity, familiarity and convenience therefore prevail. This view of the trade-off tends to be assumed rather than researched, however. Its validity will obviously tend to be model specific, but some relevant general considerations might be outlined.

The asymptotic superiority of the consistent estimators over inconsistent ordinary least squares is obvious, and of the consistent estimators full information methods have been shown to be efficient compared to limited information methods. These asymptotic properties have limited relevance in practice, of course, where sample sizes are typically small, and where the situation is often complicated by other econometric problems such as specification error, measurement errors, multicollinearity or autocorrelation. Unfortunately, the small sample properties of the various estimators are largely unestablished. Attempts to rank estimators on the basis of their small sample properties have had to rely on the evidence of Monte Carlo studies.[60] This evidence does not provide a clear-cut ranking, however, and is of restricted generality.[61] The small sample performance of estimators in the context of the dynamic models involving lagged endogenous variables commonly encountered in modelling agricultural commodity markets have had little investigation. In spite of these qualifications, the available evidence does provide some broad indications. In the estimation of individual parameters, consistent estimators, although biased, generally have smaller bias than ordinary least squares, although there is no conclusive evidence in favour of any one consistent estimator. Where any one of a variety of additional econometric problems are present, the evidence against ordinary least squares is less conclusive. Indeed, one study has found ordinary least squares to have the least bias in the face of specification error.[62] Ordinary least squares is of course fully appropriate if the model concerned is recursive, and arguably appropriate if the model is nearly so. Based largely on the Monte Carlo evidence, two-stage least squares has emerged as perhaps the most widely recommended consistent estimator.[63] It has performed well in terms of the extent of small sample bias and variance recorded, is readily computable, and has been relatively robust in the face of additional econometric problems. It avoids the inconsistency of ordinary least squares, but avoids the sensitivity to specification error and measurement error of the full-information methods.

Most of the discussion of choice of estimation technique is concerned with the statistical properties of the various estimators. It has been suggested, however, that the choice of estimator for an *economic* model should perhaps take note of the 'economic meaningfulness' of the resulting estimates in terms of economic theory or other *a priori* information.[64] The problem is, of course, that without knowledge of the true parameter values it is not easy to say whether one estimator gives more 'meaningful' estimates than another. It is only extreme divergences from prior expectations - wrong signs or totally improbable magnitudes - which might be recognised as not 'meaningful'.[65]

Where the objective of the model is simulation or prediction, it could be argued that the most appropriate estimator is that which yields the best model performance in these respects.[66] Since dynamic interactions between equations can have a significant impact on model performance, it is not certain that a ranking of estimators based on Monte Carlo evidence concerning bias and variance would be corroborated by a ranking based upon the alternative criterion of model performance in simulation and forecasting. Superior performance in these respects might prove a compelling reason for selecting a particular estimator whatever its statistical properties.[67]

Some relevant evidence on the relationship between estimation technique and model performance is available from studies made in the context of macroeconometric models.[68] These suggested gains from the application of consistent methods in preference to ordinary least squares. A similar exercise, using a fairly typical agricultural commodity market model, examined the relationship between the accuracy of the model's historical simulation performance and the estimator employed to estimate its parameters.[69] Only a limited selection of the most commonly employed estimators were considered: ordinary least squares; ordinary least squares with allowance, where appropriate, for first order autocorrelation using the Cochrane-Orcutt technique; two-stage least squares; and two-stage least squares with allowance, where appropriate, for first order autocorrelation. No one estimator gave a better simulation performance across all variables, although two-stage least squares gave the best results in the most cases. The differences between the estimators were small, however, and there was no compelling evidence in favour of any particular estimator.

It does not appear that consistent methods are necessarily uniformly superior to ordinary least squares and its extensions in terms of producing better model performance or more 'meaningful' parameter estimates. Neither does it appear that in the choice of estimation technique 'anything goes' is an acceptable methodology since the choice can have an noticeable influence upon parameter estimates and model performance. Because the appropriate choice will be model specific, one general implication for practice which might be drawn is that the choice of estimator perhaps deserves rather more consideration than it is apparently accorded by many model-builders.

Further Reading

As Peter Kennedy points out in his *Guide to Econometrics*, 2nd edn (Blackwell, Oxford, 1985), most econometrics textbooks can be regarded, at least in part, as 'catalogues' of estimators appropriate to a range of alternative estimation situations. The conventional approach is to begin with the ordinary least squares estimation of the general linear statistical model, and then relax the assumptions of this model one by one. Descriptions of the consequences of the various violations of the assumptions of the general linear model, tests for violations and some suggestions as to how to proceed when violations are revealed can be found in any econometrics textbook. The choice between them is largely a matter of personal taste, although some are not exhaustive on the estimation of simultaneous equations models, and few deal with estimation in the typical situation where more than one of the assumptions of the general linear model are violated at the same time. Kennedy provides a good brief survey in his Chapters 3, 7, 8 and 9. A more thorough treatment is given by G.G. Judge, R.C. Hill, W.E. Griffiths, H. Lütkepohl and T. Lee, *Introduction to the Theory and Practice of Econometrics*, 2nd edn (Wiley, New York, 1988), Chs. 5, 6, 8, 9, 11, 13, 14, and 15. A very detailed, though rather more difficult, discussion is available in *The Theory and Practice of Econometrics*, 2nd edn (Wiley, New York, 1985) by the same authors. This volume is perhaps the best econometrics reference book currently available for practitioners and researchers.

While most textbooks discuss estimation of simultaneous equations models, few consider anything much more complex than two-stage least squares. Besides the three books mentioned in the first paragraph, particularly good introductions to estimation of simultaneous equation models are given by R.S. Pindyck and D.L. Rubinfeld, *Econometric Models and Economic Forecasts* (McGraw-Hill, New York, 1976), Ch. 9 and appendices, and M.D. Intriligator, *Econometric Models, Techniques and Applications* (Amsterdam, North Holland, 1978), Ch. 11. R.J. and T.H. Wonnacott, *Econometrics*, 2nd edn (Wiley, New York, 1979), Ch. 20 contains some useful material on two-stage least squares and three-stage least squares, and on modifications to two-stage least squares where degrees of freedom are limited. A good simple introduction to estimation of simultaneous equations models with autocorrelated disturbances is given in the appendix to Ch. 7 of H.H. Kelejian and W.E. Oates, *Introduction to Econometrics*, 2nd edn

(Harper and Row, New York, 1981). Non-linear simultaneous equation models and their estimation using two-stage least squares are introduced in Ch. 8 and its appendix of the same book.

Possible further reading on the more specific points mentioned in this chapter is suggested in the notes below.

Notes

1. D.F. Hendry and K.F. Wallis, 'Editors' Introduction' in D.F. Hendry and K.F. Wallis (eds.), *Econometrics and Quantitative Economics* (Blackwell, Oxford, 1984), pp. 1-12.

2. An estimator, b, of a parameter, β, is unbiased if $E(b) = \beta$. Bias is measured by $E(b) - \beta$.

3. b is an efficient estimator of β if $E(b) = \beta$, and $Var(b) < Var(b^*)$, where b^* is any other unbiased estimator of β.

4. $MSE = E(b - \beta)^2 = Var(b) + (bias(b))^2$.

5. b is an asymptotically unbiased estimator if $\lim_{n \to \infty} E(b)=\beta$.

6. b is a consistent estimator of β if $plim\ (b) = \beta$.

7. G.G. Judge, R.C. Hill, W.E. Griffiths, H. Lütkepohl, and T. Lee, *Introduction to the Theory and Practice of Econometrics*, 2nd edn (Wiley, New York, 1988), pp. 214-217 gives a simple example of a Monte Carlo experiment aimed at examining the properties of the ordinary least squares estimator of the general linear statistical model.

8. Bayesian methods are not discussed here since as yet they are little used in agricultural commodity market modelling. J.D. Hey, *Data in Doubt* (Martin Robertson, Oxford, 1983) provides a simple introduction.

9. This and other *robust* estimators are described in G.S. Maddala, *Econometrics* (McGraw-Hill, New York, 1977), pp. 308-314.

10. For a survey of such methods, see A.C. Harvey, *Econometric Analysis of Time Series* (Philip Allan, Oxford, 1981), Ch. 4.

11. More formally the general linear statistical model can be expressed as follows: (i) $\mathbf{Y} = \mathbf{X}\beta + \varepsilon$, where $\mathbf{Y}$ is a nx1 vector of n observations on the dependent variable Y, $\mathbf{X}$ is a nxk matrix, each column of which is a vector of n observations on each of k independent or explanatory variables, β is a vector of k unknown parameters, and ε is a vector of n unobservable random disturbances. (ii) $E(\varepsilon) = 0$. (iii) $E(\varepsilon\varepsilon') = \sigma^2 I$. (iv) $\mathbf{X}$ has rank $k < n$. (v) $\mathbf{X}$ is fixed.

12. For a particular sample of n observations the model can be expressed $\mathbf{Y} = \mathbf{X}\mathbf{b} + \mathbf{e}$, where $\mathbf{b}$ is the kx1 vector of estimated

parameters, and **e** is the nx1 vector of sample residuals. An expression for the sum of squared residuals is derived

$$\mathbf{e'e} = (\mathbf{Y} - \mathbf{Xb})'(\mathbf{Y} - \mathbf{Xb}) = \mathbf{Y'Y} - 2\mathbf{b'X'Y} + \mathbf{b'X'Xb}$$

Differentiating the last expression with respect to **b**, and setting equal to zero for a minimum gives

$$\delta\mathbf{e'e}/\delta\mathbf{b} = -2\mathbf{X'Y} + 2\mathbf{X'Xb} = 0$$

from which

$$\mathbf{X'Xb} = \mathbf{X'Y}$$

and hence the ordinary least squares estimator is

$$\mathbf{b} = (\mathbf{X'X})^{-1}\mathbf{X'Y}$$

Using $\mathbf{Y} = \mathbf{X}\beta + \varepsilon$

$$\mathbf{b} = (\mathbf{X'X})^{-1}\mathbf{X'X}\beta + (\mathbf{X'X})^{-1}\mathbf{X'}\varepsilon = \beta + (\mathbf{X'X})^{-1}\mathbf{X'}\varepsilon$$

and taking expected values shows that the estimator is unbiased.

$$E(\mathbf{b}) = \beta + (\mathbf{X'X})^{-1}\mathbf{X'}E(\varepsilon) = \beta$$

The variances and covariances of the b's are given by

$$E[(\mathbf{b} - \beta)(\mathbf{b} - \beta)'] = E[(\mathbf{X'X})^{-1}\mathbf{X'}\varepsilon\varepsilon'\mathbf{X}(\mathbf{X'X})^{-1}]$$

or

$$(\mathbf{X'X})^{-1}\mathbf{X'}E(\varepsilon\varepsilon')\mathbf{X}(\mathbf{X'X})^{-1} = (\mathbf{X'X})^{-1}\mathbf{X'}\sigma^2\mathbf{I}\mathbf{X}(\mathbf{X'X})^{-1} = \sigma^2(\mathbf{X'X})^{-1}$$

σ^2 can be estimated from $\mathbf{e'e}/n\text{-}k$.

13. This is proved in almost any econometrics textbook. See, for example, Judge, Hill, Griffiths, Lütkepohl, and Lee, *Introduction to the Theory and Practice of Econometrics*, pp. 202-205.

14. Assumptions concerning the disturbances are summarised as $\varepsilon \sim N(\mathbf{0}, \sigma^2\mathbf{I})$.

15. Common tests are the skewness-kurtosis and Kolmogorov-Smirnov test. The Box-Cox transformation is perhaps the most common data transformation used to ensure normality. A. Spanos, *Statistical Foundations of Econometric Modelling* (Cambridge

University Press, Cambridge, 1986), pp. 451-457 has the details.

16. The likelihood function is

$$L(\beta, \sigma^2) = (2\pi\sigma^2)^{n/2} \exp[-\frac{1}{2\sigma^2}((Y - X\beta)'(Y-X\beta))]$$

or

$$L(\beta, \sigma^2) = (2\pi\sigma^2)^{n/2} \exp[-\frac{1}{2\sigma^2}(Y'Y - 2\beta'X'Y + \beta'X'X\beta)]$$

The log-likelihood function is

$$\ln L(\beta, \sigma^2) = -\frac{n}{2}\ln 2\pi - \frac{n}{2}\ln \sigma^2 - \frac{1}{2\sigma^2}(Y'Y - 2\beta X'Y + \beta'X'X\beta)$$

The maximum likelihood estimates of β, **b**, is that which maximises this function. Taking the partial derivative with respect to β and setting equal to zero for a maximum

$$\frac{\delta \ln L}{\delta\beta} = -\frac{1}{\sigma^2}(X'Y - X'Xb) = 0$$

which implies

$$-(X'X - X'Xb) = 0$$

hence

$$X'Xb = X'Y$$

from which

$$b = (X'X)^{-1}X'Y$$

which is the same as the ordinary least squares estimator, as is the maximum likelihood estimator for the variances and covariances of the b's.

Taking the partial derivative of ln L with respect to σ^2 gives

$$\frac{\delta \ln L}{\delta\sigma^2} = -\frac{n}{2\sigma^2} + \frac{1}{2\sigma^4}(Y'Y - 2\beta'X'Y + \beta'X'X\beta)$$

The maximum likelihood estimate of σ^2, s^2, is that at which this is maximised. Setting equal to zero for a maximum gives

$$-\frac{n}{2s^2} + \frac{1}{2s^4}(\mathbf{Y'Y} - 2\mathbf{b'X'Y} + \mathbf{b'X'Xb}) = 0$$

from which

$$s^2 = (\mathbf{Y'Y} - 2\mathbf{b'X'Y} + \mathbf{b'X'Xb}) / n = \mathbf{e'e} / n$$

17. Formally, the assumption $E(\varepsilon\varepsilon') = \sigma^2\mathbf{I}$ is replaced by the assumption $E(\varepsilon\varepsilon') = \sigma^2\Omega$ where Ω is a known n x n positive definite symmetric matrix. The elements on the main diagonal of $\sigma^2\Omega$ are the variances of the disturbances and the off-diagonal elements the covariances.

18. In the first order autoregressive scheme, $\varepsilon_t = \rho\varepsilon_{t-1} + \upsilon_t$, $E(\varepsilon_t) = 0$; $E(\varepsilon_t^2) = \sigma_\varepsilon^2 = \sigma_\upsilon^2/(1 - \rho^2)$; $E(\varepsilon_t\varepsilon_{t-1}) = \rho\,\sigma_\varepsilon^2$ and in general, $E(\varepsilon_t\varepsilon_{t-s}) = \rho^s\,\sigma_\varepsilon^2$.

19. D.F. Hendry and G.E. Mizon, 'Serial Correlation As a Convenient Simplification, Not a Nuisance', *Economic Journal*, vol. 88, no. 351 (1978), pp. 549-563.

20. J. Durbin, 'Testing for Serial Correlation in Least Squares Regression When Some of the Regressors are Lagged Dependent Variables', *Econometrica*, vol. 38, no. 3 (1970), pp. 410-421.

$h = r\sqrt{(n / (1 - n\,V(b_1)))}$ where r is the estimated autocorrelation coefficient, n is sample size, and $V(b_1)$ is the ordinary least squares estimate of the variance of the coefficient on the lagged dependent variable. *h* is normally distributed.

21. The autocorrelation function giving the sequence of autocorrelation coefficients for increasing lags is often plotted as a *correlogram* together with confidence intervals equal, at the 95% level, to $-(1/n) \pm (2/\sqrt{n})$.

22. H. Glejser, 'A New Test for Heteroscedasticity', *Journal of the American Statistical Association*, vol. 64, no. 325 (1969), pp. 316-323.

23. T.S. Breusch and A.R. Pagan, 'A Simple Test for Heteroscedasticity and Random Coefficient Variation', *Econometrica*, vol. 47, no. 5 (1979), pp. 1287-1294.

24. The unbiasedness of the least squares coefficient estimates can be shown as in note 12 above since their variances and covariances are not involved. Hence,

$$E(\mathbf{b}_{ols}) = \beta + (\mathbf{X'X})^{-1}\mathbf{X'}E(\varepsilon) = \beta.$$

The variances and covariances of the b's, again following note 12, are given by

$$E[(b_{ols} - \beta)(b_{ols} - \beta)'] = (X'X)^{-1}X'E(\varepsilon\varepsilon')X(X'X)^{-1}$$

which in this case, since $E(\varepsilon\varepsilon') = \sigma^2\Omega$, gives

$$(X'X)^{-1}X'\sigma^2\Omega X(X'X)^{-1} = \sigma^2(X'X)^{-1}X'\Omega X(X'X)^{-1}$$

25. Given the positive definite nxn matrix Ω, an nxn nonsingular matrix, P, will provide $P\Omega P' = I$ and $P'P = \Omega^{-1}$. Transforming the model $Y = X\beta + \varepsilon$, where $E(\varepsilon\varepsilon') = \sigma^2\Omega$, using P gives $PY = PX\beta + P\varepsilon$. The disturbances of the transformed model will have the properties $E(P\varepsilon) = PE(\varepsilon) = 0$, and $E(P\varepsilon\varepsilon'P') = PE(\varepsilon\varepsilon')P' = \sigma^2 P\Omega P' = \sigma^2 I$. The generalised least squares estimator for the unknown parameters, b_{gls}, is that which minimises the sum of the squared transformed sample residuals, Pe. The sum of squared residuals is given by

$$e'P'Pe = (PY - PXb)'(PY - PXb)$$
$$= Y'P'PY - 2b'X'P'PY + b'X'P'PXb$$

Differentiating with respect to b, and setting equal to zero for a minimum gives

$$\delta e'P'Pe/\delta b = -2X'P'PY + 2X'P'PXb = 0$$

from which

$$X'P'PXb = X'P'PY$$

and hence the generalised least squares estimator is

$$b_{gls} = (X'P'PX)^{-1}X'P'PY = (X'\Omega^{-1}X)^{-1}X'\Omega^{-1}Y$$

Using $Y = X\beta + \varepsilon$

$$b_{gls} = (X'\Omega^{-1}X)^{-1}X'\Omega^{-1}X\beta + (X'\Omega^{-1}X)^{-1}X'\Omega^{-1}\varepsilon$$
$$= \beta + (X'\Omega^{-1}X)^{-1}X'\Omega^{-1}\varepsilon$$

and taking expected values shows that the estimator is unbiased.

$$E(\mathbf{b}_{gls}) = \beta + (X'\Omega^{-1}X)^{-1}X'\Omega^{-1}E(\varepsilon) = \beta$$

The variances and covariances of the b's are given by

$$E[(\mathbf{b}_{gls} - \beta)(\mathbf{b}_{gls} - \beta)']$$

$$= E[(X'\Omega^{-1}X)^{-1}X'\Omega^{-1}\varepsilon\varepsilon'\Omega^{-1}X(X'\Omega^{-1}X)^{-1}]$$

or

$$(X'\Omega^{-1}X)^{-1}X'\Omega^{-1}E(\varepsilon\varepsilon')\Omega^{-1}X(X'\Omega^{-1}X)^{-1}$$

$$= (X'\Omega^{-1}X)^{-1}X'\Omega^{-1}\sigma^2\Omega\Omega^{-1}X(X'\Omega^{-1}X)^{-1} = \sigma^2(X'\Omega^{-1}X)^{-1}$$

σ^2 can be estimated from $e'\Omega^{-1}e/n\text{-}k$.

26. Z. Griliches and P. Rao, 'Small Sample Properties of Several Two-Stage Regression Methods in the Context of Autocorrelated Errors', *Journal of the American Statistical Association*, vol. 64, no. 325 (1969), pp. 253-272.

27. The log likelihood function is

$$\ln L = -\frac{n}{2}\ln 2\pi - \frac{1}{2}\ln|\Omega| - n\ln\sigma - \frac{1}{2\sigma^2}((Y - X\beta)'\Omega^{-1}(Y - X\beta))$$

In the case of first order autoregressive disturbances this becomes

$$\ln L = -\frac{n}{2}\ln\sigma_\upsilon^2 + \frac{1}{2}\ln(1 - \rho^2) - \frac{1}{2\sigma_\upsilon^2}((Y - X\beta)'\Omega^{-1}(Y - X\beta))$$

Maximising this yields equations nonlinear in the parameters for which they must be solved. A popular algorithm is that proposed by C.M. Beach and J.G. MacKinnon, 'A Maximum Likelihood Procedure for Regression With Autocorrelated Errors', *Econometrica*, vol. 46, no. 1 (1978), pp. 51-58.

28. For a full discussion of stochastic regressors and of the asymptotic theory needed in establishing their consequences and the properties of different estimators, see Judge, Hill, Griffiths, Lütkepohl and Lee, *Introduction to the Theory and Practice of Econometrics*, Ch.13.

29. The unbiasedness of ordinary least squares can be shown as in Note 12 above, except that where X is stochastic but distributed independently of X, $E(\mathbf{b}_{ols}) = \beta + E[(X'X)^{-1}X']E(\varepsilon) = \beta$, since $E(\varepsilon) =$

0. $s^2E[(X'X)^{-1}]$ is an unbiased estimator for $E[(b - \beta)(b - \beta)']$, and $s^2 = (e'e)/n\text{-}k$ is an unbiased estimator for σ^2.

In the maximum likelihood case, the log likelihood function is

$$\ln L = -\frac{n}{2}\ln 2\pi - \frac{n}{2}\ln \sigma^2 - \frac{1}{2\sigma^2}(Y - X\beta)'(Y - X\beta) + \ln f(X)$$

where f(X) describes the distribution of X. The partial derivatives of ln L with respect to β and σ^2, and hence the maximum likelihood estimators for these, are not affected by the presence of f(X).

30. Provided that X is contemporaneously uncorrelated with ε, plim $(1/nX'\varepsilon) = 0$. plim $b_{ols} = \beta + \text{plim } [(1/nX'X)^{-1}(1/nX'\varepsilon)] = \beta$, and so ordinary least squares is consistent.

31. In the case of contemporaneous correlation between an explanatory variable and the disturbance, plim $(1/nX'\varepsilon) \neq 0$. Consequently, plim $b_{ols} = \beta + \text{plim } [(1/nX'X)^{-1}(1/nX'\varepsilon)] \neq \beta$, and so ordinary least squares is not consistent.

32. Instrumental variables estimation of the model $Y = X\beta + \varepsilon$ relies on the matrix of instrumental variables Z, which may have some columns in common with X. Z should have the properties plim $(1/n\ Z'\varepsilon) = 0$, plim $(1/n\ Z'X) = \Sigma_{ZX}$ exists and is non-singular, plim $(1/n\ Z'Z) = \Sigma_{ZZ}$ exists and is non-singular. The instrumental variables estimator is derived by premultiplying the original model by Z' to obtain

$$Z'Y = Z'X\beta + Z'\varepsilon$$

from which

$$b_{IV} = (Z'X)^{-1}Z'Y$$

This is consistent since

$$b_{IV} = (Z'X)^{-1}(Z'X)\beta + (Z'X)^{-1}(Z'\varepsilon) = \beta + (Z'X)^{-1}(Z'\varepsilon)$$

and

$$\text{plim } b_{IV} = \beta + \text{plim } [(Z'X)^{-1}(Z'\varepsilon)]$$

$$= \beta + \text{plim } [(1/n\ Z'X)^{-1}(1/n\ Z'\varepsilon)] = \beta$$

since plim $(1/n\ \mathbf{Z}'\varepsilon) = \mathbf{0}$. A consistent estimator of the asymptotic variances and covariances of β is given by $s^2(\mathbf{Z}'\mathbf{X})^{-1}(\mathbf{Z}'\mathbf{Z})(\mathbf{X}'\mathbf{Z})^{-1}$, where s^2 is a consistent estimator of σ^2 given by $((\mathbf{Y} - \mathbf{X}\mathbf{b}_{IV})'(\mathbf{Y} - \mathbf{X}\mathbf{b}_{IV}))/n\text{-}k$.

33. J. Johnston, *Econometric Methods*, 3rd edn (McGraw- Hill, New York, 1984), pp. 364-371 provides a survey.

34. The inconsistency of ordinary least squares is explored and maximum likelihood estimation is discussed by H.E. Doran and W.E. Griffiths, 'Inconsistency of the OLS Estimator of the Partial Adjustment-Adaptive Expectations Model', *Journal of Econometrics*, vol. 7, no. 1 (1978), pp. 133-146.

35. The structural form of the simultaneous equations model is conventionally expressed as $\mathbf{YB} + \mathbf{XA} = \mathbf{E}$. $\mathbf{Y}$ is an nxg matrix of n observations on each of g endogenous variables. $\mathbf{X}$ is an nxk matrix of n observations on each of k predetermined variables. $\mathbf{B}$ is a gxg matrix of coefficients on the current endogenous variables, each column of which is a vector of the coefficients from one equation. Conventionally the diagonal elements of $\mathbf{B}$ are set equal to one, implying that, for example, the first endogenous variable is dependent in the first equation and so on. Some elements will be zeros implying that the corresponding endogenous variables do not appear in a particular equation. $\mathbf{A}$ is a kxg matrix of coefficients on the predetermined variables, again with each column containing the coefficients from a particular equation, and zeros indicating that the corresponding predetermined variables do not appear in a particular equation. E is an nxg matrix of unobservable stochastic disturbances, with each column being a vector of disturbances for one particular equation. The disturbances are assumed to have the properties $E(\varepsilon_i) = 0$ for all i = 1,2 ... g, and $E(\varepsilon_i\varepsilon_j) = \sigma_{ij}\mathbf{I}$ for all i,j = 1,2 ... g.

One particular equation, the first, for example, can be isolated from the system by partitioning $\mathbf{Y}$ and $\mathbf{X}$: $\mathbf{Y} = (\mathbf{y}_1 \mid \mathbf{Y}_1 \mid \mathbf{Y}_2)$ and $\mathbf{X} = (\mathbf{X}_1 \mid \mathbf{X}_2)$ where $\mathbf{y}_1$ is the nx1 vector of n observations on the endogenous variable taken to be dependent in the equation, $\mathbf{Y}_1$ is the nxg_1-1 matrix of n observations on those g_1 endogenous variables except y_1 appearing in the equation, $\mathbf{Y}_2$ is the nxg-g_1 matrix of n observations on the g-g_1 endogenous variables not appearing in the equation, $\mathbf{X}_1$ is the nxk_1 matrix of n observations on k_1 predetermined variables appearing in the equation, and $\mathbf{X}_2$ is the nxk-k_1 matrix of n observations on the k-k_1 predetermined variables not appearing in the equation. The coefficient and disturbance matrices can be partitioned comformably to obtain

$$\begin{bmatrix} y_1 \mid Y_1 \mid Y_2 \end{bmatrix} \begin{bmatrix} 1 \\ -- \\ \beta_1 \\ -- \\ 0 \end{bmatrix} + \begin{bmatrix} X_1 \mid X_2 \end{bmatrix} \begin{bmatrix} \alpha_1 \\ — \\ 0 \end{bmatrix} = \begin{bmatrix} \varepsilon_1 \end{bmatrix}$$

and rearranging gives

$$y_1 = - Y_1\beta_1 - X_1\alpha_1 + \varepsilon_1$$

36. J.C.S. Tang, 'Estimating the Demand Functions for Fresh Citrus', *European Review of Agricultural Economics*, vol. 7, no. 3 (1980), pp. 341-346.

37. The SURE model consists of g equations linked via their disturbances. Each equation can be written as $Y_i = X_i\beta_i + \varepsilon_i$, i = 1,2, ... g, where Y_i is an nx1 vector of n observations on the dependent variable in the ith equation, X_i is an nxk_i matrix of n observations on each of the k_i explanatory variables appearing in the ith equation, β_i is a k_ix1 vector of unknown parameters in the ith equation, and ε_i is an nx1 vector of disturbances in the ith equation. The complete system of g equations can be written

$$\begin{bmatrix} Y_1 \\ Y_2 \\ . \\ . \\ Y_g \end{bmatrix} = \begin{bmatrix} X_1 & 0 & . & . & 0 \\ 0 & X_2 & . & . & 0 \\ . & . & . & . & . \\ . & . & . & . & . \\ 0 & 0 & . & . & X_g \end{bmatrix} \begin{bmatrix} \beta_1 \\ \beta_2 \\ . \\ . \\ \beta_3 \end{bmatrix} + \begin{bmatrix} \varepsilon_1 \\ \varepsilon_2 \\ . \\ . \\ \varepsilon_g \end{bmatrix}$$

or $Y = X\beta + \varepsilon$, where Y is an ngx1 vector, X is an ngxΣk_i matrix, β is a Σk_ix1 vector and ε is an ngx1 vector. Variances of the disturbances in each equation and covariances between the disturbances of any pair of equations, σ_{ij}, i,j = 1,2 ... g, are assumed to be constant. Covariances of the disturbances for different periods within or across equations are assumed to be zero. These assumptions are summarised by the matrix Ω

$$\Omega = E(\varepsilon\varepsilon') = \begin{bmatrix} \sigma_{11}I & \sigma_{12}I & . & . & \sigma_{1g}I \\ \sigma_{21}I & \sigma_{22}I & . & . & \sigma_{2g}I \\ . & . & . & . & . \\ . & . & . & . & . \\ \sigma_{g1}I & \sigma_{g2}I & . & . & \sigma_{gg}I \end{bmatrix}$$

where **I** is an nxn identity matrix. Using this in the generalised least squares estimator, $\mathbf{b} = (\mathbf{X}'\Omega^{-1}\mathbf{X})^{-1}\mathbf{X}'\Omega^{-1}\mathbf{Y}$, and $E[(\mathbf{b} - \beta)(\mathbf{b} - \beta)'] = (\mathbf{X}'\Omega^{-1}\mathbf{X})^{-1}$. The Zellner two-stage Aitken estimator estimates the σ_{ij} where these are unknown. $s_{ij} = (e_i e_j)/\sqrt{((n-k_i)(n-k_j))}$ where $\mathbf{e}_i$ and $\mathbf{e}_j$ are the ordinary least squares residuals from the ith and jth equations , provides an unbiased and consistent estimator for σ_{ij}.

38. A. Zellner, 'An Efficient Method of Estimating Seemingly Unrelated Regressions and Tests of Aggregation Bias', *Journal of the American Statistical Association*, vol. 57, no. 298 (1962), pp. 348-368.

39. The reduced form is obtained by multiplying through the structural form by $\mathbf{B}^{-1}$ to obtain $\mathbf{YBB}^{-1} + \mathbf{XAB}^{-1} = \mathbf{EB}^{-1}$, and rearranging gives $\mathbf{Y} = -\mathbf{XAB}^{-1} + \mathbf{EB}^{-1}$, or $\mathbf{Y} = \mathbf{X}\Pi + \mathbf{V}$, where $\Pi = -\mathbf{AB}^{-1}$ is the kxg matrix of reduced form coefficients, and $\mathbf{V} = \mathbf{EB}^{-1}$ is the nxg matrix of reduced form disturbances.

40. See M.D. Intriligator, *Econometric Models, Techniques and Applications* (North Holland, Amsterdam, 1978), pp. 499-506.

41. Identification conditions in non-linear models can be complex. H.H. Kelejian and W.E. Oates, *Introduction to Econometrics*, 2nd edn (Harper and Row, New York, 1981), pp. 288-299, provides a simple introduction.

42. Formal conditions for identification are derived and discussed in most econometrics texts. See, for example, R.S. Pindyck and D.L. Rubinfeld, *Econometric Models and Economic Forecasts* (McGraw-Hill, New York, 1976), pp. 292-298.

43. Identification can be secured by other means - restrictions on the covariances of the disturbances of different equations, for example. J. Johnston, *Econometric Methods*, pp. 452-467 provides a review of the alternatives.

44. W.C. Labys, *Dynamic Commodity Models: Specification, Estimation, and Simulation* (D.C. Heath, Lexington, 1973), p. 133.

45. T.C. Liu, 'Underidentification, Structural Estimation and Forecasting', *Econometrica*, vol. 28, no. 4 (1960), pp. 338-348.

46. Two-stage least squares estimation of, say, the first equation in a system,

$$y_1 = - Y_1\beta_1 - X_1\alpha_1 + \varepsilon_1$$

or

$$y_1 = \begin{bmatrix} Y_1 & X_1 \end{bmatrix} \begin{bmatrix} \beta_1 \\ \alpha_1 \end{bmatrix} + \varepsilon_1$$

proceeds by estimating fitted values, for the endogenous variables in Y_1 from the estimated reduced form $Y_1 = X\Pi + V$. Π is estimated by $P = (X'X)^{-1}X'Y_1$, and the fitted values of Y_1, Y_1^*, from $X(X'X)^{-1}X'Y_1$. Y_1^* is then used, together with X_1, as instrumental variables in the equation for y_1.

$$\begin{bmatrix} Y_1^{*\prime} \\ X_1' \end{bmatrix} y_1 = \begin{bmatrix} Y_1^{*\prime} \\ X_1' \end{bmatrix} \begin{bmatrix} Y_1 & X_1 \end{bmatrix} \begin{bmatrix} \beta_1 \\ \alpha_1 \end{bmatrix} + \begin{bmatrix} Y_1^{*\prime} \\ X_1' \end{bmatrix} \varepsilon_1$$

or

$$\begin{bmatrix} Y_1^{*\prime}y_1 \\ X_1'y_1 \end{bmatrix} = \begin{bmatrix} Y_1^{*\prime}Y_1 & Y_1^{*\prime}X_1 \\ X_1'Y_1 & X_1'X_1 \end{bmatrix} \begin{bmatrix} \beta_1 \\ \alpha_1 \end{bmatrix} + \begin{bmatrix} Y_1^{*\prime}\varepsilon_1 \\ X_1'\varepsilon_1 \end{bmatrix}$$

from which

$$\begin{bmatrix} Y_1{*}'Y_1 & Y_1{*}'X_1 \\ X_1'Y_1 & X_1'X_1 \end{bmatrix}^{-1} \begin{bmatrix} Y_1{*}'y_1 \\ X_1'y_1 \end{bmatrix} = \begin{bmatrix} \beta_1 \\ \alpha_1 \end{bmatrix} + \begin{bmatrix} Y_1{*}'Y_1 & Y_1{*}'X_1 \\ X_1'Y_1 & X_1'X_1 \end{bmatrix}^{-1} \begin{bmatrix} Y_1{*}'\varepsilon_1 \\ X_1'\varepsilon_1 \end{bmatrix}$$

The last term on the right is equal to zero in the probability limit, and hence the two-stage least squares estimator for β_1 and α_1, $\mathbf{b}_1$ and $\mathbf{a}_1$ is given by

$$\begin{bmatrix} Y_1{*}'Y_1 & Y_1{*}'X_1 \\ X_1'Y_1 & X_1'X_1 \end{bmatrix}^{-1} \begin{bmatrix} Y_1{*}'y_1 \\ X_1'y_1 \end{bmatrix} = \begin{bmatrix} \mathbf{b}_1 \\ \mathbf{a}_1 \end{bmatrix}$$

In practice there is no need to estimate $\mathbf{Y}_1{*}$ separately since it can be substituted throughout by $\mathbf{X}(\mathbf{X}'\mathbf{X})^{-1}\mathbf{X}'\mathbf{Y}_1$. A consistent estimator of $E[(\mathbf{b}-\beta)(\mathbf{b}-\beta)']$ is obtained by multiplying s^2 into the inverse above, where $s^2 = \mathbf{e}_1'\mathbf{e}_1/(n - (g_1-1+k_1))$.

47. Kelejian and Oates, *Introduction to Econometrics*, pp. 299-315, provides an introduction to the estimation of non-linear simultaneous equations models.

48. Some alternatives are reviewed in R.J. Wonnacott and T.H. Wonnacott, *Econometrics*, 2nd edn (Wiley, New York, 1979), pp. 294-296 and pp. 511-516.

49. See, for example, R.C. Fair, 'The Estimation of Simultaneous Equation Models With Lagged Endogenous Variables and First Order Serially Correlated Errors', *Econometrica*, vol. 38, no. 3 (1970), pp. 507-516.

50. The three-stage least squares estimator involves simultaneous generalised least squares estimation of a simultaneous equations model. It begins, however, with the two-stage least squares estimation of each equation in turn. From this application of two-stage least squares the fitted values from the reduced form equations of the first stage are retained and the residuals from each equation are estimated. The two-stage least squares estimates of the parameters of the model are of no further interest. Each equation, the ith for example, of the model can be written

$$\mathbf{y}_i = \mathbf{Y}_i{*}\beta_i + \mathbf{X}_i\alpha_i + \varepsilon_i$$

where the matrices and vectors are as defined in note 35 above, but in particular $\mathbf{Y}_i^*$ is a matrix of fitted values of the endogenous variables appearing on the right-hand side of the ith equation obtained from the reduced form equations in the first stage of two-stage least squares. The equations can be written more compactly as

$$y_i = Z_i\delta_i + \varepsilon_i$$

where $\mathbf{Z}_i = [\ \mathbf{Y}_i^* \quad \mathbf{X}_i\ ]$, and $\delta_i = [\ \beta_i \quad \alpha_i\ ]'$. The complete model can be written, as in the seemingly unrelated regressions model, as

$$\begin{bmatrix} y_1 \\ y_2 \\ . \\ . \\ y_g \end{bmatrix} = \begin{bmatrix} Z_1 & 0 & . & . & 0 \\ 0 & Z_2 & . & . & 0 \\ . & . & . & . & . \\ . & . & . & . & . \\ 0 & 0 & . & . & Z_g \end{bmatrix} \begin{bmatrix} \delta_1 \\ \delta_2 \\ . \\ . \\ \delta_g \end{bmatrix} + \begin{bmatrix} \varepsilon_1 \\ \varepsilon_2 \\ . \\ . \\ \varepsilon_g \end{bmatrix}$$

or $\mathbf{Y} = \mathbf{Z}\delta + \varepsilon$. This is estimated using the generalised least squares estimator $\mathbf{d} = (\mathbf{Z}'\Omega^{-1}\mathbf{Z})^{-1}\,\mathbf{Z}'\Omega^{-1}\mathbf{Y}$ where $\Omega = E(\varepsilon\varepsilon')$ is the matrix of variances and covariances of the disturbances, and again as in the seemingly unrelated regressions case, takes the form

$$\Omega = \begin{bmatrix} \sigma_{11}I & \sigma_{12}I & . & . & \sigma_{1g}I \\ \sigma_{21}I & \sigma_{22}I & . & . & \sigma_{2g}I \\ . & . & . & . & . \\ . & . & . & . & . \\ \sigma_{g1}I & \sigma_{g2}I & . & . & \sigma_{gg}I \end{bmatrix}$$

The σ_{ij}, $i,j = 1,2 \ldots g$, will not be known but can be estimated using the two-stage least squares residuals from $s_{ij} = e_i'e_j/n$. The three stage least squares estimator of $E[(\mathbf{d} - \delta)(\mathbf{d} - \delta)']$ is given by

$(Z'\Omega^{-1}Z)^{-1}$. For a proof of the consistency and asymptotic efficiency of three-stage least squares see Judge, Hill, Griffiths, Lütkepohl, and Lee, *Introduction to the Theory and Practice of Econometrics*, pp. 649-651.

51. For a discussion of full information maximum likelihood estimation see Johnston, *Econometric Methods*, pp. 490-492.

52. R.B. Miller, *Minitab Handbook for Business and Economics* (PWS-Kent, Boston, 1988), Chs. 11 and 12.

53. TSP International, *TSP User's Manual*, Version 4.0B (TSP International, Stanford, 1983).

54. Quantitative Micro Software, *MicroTSP*, Version 5.0 (Quantitative Micro Software, Irvine, 1988).

55. Model solution and the difficulties caused by non-linearities are discussed in Chapter 5 below.

56. More formally, the endogenous variables coefficients matrix remains sparse.

57. See, for example, the summing up on a series of sector models by S.R. Johnson, 'Discussion', *American Journal of Agricultural Economics*, vol. 59, no. 1 (1977), pp. 133-136.

58. Fair, 'The Estimation of Simultaneous Equation Models With Lagged Endogenous Variables and First Order Serially Correlated Errors' suggests a means of easing pressure on degrees of freeedom by combining current and lagged values of those predetermined variables excluded from the structural equation to be estimated into generalised differences for use in the first-stage regressions. In practice this does not always provide much relief.

59. T. Young, *The Position of the UK Cereals Market Within the EEC* , University of Manchester Department of Agricultural Economics Bulletin 170, 1979, p. 55, for example argues that '. . . despite the built-in biases which occur when using ordinary least squares on a simultaneous system, the gains in efficiency from more sophisticated methods are insufficient to outweigh the convenience of estimating a large model equation by equation'.

R.L. Carter, 'Least Squares as an Exploratory Estimator', *Canadian Journal of Economics*, vol. 6, no. 1 (1973), pp. 108-114, found ordinary least squares preferable to two-stage least squares for exploratory stages of model construction using the conventional t-test for variable selection in that the probability of Type II errors - accepting a null hypothesis that a parameter is equal to zero when it is false - is reduced. Once an acceptable model is selected, however, re-estimation using two-stage least squares to reduce the probability of Type I errors is suggested.

60. Monte Carlo evidence is reviewed in D.W. Challen and A.J. Hagger, *Macroeconometric Systems* (Macmillan, London, 1983), Ch. 5.

61. A. Zellner, 'Statistical Analysis of Econometric Models,

Journal of the American Statistical Association, vol. 74, no. 367 (1979), pp. 62[illegible] 651.

62. G.F. Rhodes and M.D. Westbrook, 'A Study of Estimator Densities Under Misspecification', *Journal of Econometrics*, vol. 16, no. 2 (1981), pp. 311-337.

63. See, for example, J.G. Cragg, 'On the Relative Small Sample Properties of Several Structural Equation Estimators', *Econometrica*, vol. 35, no. 1 (1967), pp. 89-109, or Intriligator, *Econometric Models, Techniques and Applications*, p. 420.

64. M.H. Salmon and J.R. Eaton, 'Estimation Problems in Large Econometric Models: An Application of Various Estimation Techniques to the London Business School Model' in G.A. Renton (ed.), *Modelling the UK Economy* (Heinemann, London, 1975), pp. 323-348.

65. The benefits or otherwise in terms of 'economic meaningfulness' of estimates from using different estimators might be inferred indirectly. The direction of bias in ordinary least squares estimates can sometimes be predicted. If the relationship between ordinary least squares and consistent estimates of the same parameter was as would be predicted on the basis of simultaneity bias, this might be taken to imply that the consistent estimate was more acceptable in that it was reducing an expected bias. D. Hallam, *The Neglect of Simultaneity in Agricultural Market Models*, University of Reading Department of Agricultural Economics Discussion Paper 86/1, 1986, for example, compares estimates of milk supply elasticity obtained using different estimators and notes that the differences between the estimates are indeed as would have been expected. Whether these differences can be attributed solely to differences in estimator used is uncertain, however.

66. L.R. Klein, 'Estimation of Interdependent Systems in Macroeconometrics', *Econometrica*, vol. 37, no. 1 (1969), pp. 171-192; R.C. Fair, 'A Comparison of Alternative Estimators of Macroeconomic Models', *International Economic Review*, vol. 14, no. 2 (1973), pp. 261-277.

67. Salmon and Eaton, 'Estimation Problems in Large Econometric Models: An Application of Various Estimation Techniques to the London Business School Model'.

68. Klein, 'Estimation of Interdependent Systems in Macroeconometrics'; Fair, 'A Comparison of Alternative Estimators of Macroeconomic Models'.

69. D. Hallam, *The Estimation of Dynamic Commodity Models*, University of Reading Department of Agricultural Economics Discussion Paper 83/3, 1983.

5
Model Solution

... give me your answer, do!

(Harry Dacre, *Daisy Bell*)

'Model solution' involves the computation of values, for one or more often a sequence of time periods, of the endogenous variables of an estimated econometric model for given values of its predetermined variables and stochastic disturbances. This process is sometimes referred to as 'simulation'[1] although that term is perhaps best reserved for solution in more specific contexts - the analysis of policy options, for example, discussed in Chapter 7. Most practical applications of a model will entail solution for the values of its endogenous variables. Different types of solution can be defined according to the historical time period to which the solution corresponds. Solution over periods for which the actual values of the endogenous variables are known, and hence can be compared with a model's predictions, plays a central role in model validation. Such solutions are referred to as *historical simulations* or *ex post forecasts* depending upon whether the solution period falls within that from which data are drawn for estimation of the model or not. Solutions over a period for which actual values of endogenous variables are known also allow counterfactual analyses, sometimes referred to as *simulation experiments*, aimed at ascertaining the differential effects of, for example, policies alternative to those actually pursued. Solutions for future time periods, or at least periods for which actual values of endogenous variables are not yet known, constitute *ex ante forecasts* .

Solution of a single equation model, where all explanatory variables can be regarded as predetermined - an estimated demand or supply function, for example - for a particular time period is clearly trivial. The solution value for the dependent variable is simply the fitted value routinely obtained from the estimated equation. In the case of recursive models, solution for a particular time period is similarly straightforward. A recursive model can be considered as a sequence of individual equations to be solved in turn. Solution progresses with the value of each endogenous variable substituted as it becomes available into equations subsequent in the causal ordering. Solution of simultaneous equation models is more problematic since the solution value for each endogenous variable depends upon the corresponding solution values for other endogenous variables. In the case of the agricultural commodity market model introduced in Chapter 2,

$$S_t = \alpha_0 + \alpha_1 P_t + \alpha_2 S_{t-1} + \alpha_3 W_t + u_t$$

$$D_t = \beta_0 + \beta_1 P_t + \beta_2 Y_t + \upsilon_t$$

$$I_t = I_{t-1} + S_t - D_t$$

$$P_t = \delta_0 + \delta_1 I_t + \delta_2 D_t + \varpi_t$$

the solution values for the endogenous variables, S_t, D_t, I_t, and P_t, would clearly be mutually dependent: by the second equation, current demand depends upon current price, but by the final equation, current price depends upon current demand, for example. Solution of the model entails solution of a set of simultaneous difference equations. The problems and methods of solution for this type of model are the primary concern of this chapter.

Treatment of Predetermined Variables

Solution of an estimated model for the values of its endogenous variables requires that values first be assigned to the predetermined variables. In the case of historical simulations or *ex post* forecasts actual values, at least for the exogenous variables concerned, are commonly employed. Where the solution is an *ex ante* forecast the current values of predetermined variables may be unknown. Since the forecast is conditional upon the values assigned these will be crucial in determining its accuracy. Deciding upon appropriate time paths for the exogenous variables over the forecast period can therefore account for a major portion of the time and effort involved in a forecasting exercise.

Where solution is for a sequence of time periods, current solved values for the endogenous variables for each period can be fed back into the model as values for the lagged endogenous variables in subsequent periods, generating what is sometimes referred to as a *dynamic solution* or *dynamic simulation*. This procedure is inevitable for *ex ante* forecasts where the actual time paths of the endogenous variables are unknown. Dynamic solutions provide a more complete picture of a model's dynamic properties and 'tracking' abilities, however, and hence are also commonly employed in historical simulations and *ex post* forecasting for the purposes of model validation.

Where they are known, the actual values of exogenous variables can be used in generating a solution. Where ascertaining the effect of a particular exogenous variable - a policy instrument, for example - is the object of a simulation exercise, however, a range of alternative hypothetical values may be used, whether the actual values are known or not.

Even for future time periods, the values of certain exogenous variables will be known. In the case of time trends used as proxies for technical progress or taste changes, for example, the appropriate values follow a known progression. In the case of dummy variables used for seasonal adjustment their values are known to follow a repeating pattern of zeros and ones. Some exogenous variables, such as population, follow relatively stable time paths. Others, some guaranteed producer prices, for example, may have their future values fixed one period in advance by decree. In such cases, their values might be regarded as 'known' for all practical purposes, at least where a relatively short forecast horizon is involved. There will remain, however, in any model a number of exogenous variables whose time paths over a forecast period are uncertain. For agricultural commodity market models these will typically include income or the level of economic activity influencing consumption, the prices of inputs and of other products which are substitutes or complements in production or consumption, the range and settings of policy instruments, and, perhaps most uncertain of all, weather.

In spite of the sometimes overriding influence of weather conditions on crop yields, the treatment of climatic variables in agricultural commodity market models remains unsatisfactory. The typically detailed climatic data and typically generalised forecasts can be difficult to incorporate into the estimation and solution of an econometric model. Dummy variables are perhaps the most common device for picking up the effects of abnormal climatic conditions in particular years to produce a better fit of the estimated model. In the absence of information to the contrary the forecast values of such variables are set at zero implying 'normal' weather conditions over the forecast period. The extent of yield uncertainty resulting from climatic variations can be described by the inclusion of stochastic variations in the solution procedure.[2] Stochastic solutions are discussed below. Solution for 'good', 'bad' and 'normal' yield scenarios allows consideration of a more restricted set of alternative weather conditions.

The future policy framework can represent another fundamental uncertainty in model solution, particularly where the forecast horizon is long. Resort is typically made to assumptions concerning the settings of particular relevant policy instruments or the general policy stance. Alternative assumptions can provide a range of scenarios of future market developments. Where ascertaining the impact of possible future policy changes is not a central object of the modelling exercise, the most common assumption made is that the policy framework will remain unchanged over the forecast period. Given the extent of policy interventions in agricultural commodity markets, their significant influence on output and prices, and the widespread discussion of agricultural policy reform, an assumption of 'no-change' may be unsatisfactory. Recently, there has been a growing interest in endogenising policy to commodity market models. This rests on the possibility that not only are commodity market developments conditioned by policy as almost all models assume, but policy is conditioned by market developments. Policy therefore becomes endogenous to the model to be determined along with the other endogenous variables.[3]

Expert economic and technical opinion may provide future values for some variables. 'Situation and outlook' publications from interested institutions can provide at least broad suggestions as to how quantities and prices of agricultural inputs and outputs might develop in the short to medium term. Forecasts of some exogenous variables may be available from other econometric models. Forecasts of macroeconomic variables, such as GDP used as a proxy for income in final consumption equations, or indices of industrial production used as indicators of the level of economic activity in demand equations for agricultural raw materials, are available from a variety of national and international sources. The output of other models may require some manipulation, however, to translate it into a form consistent with the variable definitions employed in the model to be solved.

In some cases an assumption of 'no change' either in the levels or recent trends of exogenous variables is made for the forecast period. FAO projections of food demand, for example, have assumed constant relative prices.[4] Such an assumption can be over-simplistic, particularly where extended time intervals are concerned: the relative price of poultrymeat, for example, declined dramatically over a period of years. The future time path of exogenous variables might also be characterised as a continuation of recent trends, and seasonal and cyclical patterns. Models of varying degrees of sophistication from simple linear time trends to Box-Jenkins time series models can be used to establish and predict such regularities.

Deterministic and Stochastic Solutions

Solutions can be further classified according to the treatment of the stochastic components of the model. In a *deterministic* solution the additive disturbance in each equation is set at its expected value of zero, the values of the predetermined variables are assumed to be fixed and known with certainty, and the parameters are assumed to be known constants rather than random variables dependent upon the particular sample of observations from which they are estimated. A deterministic solution provides unique values for each endogenous variable which is desirable in historic simulations and *ex post* forecasts used for model validation. In fact, their straightforward computation and interpretation make deterministic solutions a popular choice for a variety of purposes.

A *stochastic* solution acknowledges and attempts to incorporate one or more of the stochastic elements of the relationships specified within a model. The simplest means of incorporating a stochastic element is to assign non-zero values to the additive disturbance of each equation. These non-zero values are drawn from appropriate probability distributions. In the simplest case these would be normal distributions with means zero and variances equal to the estimated residual variances of the equations under consideration. Where the model is simultaneous, and hence the disturbances are correlated across equations, disturbance values can be drawn from a joint normal distribution. Stochastic components can also be added to the parameter values, again using values drawn from joint normal distributions with means, variances and covariances equal to the estimated values for the parameters concerned. Replication of a stochastic solution, typically one hundred times, drawing different values for the disturbances generates a probability distribution of values of each endogenous variable for each time period in the solution. The replications of a stochastic solution procedure can entail greater computational expense than a deterministic solution, although depending upon the solution method employed, the computational effort required need not be prohibitive. Decision-makers may not obtain an immediately obvious general picture from the multiplicity of raw results generated by stochastic solutions, a problem compounded where stochastic simulations of a range of policy alternatives are under consideration.[5] Presentation of results in the more helpful summary form of means and standard errors or confidence intervals is therefore common.

Uncertainty surrounding the precise nature of market relationships and the time paths of exogenous variables can be captured in a stochastic solution. The inclusion of stochastic elements can also provide a more informative description of possible market behaviour. The possibility of extreme fluctuations resulting from the superimposition of stochastic factors such as exceptionally adverse weather upon more systematic movements in prices and quantities is overlooked by a deterministic solution. The possible extent and effects of such extreme fluctuations are of some importance, however, for the design and administration of market stabilisation policies. Furthermore, control of policy variables such as stocks may itself be imperfect, making the outcome of a policy stochastic rather than certain. Stochastic simulations can provide information on the possible margins of error.

Solution Methods

The reduced form can be used in the solution of small linear simultaneous equation models like the simple market model above.

$$S_t = \pi_{10} + \pi_{11}Y_t + \pi_{12}S_{t-1} + \pi_{13}W_t + \pi_{14}I_{t-1} + v_{1t}$$

$$D_t = \pi_{20} + \pi_{21}Y_t + \pi_{22}S_{t-1} + \pi_{23}W_t + \pi_{24}I_{t-1} + v_{2t}$$

$$I_t = \pi_{30} + \pi_{31}Y_t + \pi_{32}S_{t-1} + \pi_{33}W_t + \pi_{34}I_{t-1} + v_{3t}$$

$$P_t = \pi_{40} + \pi_{41}Y_t + \pi_{42}S_{t-1} + \pi_{43}W_t + \pi_{44}I_{t-1} + v_{4t}$$

Given the values of the reduced form parameters, the π's, assignment of suitable values to the predetermined variables allows computation of the corresponding values of the endogenous variables.[6] The problem of precedence in solving for the endogenous variables does not arise since only predetermined variables appear on the right-hand sides of the reduced form equations. The particular obstacle in solution via the reduced form is the need first to obtain the reduced form parameters from the estimated structural parameters. For very small models the necessary algebraic manipulation may be straightforward. In general, however, it involves operations on the structural parameters arranged in matrices, notably the inversion of the matrix of estimated structural parameters on the endogenous variables. The greater the number of endogenous variables, the greater the dimension of the corresponding parameter matrix, and hence the greater the computational burden involved in its inversion. While this may not be prohibitive, the procedure can be cumbersome. Simulation of the impact of possible changes in the values of a particular structural parameter on an endogenous variable, for example, requires derivation of a revised reduced form for each alternative parameter value. Perhaps the most significant limitation on solution via the reduced form is that its applicability is confined to models which are linear. A unique reduced form cannot be derived for non-linear models.[7] As Chapter 2 indicated, non-linearities involving endogenous variables are commonplace in agricultural commodity market models. Non-linear relationships within a model can be linearised approximately using the first two terms of a *Taylor's Series expansion.*[8] The accuracy of the linear approximation will depend upon the nature of the time paths of the variables involved and the choice of reference values or *expansion point* around which the relationship is linearised.[9] Linearisation may not provide a particularly accurate reflection of an underlying non-linear model, and imposes an additional burden on the model-builder. Consequently, there have been few, if any, recent applications. Indeed, for the reasons mentioned here, solution of models via their reduced forms is increasingly uncommon.

Solution directly using the estimated structural form of a model offers a more flexible and mathematically less complex alternative. Because the structural parameters are explicit, resolving a model for different sets of parameter values, perhaps as part of a simulation exercise, is rapid and straightforward. The *Gauss-Seidel method* for solving sets of simultaneous equations has been appropriated by econometric model-builders, and is perhaps the most widely used solution algorithm.[10] It is applicable to any model, including non-linear systems. The method consists of a simple iterative procedure which does not involve a need for matrix inversion, and hence is readily implemented on microcomputers of relatively limited capacity. The method can be illustrated using the market model above. Assuming that the values of the predetermined variables are given and that the disturbances are set at zero, the problem in solving the equations is the presence of simultaneously determined endogenous variables on their right-hand sides. The Gauss-Seidel method proceeds by setting starting values for the unknown endogenous variables. The choice of appropriate starting values depends on the context of the solution. Where the actual values of the variables concerned are known, as they would be for historical simulations, these might be used. Where the actual values are unknown, as they would be in the case of *ex ante* forecasting, the lagged values might be used. Given a starting value for P_t, P_t^0, the first equation can be solved to obtain a first round estimate of S_t, S_t^1,

$$S_t^1 = \alpha_0 + \alpha_1 P_t^0 + \alpha_2 S_{t-1} + \alpha_3 W_t$$

and the second equation can be solved to obtain a first round estimate of D_t, D_t^1,

$$D_t^1 = \beta_0 + \beta_1 P_t^0 + \beta_2 Y_t$$

Given these estimates of S_t and D_t, a first round estimate of I_t, I_t^1, can be obtained from the identity

$$I_t^1 = I_{t-1} + S_t^1 - D_t^1$$

and finally, a first round estimate of P_t, P_t^1, can be obtained from the fourth equation

$$P_t^1 = \delta_0 + \delta_1 I_t^1 + \delta_2 D_t^1$$

The process is then repeated using these first round estimates of the endogenous variables in place of the starting values to obtain second round estimates and so on. The iterative procedure continues until the proportionate differences between successive estimates of each endogenous variable are less than some preassigned value. Convergence is assessed by evaluating a *stopping rule* in respect of each endogenous variable after each iteration. The stopping rule takes the form, for example in the case of the supply equation,

$$\left| \frac{S_t^r - S_t^{r-1}}{S_t^{r-1}} \right| \leq c$$

where r is the iteration number, and c is the preassigned tolerance level, usually 0.001, for proportionate differences between values obtained for each variable in successive iterations. Once the stopping rule is satisfied for all the endogenous variables, convergence is assumed to have been reached and the iterations cease. In the absence of serious misspecification, solutions for a typical agricultural market model should converge rapidly. Non-convergence can be a problem if equations are incorrectly *normalised* - the choice of dependent variable is inappropriate - or if their sequence for solution is not an appropriate reflection of the chains of causation or *causal ordering* within the model.[11] Once convergence is achieved, solution can move on to the next period, with, if desired, the solved values of the endogenous variables for period t becoming the values for the lagged endogenous variables in the solution for period t+1.

Further Reading

Since solution of models is a fairly mechanical procedure, there is little in the way of further reading which might be recommended. The algebra of the various solution methods is reviewed in more detail by L.R. Klein, *Lectures in Econometrics* (North Holland, Amsterdam, 1983), Ch. 2. A mathematically simpler treatment is given by D.W. Challen and A.J. Hagger, *Macroeconomic Systems: Construction, Validation and Applications* (Macmillan, London, 1983), Ch. 2.

Notes

1. See, for example, L.R. Klein, *Lectures in Econometrics* (North Holland, Amsterdam, 1983), Ch. 2.

2. See, for example, J. Anderson, C. Blitzer, T. Cauchois, and E. Grilli, 'A Dynamic Simulation Model of the World Jute Economy' in World Bank, *World Bank Commodity Models*, vol. 1, World Bank Staff Commodity Working Paper No. 6 (World Bank, Washington, 1981).

3. See G.C. Rausser, E. Lichtenberg and R. Lattimore, 'New Developments in the Theory and Empirical Applications of Endogenous Governmental Behaviour' in G.C. Rausser (ed.), *New Directions in Econometric Modeling and Forecasting in US Agriculture* (North Holland, Amsterdam, 1982), pp. 547-614, for a review.

4. See, for example, FAO, *Agriculture: Toward 2000* (FAO, Rome, 1979).

5. See, for example, the spaghetti-like plots of stochastic solutions in Figs. 11.7 and 11.8 in R.S. Pindyck and D.L. Rubinfeld, *Econometric Models and Economic Forecasts* (McGraw-Hill, New York, 1976), pp. 364-365.

6. Given the estimated structural form, $\mathbf{YB} + \mathbf{XA} = \mathbf{E}$, the reduced form is obtained by multplying through by the inverse of the gxg matrix of endogenous variable parameters, $\mathbf{B}^{-1}$ to obtain $\mathbf{YBB}^{-1} + \mathbf{XAB}^{-1} = \mathbf{EB}^{-1}$, and rearranging to obtain $\mathbf{Y} = -\mathbf{XAB}^{-1} + \mathbf{EB}^{-1}$, or $\mathbf{Y} = \mathbf{X\Pi} + \mathbf{V}$, where $\Pi = -\mathbf{AB}^{-1}$ is the kxg matrix of reduced form parameters, and $\mathbf{V} = \mathbf{EB}^{-1}$ is the nxg matrix of reduced form disturbances. Assuming that the reduced form disturbances are set at zero, a 1xg vector of solution values for the endogenous variables can be obtained from this reduced form by specifying an appropriate 1xk vector of values for the predetermined variables.

7. W.C. Labys, *Dynamic Commodity Models: Specification, Estimation, and Simulation* (D.C. Heath, Lexington, 1973), pp. 203-206 illustrates the difficulties caused by the introduction of a price ratio involving an endogenous price variable, for example. In this case the values of the reduced form parameters are dependent on the values taken by the deflating price.

8. The algebra of Taylor's Series expansions is described in S. Glaister, *Mathematical Methods for Economists*, 3rd edn (Blackwell, Oxford, 1984), pp. 152-155. The method is demonstrated with an application to a non-linear demand function for oranges by A.W. Womack and J.L. Matthews, 'Linear Approximations of Nonlinear Relationships by the Taylor's Series Expansion Revisited', *Agricultural Economics Research*, vol. 24, no. 4 (1972), pp. 93-101.

9. Womack and Matthews, 'Linear Approximations of Nonlinear

Relationships by the Taylor's Series Expansion Revisited' examines some possibilities: for irregular series with no trend, the mean is the most appropriate expansion point; for series with irregular variation around a trend, a moving average of past values should be used; and for smooth series with trend the previous period's value should be used.

10. The *Newton-Raphson method* is also used for solving econometric models, and again is applicable to non-linear systems. It has certain disadvantages relative to the Gauss-Seidel method, however, notably the repeated matrix inversion involved, and is less frequently used. The method is described and discussed in D.W. Challen and A.J. Hagger, *Macroeconomic Systems: Construction, Validation and Applications* (Macmillan, London, 1983), pp. 37-43.

11. The consequences of errors in normalisation and causal ordering are discussed by D. Heien, J. L. Matthews, and A.W. Womack, 'A Methods Note on the Gauss-Seidel Algorithm for Solving Econometric Models', *Agricultural Economics Research*, vol. 25, no. 3 (1973), pp. 71-80.

6
Validation Procedures

. . . there can be no demonstrative arguments to prove that those instances of which we have had no experience resemble those of which we have had experience.

(David Hume, *A Treatise of Human Nature*)

Some confidence in a model's adequacy to the purpose at hand is clearly essential for any meaningful application in simulation or forecasting. The battery of tests outlined in Chapter 2 can be employed to examine the possibility of misspecification in individual equations, the appropriateness of restrictions on their specification, the stability of the estimated parameters, and their consistency with relevant economic theory or other *a priori* information. Assuming that the results of these tests are satisfactory, attention focuses on the ability of the model as a whole to generate time paths for its endogenous variables in historical simulations or *ex post* forecasts which approximate, to an acceptable degree, the actual time paths of the variables concerned. '*Tracking*' capability is the central concern of model validation. Various techniques are available to accomplish the relevant comparisons, from simple graphical methods to spectral analysis. The ability of the model to mirror the behaviour of the real market in response to exogenous shocks is also relevant, particularly where a major use is to be simulation. Evidence on this is collected via *multiplier* analysis. A range of validation procedures is applied routinely as part of the model-building process. A model's validity is, or should be, challenged continuously throughout its life, however: its performance in each new application provides information of value in model development or reformulation.

Apparent success in tracking the salient features of the historical time paths of variables of interest may not be a guarantee of equal success in the changed circumstances of actual simulation or forecasting applications. The belief that it may be is largely a matter of judgement and faith. Validation procedures can, however, provide information concerning the behaviour of the model useful in identifying areas for improvement, or in interpreting its results.

Tracking Performance

The basis of most validation procedures is simple comparison of the 'fitted' time paths of the endogenous variables generated by a model with the actual time paths. Historical simulations or *ex post* forecasts allow such comparisons. Dynamic solutions provide the most rigorous test of a model's tracking ability since feeding back solved values of endogenous variables into the solution for the next period as the values for lagged endogenous variables admits the possibility of cumulative errors. Actual values for the exogenous variables are known, of course, and used in generating the solution.

The tracking ability of a model is assessed in terms of the correspondence of absolute values, trends and turning points in the fitted and actual time paths for each endogenous variable. Ideally, a model should replicate the timing, direction and magnitude of changes in the endogenous variables. Any divergences or 'errors' between the fitted and actual series should be random and small. Simple regression of the actual on the fitted values should produce an estimated intercept not significantly different from zero and an estimated slope coefficient not significantly different from one. Comparisons of fitted and actual percentage changes can be helpful in assessing the quantitative importance of divergences between the fitted and actual series. An error of one hundred tonnes in simulating supply of some commodity, for example, is rather more serious if the level of supply is a thousand tonnes than if it is a million tonnes. Simple comparisons of the corresponding figures in fitted and actual series, and consideration of the errors between them, may not always provide an immediately obvious picture of a model's tracking ability. A plot of the two series gives a more immediate impression, and is perhaps the most frequently presented demonstration of model 'validity'.

Figure 1.2 gave an example of such a diagram, showing fitted and actual values of world cocoa supply from a historical simulation with the cocoa market model discussed in Chapter 1. Figures 6.1, 6.2, and 6.3 give corresponding plots for the other endogenous variables in the model: world demand; world inventories; and real world price.

Broad trends in supply, demand, inventory and price appear to

Figure 6.1: Historical Simulation of World Cocoa Demand

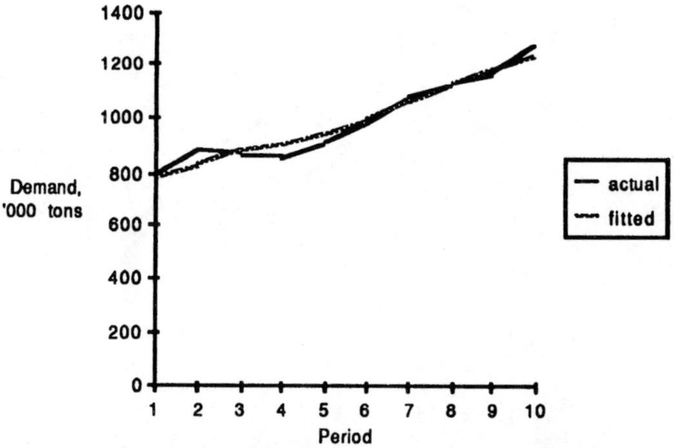

Source: Derived from F.G. Adams and J.R. Behrman, *Econometric Models of Agricultural Commodity Markets* (Ballinger, Cambridge, Mass., 1976), Appendix B and Table 4-2.

Figure 6.2: Historical Simulation of World Cocoa Inventories

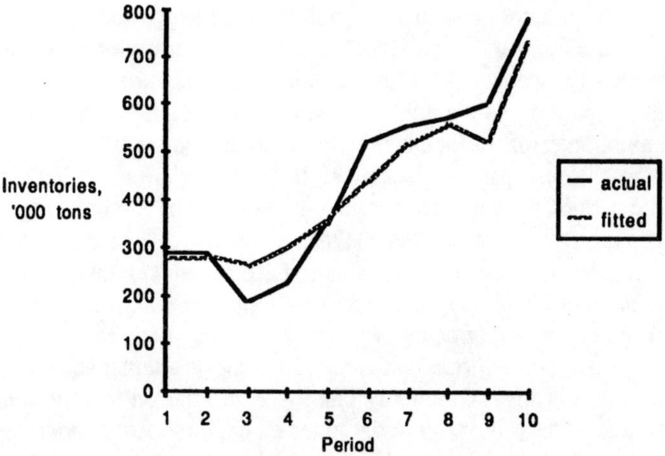

Source: Derived from Adams and Behrman, *Econometric Models of Agricultural Commodity Markets*, Appendix B and Table 4-2.

Figure 6.3: Historical Simulation of Real World Cocoa Price

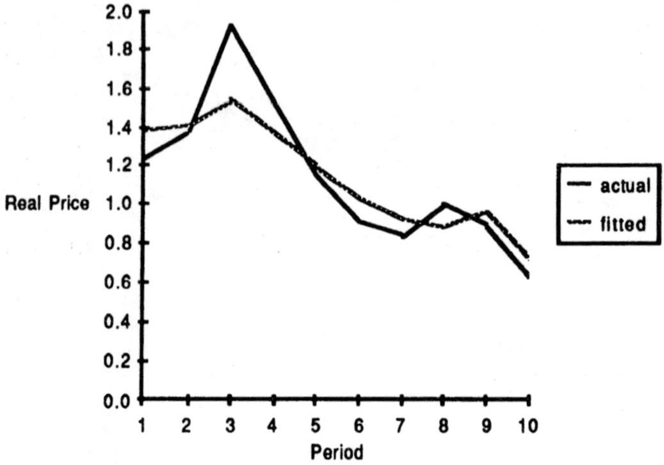

Source: Derived from Adams and Behrman, *Econometric Models of Agricultural Commodity Markets*, Appendix B and Table 4-2.

be simulated reasonably well, but the model's performance in capturing turning points is less acceptable. Overall, the ability of the model as a whole to 'explain' movements in the endogenous variables is rather less than might have been suggested by the high R^2 values attached to individual equations. The inventory simulation is clearly weak. To some extent this may be due to the determination of inventories by an identity which will accumulate simulation errors of the other variables in the model.

As might be expected, tracking ability is better the more stable the time path of the variable in question: demand, for example, appears to be more accurately shadowed than price. The differences between the historical simulation performance for different variables illustrate the difficulties of coming to an overall view of whether a model is acceptable or not, or better or worse than its competitors.

Prediction-realisation diagrams provide an alternative graphical presentation most commonly employed in relation to forecasting accuracy analysis.[1] Figure 6.4 gives an example for *ex post* price forecasts from a simple model of the United Kingdom egg market.[2]

Prediction-realisation diagrams have the advantage that the nature of errors is clearly shown. The diagram plots actual against predicted percentage changes for the variable of interest. Perfect predictions, where the predicted change is equal to the actual change give points on the broken line which bisects the origin at 45°. Points above the broken line in the north-east quadrant or below the broken line in the south-west quadrant show that the direction of change is correctly predicted, but its magnitude is overestimated. Points below the broken line in the north-east quadrant or above the broken line in the south-west quadrant show that the direction of change is correctly predicted, but its magnitude is underestimated. Points in the north-west or south-east quadrants indicate turning-point errors where predicted and actual changes are in opposite directions.

Figure 6.4: Prediction-Realisation Diagram for *Ex Post* Forecasts of UK Egg Prices

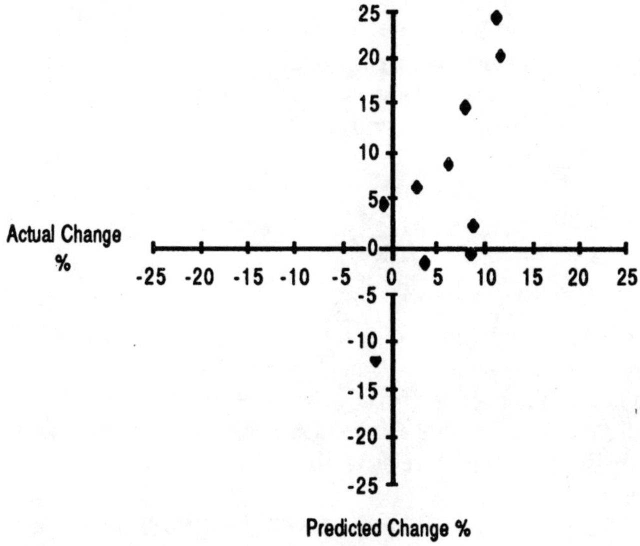

Source: D. Hallam, *Econometric Forecasting in the UK Egg Market* (Eggs Authority, Tunbridge Wells, 1981).

It appears from Figure 6.4 that the model involved tends to overestimate changes in egg prices, although there are perhaps too few observations to be conclusive. Random errors might be expected to make over- and underestimates equally likely - a hypothesis which might be tested using the Binomial distribution.[3] Rather more seriously, in two cases the model makes turning-point errors in failing to predict what are presumably continuations of an apparently fairly steady upward trend.

While graphical presentations of historical simulation or *ex post* forecasting results may provide an immediate visual impression of model performance, the broadness of this impression may not be particularly helpful to more detailed decisions concerning respecification or model selection.[4] A range of summary measures allows comparisons between alternative models. The simplest of such measures is *Mean Square Simulation Error*, MSE

$$MSE = \frac{1}{N}\sum_{n=1}^{N}(Y_n^f - Y_n^a)^2$$

where Y^f_n and Y^a_n are the nth fitted and actual values from an historical simulation or *ex post* forecast over N periods. The square root of MSE gives perhaps the most widely used measure, *Root Mean Square Simulation Error*, RMSE

$$RMSE = \sqrt{\frac{1}{N}\sum_{n=1}^{N}(Y_n^f - Y_n^a)^2}$$

which has the advantage of being measured in the same units as the particular variable involved, and hence being directly comparable to the mean of the series. Broadly the same comparison can be made with *Root Mean Square Percentage Simulation Error* obtained by expressing each error relative to the actual value for the period concerned.

Some illustrative figures of MSE and RMSE for simulations and forecasts of UK egg prices and supplies are shown in Table 6.1. Clearly, the smaller the MSE's or RMSE's the better the simulation or forecast performance. Comparisons of MSE's or RMSE's from alternative models might therefore serve as a basis for model selection. In the absence of such an objective comparator, judgement of whether a model is adequate must rely on subjective determination of acceptable values. What is acceptable in terms of error may vary from one variable to another according to the objectives and priorities of the modelling exercise.

Table 6.1: Summary Statistics of Historical Simulation and *Ex Post* Forecast Performance for UK Egg Prices and Supplies

	Mean	MSE	RMSE	RMSE%	U
Price	0.81	0.01	0.10	12.6	0.76
Supplies	9.275	0.09	0.29	3.2	0.61

Source: Derived from Hallam, *Econometric Forecasting in the UK Egg Market*.

Theil's *Inequality Coefficient*, U,

$$U = \frac{\sqrt{\frac{1}{N}\sum_{n=1}^{N}(P_n - A_n)^2}}{\sqrt{\frac{1}{N}\sum_{n=1}^{N}A_n^2}}$$

where P_n and A_n are predicted and actual changes from a simulation, or more commonly an *ex post* forecast over N periods, provides yardstick values of zero for perfect forecasts where predicted change equals actual change, and unity for the 'naive' forecast of 'no-change' where P would always be zero.[5] Some illustrative figures are given in Table 6.1. Values of U lower than unity are sometimes presented as evidence of forecasting accuracy. It might be argued, however, that a model which fails to improve significantly on the accuracy of a naive 'no-change' prediction cannot be regarded as a particularly useful forecasting device. Less naive yardstick forecasts, perhaps based on autoregressive models, might provide a more testing and meaningful standard for comparison.

The summary statistics described above do not provide information on all relevant aspects of a model's tracking ability. In particular RMSE's may be low, for example, even when turning points are simulated or predicted badly. Ability to explain or predict the turning points in a variable's time path may be of great strategic importance to decision-makers.[6] Consequently, turning point performance is often accorded special consideration. Two types of turning point error are possible: a failure to predict a turning point which actually occurs; and a prediction of a turning point which does not actually occur. Two indices of turning point performance can be calculated accordingly.[7] These measure the proportion of actual turning points the model fails to predict, and the proportion of predicted turning points which are false. In both cases, the limiting values are zero where all turning points are correctly predicted, and one where no turning points are correctly predicted. Values of these indices derived from the egg market model are 0.6 and 0.5 for prices, and 0.25 and 0.5 for output. One problem with such indices is the need to define turning point error precisely with respect to timing, direction and magnitude.[8] Thus, if a model correctly predicts the direction of change but misses the timing by one period, should that be regarded as one turning point error or two? In a quarterly model a one period error in the prediction of the timing of a turning point may be less serious. Turning point performance may appear rather worse than it actually is by the zero-one scoring system used by the indices which takes no account of the magnitude of errors. A prediction of 'no change' in the face of an actual downturn of, say, 0.5%, would be scored as a turning point error with the same weight as would a predicted upturn of 20%.

Multiplier Analysis

Clearly, a model should be capable, given the known values for its exogenous variables, of generating time paths for its endogenous variables which are an adequate approximation to actual market behaviour. It should also be the case that dynamic responses in the time paths of endogenous variables elicited by the imposition of exogenous shocks in model solution are consistent with those which would be expected in the real market. Validation, therefore, may include an investigation of these *multipliers* - the dynamic responses in the endogenous variables to changes in the exogenous variables.

Consideration of the signs and magnitudes of estimated parameters in individual equations overlooks the possibility of dynamic interactions between equations, and hence will not usually provide a complete picture of the likely nature and size of multipliers. They can be determined from dynamic solutions of a model for alternative exogenous data sets. A historical simulation using actual values for the exogenous variables establishes a baseline solution. One period, or sometimes sustained, small percentage changes in the value of each exogenous variable are made in turn and 'shocked' solutions generated. Comparison of the shocked and baseline solutions for each endogenous variable provides measurements of the dynamic multipliers showing the effects on that endogenous variable of changes in the exogenous variable concerned. Figure 1.3 in Chapter 1 showing a baseline solution for real cocoa prices and a shocked solution consequent upon an exogenous five per cent increase in world cocoa demand illustrates multiplier effects. As might have been expected, the dramatic initial increase in price gradually chokes off demand giving a stable return to the baseline price time path. An unstable response involving cumulative divergence from the baseline solution would represent cause for concern implying a failure to capture expected feedback effects between the endogenous variables.

The Meaning of Validation

The kind of validation procedures described here can provide information useful in selecting a model from among alternatives,[9] in interpreting its results - a tendency to over- or underpredict, for example - and above all, in indentifying its weaknesses. Since actual values of exogenous variables are used in generating model solutions for validation purposes, errors can be attributed to misspecification or doubtful parameter estimates in the model itself. Likely sources of error in these respects can be identified by a progressive decomposition of the discrepancies between actual and fitted series. This can be accomplished by resolving the model using actual values for alternative sets of variables appearing on the right-hand sides of the equations of the model, and comparing the resulting fitted values with the corresponding actual values. A solution using actual values for all variables - endogenous and lagged endogenous as well as exogenous - where they appear on the right-hand side yields the residuals for each equation individually. These can be used as described in Chapter 2 to test for misspecification and remedial action directed accordingly. The possibility that simulation or forecasting of one endogenous variable is a weak link in the model as a whole can be examined by exogenising that particular variable and observing the effect on the RMSEs for the remaining endogenous variables. Solution using actual values for all predetermined variables - lagged endogenous as well as exogenous - permits errors arising from misspecification of the causal structure of the model. Any increment in errors over and above those recorded as single-equation residuals can be attributed to incorrect assumptions regarding the nature of simultaneity. Finally, any increment in errors between this solution and the conventional dynamic solution, where only exogenous variables are given their actual values, can be attributed to misspecification in the dynamic structure of the model.

A satisfactory outcome to the various procedures described above might give rise to greater confidence in a model's capabilities, but validation of a model in terms of a favourable assessment of historical simulation or *ex post* forecasting performance cannot be regarded as a guarantee that a model will yield informative simulation results or accurate *ex ante* forecasts in real practical applications. The assumption that it will is a matter of judgement and faith. The performance of a model in historical simulations *should* be good since it is assessed against the data on which the model is based. The constancy of change in the behaviour patterns of market participants, technology, policies and institutions, however, will work towards limiting a model's temporal range of applicability, and, incidentally, impose a requirement for frequent updating of specification and parameter estimates.[10] *Ex post* forecasts are not subject to error arising from inaccurate forecasts of exogenous variables, although in practice these might be a major source of error in true *ex ante* forecasting. While satisfactory validation results may be no guarantee of success in real applications, there must be few models which have been rejected out of hand because of validation results which were unsatisfactory.

Further Reading

Validation procedures do not feature regularly in the contents of econometrics texts. L.R. Klein, *Lectures in Econometrics* (North Holland, Amsterdam, 1983), Ch. 3, however, provides a detailed review. In actual econometric studies of agricultural commodity markets validation is similarly frequently under-reported. Two illustrative examples are: D. Hallam, *Econometric Forecasting in the UK Egg Market* (Eggs Authority, Tunbridge Wells, 1981) referred to in this chapter; and W.C. Labys, *Dynamic Commodity Models: Specification, Estimation, and Simulation* (D.C. Heath,

Lexington, 1973), pp. 227-239 which describes the validation of a model of the world lauric oils market.

Notes

1. Originated by Henri Theil. See, for example, H. Theil, *Applied Economic Forecasting* (North Holland, Amsterdam, 1966).

2. D. Hallam, *Econometric Forecasting in the UK Egg Market* (Eggs Authority, Tunbridge Wells, 1981).

3. J.C.K. Ash and D.J. Smyth, *Forecasting the UK Economy* (Saxon House, Farnborough, 1973).

4. In fact, the extent to which such results are helpful in this context however expressed may be limited. See D.F. Hendry and J. Richard, 'On the Formulation of Empirical Models in Dynamic Econometrics', *Journal of Econometrics*, vol. 20, no. 1 (1982), pp. 3-33.

5. Theil, *Applied Economic Forecasting*.

6. In a quarterly model, many 'turning points' may in fact be regular seasonal fluctuations, which should be simulated or predicted accurately. In such models it may be more relevant to assess turning point performance defining turning points in terms of changes between corresponding quarters of successive years.

7. J.C.K. Ash and D.J. Smyth, *Forecasting the UK Economy* (Saxon House, Farnborough, 1973).

8. Ash and Smyth, *Forecasting the UK Economy*.

9. Although use of validation statistics such as RMSE for model selection is clearly problematic where the alternatives differ in terms of variables classed as exogenous. See D.F. Hendry and J. Richard, 'On the Formulation of Empirical Models In Dynamic Econometrics', *Journal of Econometrics*, vol. 20, no. 1 (1982), pp. 3-33.

10. T.W. Hutchison, *Knowledge and Ignorance in Economics* (Blackwell, Oxford, 1977), Ch. 2.

7
The Uses of Econometric Modelling

Say from whence you owe this strange intelligence . . .

(*Macbeth*)

Applications of econometric models of agricultural commodity markets are conventionally categorised into three rather arbitrary and overlapping groups: market analysis concerned with explaining historic market behaviour and hence contributing to an understanding of current developments; forecasting future market prices and quantities; and policy analysis aimed at ascertaining the impact of policy instruments or identifying the optimal policy mix to achieve specified targets or goals. Clearly, all these applications add to the decision-maker's information set, in particular by providing a quantitative dimension, and therefore have a potentially beneficial effect on the efficiency of decisions made.

The potential for success in these applications is constrained by certain methodological problems. These arise both from the nature of the markets under study, which are elements of an evolving and shifting economic system, and the nature of the research method itself, which centres around description of historic behaviour based upon data which may be limited in quantity and quality. While these factors may be beyond the control of the model-builder, the specification and estimation of the model, over which the model-builder does have control, should at least be such as to mitigate rather than exacerbate their worst effects. Certainly specification and estimation choices should not introduce additional problems.

The human element in the success or otherwise of a model is not confined to the technical decisions in model construction. The usefulness of a model depends not only upon how it is constructed, but also upon how it is used. Of particular importance in this respect is the sometimes uneasy relationship in the management and administration of econometric modelling between those responsible for building a model and those responsible for commissioning and using it.

This chapter discusses some of these broad issues concerning the use and potential of econometric models of agricultural commodity markets.[1]

Market Analysis

Market analysis obtains or adds to quantitative knowledge of how a market works, or at least has worked. As noted in Chapter 1, the necessity in econometric model-building for detailed scrutiny of relevant data series and for rigorous and formal presentation of perceptions of market behaviour can in themselves be valuable in improving understanding. Market analysis, however, centres around quantification of relationships between variables of interest, and in particular measurement of the response in endogenous variables to exogenous shocks.

The range and validity of such measurements depend upon the specification adopted. The need to capture all relevant features of the dynamic causal relationships describing the operation of a market usually calls for models rather more complex than the simple illustrative model referred to in the preceding chapters. The underlying assumptions of a competitive equilibrium model may themselves not be an adequate approximate description of the nature of agricultural commodity markets.[2] Any serious attempt at modelling agricultural markets typically involves a more disaggregated and detailed specification. Different production and consumption conditions may call for disaggregation by country or region in international market models. Interrelationships between markets - livestock and cereals, for example - may call for multicommodity models, extending in the limit to coverage of an entire agricultural sector. Detail concerning the biology and technology of production may be required, particularly where livestock products or perennial crops are involved, to provide a complete description of the determination of supply and its response to price changes. Uncertainty on the part of consumers and producers concerning future prices requires the incorporation of assumptions as to how expectations are formed. The more naive extrapolative expectations models remain the most commonly employed, although rational expectations models, which are appearing more frequently, may be a promising, if somewhat delayed, development. Risk and uncertainty engendered by price variability are compounded by those stemming from yield variability as a result of climatic variations. It is perhaps surprising that despite the acknowledgement of the importance of such climatic variations in agricultural production, allowances for risk and uncertainty in supply relationships are not more common.[3] Changes in market behaviour patterns, policy measures and technology work towards the invalidation of any particular set of parameter estimates. Specification of varying parameter models can limit the disruptive effects. Policy changes might be endogenised.[4] It is unlikely, particularly where such additional detail is considered, that the relationships of an agricultural commodity market model can suitably be set against the general linear statistical model and estimated by ordinary least squares. The resulting parameter estimates may be biased, inefficient or inconsistent, and analyses based on them may be correspondingly misleading or unreliable.

Clearly, parameter estimates themselves contain much of the information relevant to market analysis. Elasticities and flexibilities derived from them can provide a more convenient summary with an immediate economic interpretation of the nature and strength of direct relationships between variables. Reduced form parameters, or *impact multipliers*, can be derived from the estimated structural form of a linear model to quantify both the direct and indirect effects of changes in exogenous variables on endogenous variables. These can be alternatively expressed as *total elasticities*.[5]

The dynamic effects of a change in an exogenous variable on the endogenous variables of a model are of particular interest. Also of interest are the time paths of the endogenous variables following such a change - whether these lead back to equilibrium, and whether they are oscillatory. A model which displays instability with cumulative divergence from equilibrium in these time paths is unlikely to be considered an acceptable representation of real market behaviour. Reduced from parameters or the corresponding elasticities and flexibilities show the immediate effect of change in exogenous variables on endogenous variables, and can be manipulated to show the dynamic effects after one, two, or more periods.[6] The stability or otherwise of a model can also be ascertained by analysis of the reduced form parameters in the case of a linear deterministic model.[7] Analyses for more complex models involving non-linearities have relied upon the simulation approach to determine the dynamic response to changes in exogenous variables. These responses are measured by divergences between control and shocked solutions of the model as described in Chapter 6.

Forecasting

Forecasts can be generated from either the reduced form or the structural form of a model as described in Chapter 5. In either case the necessary actual computations are straightforward and routine. Future values for the exogenous variables - known, forecast or assumed - are incorporated into the estimated model, and the model is solved for as many periods as the forecast is to run. Obviously for *ex ante* forecasts the solution must be 'total' with the forecast values of the endogenous variables being fed back into the model as values for the lagged endogenous variables to forecast the next period. The major effort involved in an econometric forecasting exercise is in the preparatory stages. Data sets including the most recent observations available for all variables in the model must be assembled. Re-estimation of the parameters of the model using this most recent data, and re-evaluation of the specification are desirable to check for and keep abreast of changes in the economic structure. The residuals from the re-estimated equations for most recent periods should be examined for any systematic variation. Information concerning such variation might be used to improve forecast accuracy as described below. Finally, as described in Chapter 5, appropriate values must be specified for the exogenous variables over the forecast period.

Errors in values assigned to exogenous variables are one source of forecast error. Uncertainty as to the appropriate values may favour the presentation of a series of scenarios based on different assumptions concerning the future time paths of exogenous variables. Responsibility for assigning probabilities to the alternative scenarios rests with the decision-maker. The other source of forecast error is the model itself. Thorough model testing and validation should limit the possibility of forecast error originating in biased parameter estimates or specification error. Deficiencies in these respects can arise passively, however, through changes in the nature of the market, and hence the obsolescence of the model structure, during the forecast period. Forecasting using an econometric model based on historic data assumes, usually implicitly, that the statistical relationships and their estimated parameters observed in the past, will continue to be relevant into the forecast period. Unfortunately, the logical grounds for this assumption are not strong, whatever the evidence of regularity in the past in its favour. Some relationships might, of course, be expected to remain relatively stable through time. It would be surprising, for example, if the number of calves born did not bear some close relationship to the size of the breeding herd. It would not be so surprising if the relationship between the size of the breeding herd and beef prices was unstable. Chapter 6 referred to the instability in economic relationships arising from random elements in human behaviour patterns, shifts in the policy framework, and technological change. The temporal relevance of the descriptions of transient 'trends, tendencies and patterns' embodied in an econometric model may therefore be limited, calling for regular updating and re-estimation.[8] In cases where structural change is itself predictable, allowance might be made through the specification of varying parameter models. Paradoxically, it is often where circumstances are known to be changing that the predictions of econometric models are particularly considered: in examining the likely effects of planned policy changes, for example. This problem is discussed further below.

Forecast errors can be reduced by arbitrary adjustment based on an analysis of residuals from each estimated equation for periods immediately prior to the start of the forecast. A run of positive or negative residuals may imply a corresponding tendency towards over- or under-prediction of the endogenous variable concerned. Forecast error may be reduced by the addition or subtraction as appropriate of projected values for these residuals to the forecast for each period. These *intercept adjustments* may be constant, equal perhaps to the average recent residual from the appropriate estimated equation, or may be some function of time, depending upon the sort of pattern, if any, discerned in the estimated residuals.

Less arbitrary forecast adjustments can be made. The raw output of an econometric model rarely forms the the actual forecast used. Rather it is subject to modification and adjustment by expert opinion or judgement concerning, for example, the likely effects of extraneous factors. Such modifications and adjustments can also be made to the estimated parameters of the model from which the forecast is derived. The explicit and obvious description of the market provided by the structural form of an econometric forecasting model facilitates the incorporation of expert opinion.

Econometric models are not the only, and certainly not

necessarily the best, means of generating forecasts of economic variables. In fact, in the few comparative studies which have been made, econometric forecasting models have not emerged as uniformly superior in terms of accuracy to the alternatives such as Box-Jenkins time series models, futures market quotations, or pure expert judgement.[9] Neither does there appear to be strong general support for the common belief that the relative accuracy of econometric forecasts improves with the length of forecast horizon. As might be expected, the performance of econometric models differs from one commodity to another, and may be superior the more volatile the behaviour of the forecast variable.[10] It is difficult to draw general conclusions from this evidence concerning the value of econometric models in forecasting. The results themselves are not compelling in favour of any particular methodology. At the same time, however, the econometric models employed and the way in which forecasts were generated from them might, in some of these studies, be considered rather crude.

Policy Analysis

Although it is only the last of the three roles of econometric modelling identified above which mentions policy explicitly, all three are relevant in the policy-making process since all three provide relevant information to the policy-maker and hence have a potential impact upon policy decisions. Indeed, the importance of the first two may outweigh that of the third in this respect. Forewarning provided by econometric forecasts, for example, allows the policy-maker to be forearmed against and possibly to avert undesirable developments and in general can reduce intertemporal uncertainty involved in policy decision-making. Such forecasts have therefore been used by many governments in support of their agricultural policy-making. In some cases, forecasts might *be* the policy where they are disseminated with the express desire to influence economic behaviour. In theory, publicly announced forecasts, even when these are not completely accurate, can under certain circumstances lead to a reduction in price instability.[11]

In explicitly policy-oriented applications, econometric models can be decisive in identifying policies to be adopted, supplanting, at least in theory, rather than aiding the policy-makers deliberations. Such policy decision modelling involves the application of mathematical optimisation methods - optimal control, for example -

to determine optimum values for policy instruments to achieve the policy-maker's formally expressed objectives. A major difficulty, and this may be prohibitive, lies in persuading the policy-maker to define these objectives in the necessary form or to specify target values for variables of concern. In some cases - the operation of an international buffer stock to achieve price or earnings stability, for example - the objectives might be unexceptionable.[12] Alternatively the approach might be employed to trace the policy implications of a range of objectives and thus assist in the selection of the appropriate objective as well as the means to its achievement.[13]

Simulation experiments are a more common vehicle for policy analysis. Alternative policy assumptions define a series of shocked solutions. Comparisons of these with the baseline control solution informs the policy-maker as to the effects of alternative policy choices. A simple example investigating the impact of one particular level of buffer stock acquisition of cocoa on world prices was given in Chapter 1. In practice, such an exercise might consider a wider range of policy options, perhaps involving combinations of policy instruments, and might more realistically involve stochastic rather than deterministic solutions. A criticism sometimes made of simulation analyses is that a thorough exploration of all feasible policy alternatives may generate more information than can comfortably be absorbed by policy-makers.

The possibility that changes in the economic environment and human behaviour patterns persistently reduce the validity of estimated model structures has been commented upon at several points. A 'special case'[14] of this view is the *Lucas critique* of econometric policy simulations, which although proposed in the context of macroeconomic models may be equally relevant to agricultural commodity market models.[15] It originates in the 'rational expectations' school of macroeconomics. Individuals' expectations regarding the economic future are assumed to be formed 'rationally', taking into account all relevant aspects of the economic environment. On average, such expectations will be matched by actual events, with any divergences between the two being purely random. The 'Lucas critique' argues that 'rational' individuals will anticipate the effects of any policy changes and modify their behaviour accordingly. The structure of existing econometric models which describe previous behaviour patterns, no matter how accurately, will thus be rendered obsolete. Lucas therefore concludes that simulation results cannot provide any useful information as to the actual consequences of alternative economic policies.[16]

Rather ironically, therefore, the advice of econometric policy simulations is necessarily misleading just when the policy-maker is most in need of it. The 'Lucas critique' has itself been criticised as being exaggerated.[17] Behavioural adaptations might themselves be predicted and modelled.[18] It has also been argued that while the critique might apply where quantum leaps in policy are contemplated, it would not apply in the more normal circiumstances of variations in the levels of existing policy instruments.[19] Most agricultural policy changes might fall into the latter category, although occasional quantum leaps do occur - the introduction of EEC milk quotas might represent such a discontinuity, for example. It might in any case be asked whether agricultural producers really are 'rational' in the sense of the 'Lucas critique'. There has been little research into this, and what evidence exists is conflicting. As noted in Chapter 2, a study of the US broiler industry concluded that producers did indeed form expectations rationally.[20] Whether the US broiler industry can be considered to be typical of agriculture in general is open to question, however. On the other hand, a not very convincing game-based test of various models of expectations formation found that the rational expectations model 'performed badly'.[21]

Irrespective of any displacement in time, space or policy environment, an econometric model cannot be identified with the real world system it is intended to represent. The conditional predictions of a model need not correspond to real world outcomes even given the same conditions. Extravagant claims for econometric simulation models and the transferability of their results to the real world should be approached with some caution. Parallels are sometimes drawn between simulation experiments with econometric models and the kind of laboratory experiments performed in the physical sciences.[22] This type of view implies a parity between economists and physical scientists in methodology of experimentation which in turn might be taken to imply equal validity of generalisation from experimental results to the real world. To say that the 'only difference'[23] between simulation experiments and 'real world' experiments is that the one uses a mathematical model of a system rather than a physical system is perhaps to minimise the methodological gap between the two. While a parallel might be drawn in terms of experimental design, the extent to which this can be stretched to include equal transferability of experimental results to a real world application is uncertain. An econometric model is not governed by any physical laws which make it similar in operation to the system being modelled.[24] Indeed, some would argue that there are no laws of any sort governing economic systems. The behaviour of physical models, such as pilot chemical plants or aeroplane models in wind tunnels, however, are governed by the same physical laws as the full-scale plant or aeroplane. It might be added that the results of many physical experiments can be reproduced in the real world since 'experimental conditions' can be recreated, albeit perhaps with some difficulty and expense. The 'experimental conditions' of an econometric model can never be recreated in the real world.

Management and Administration of Econometric Models

An ostensibly adequately specified, estimated and validated model can turn out to have a disappointing performance in practice. Some potential sources of disappointment have been suggested above, notably the limited guidance to the actual performance of a model in real applications provided by conventional validation procedures. Performance loss can also originate in inefficient operation and maintenance of models which arises particularly from an inappropriate division of labour between model-builders and model-users. Broadly speaking, the specification, estimation and validation stages of econometric modelling are the preserve of the specialist model-builder. Real world applications of the model and use of its results are the preserve of the model-user. This functional separation of builder and user is exacerbated in many cases by their institutional and geographical separation. Model-building is often the subject of a research programme commissioned by a policy-making institution from an academic or research institution. The genesis of even more 'policy models' is less purposive. The majority of models, even when of obvious and explicit policy relevance are the unsolicited product of purely academic research, frequently funded, if at all, by some independent body such as a research foundation removed from the policy process. The specification and estimation of the model may be an end in itself for such research, potential applications of the model being of less interest.[25]

It has been suggested as a 'principle' of model-building, that the ultimate user should be involved in model design and development.[26] This is a sound principle and to be recommended although users may not always have sufficient knowledge to be able to contribute constructively at this stage to the mutual benefit of the model-builders and themselves. While users' involvement at the model-building stage may help to ensure that their requirements are better met, it is not always conducive to the production of an adequate econometric model. Useful dialogue between builders and users can be hampered by differences in technical knowledge which model-builders have some responsibility to reduce. Users are unlikely to accept a model whose mechanics and logic are obscure. At worst, users may only be willing to accept a model which confirms their prior prejudices, beliefs, and experience. The dialogue is obviously potentially important, but it is unlikely to be constructive if conducted in terms of the lowest common denominator. The requirement frequently expressed by users that models should be 'simple' is a case in point. By 'simple' is usually meant models which are highly aggregated across economic units, grouping together mixed and specialist farms for example, and close bounded, 'explaining' only a restricted set of variables. Paradoxically, such models are often far from simple to use and interpret. It is a basic principle of policy-model specification that the level of aggregation and the boundaries of the model should be those appropriate to the policy maker's domain. This may be more complex and wider than the policy maker assumes, although upper limits will obviously be set by the data and resources available. Different types of economic units may react differently to a given policy. Sometimes policy is directed at particular groups of producers or consumers. Disaggregation may therefore be essential to obtain results of any practical value. Furthermore, the parameters of highly aggregated models represent amalgams of the parameters of more disaggregated models, making their interpretation difficult. It may also be the case that there is a positive correlation between disaggregation and predictive accuracy. If useful policy information is to be provided, the boundaries of the model, that is the range of variables it seeks to 'explain', must be sufficient to at least encompass all variables upon which policy instruments have an actual or potential impact and which have an actual or potential effect upon the target variables.

While it may be desirable that users be involved in model construction, it is perhaps equally desirable that model-builders should be involved in model usage. As noted above, econometric models are impressions of transient relationships which shift with the passage of time. If they are not to be by-passed by events and changed circumstances, models require regular updating. Indeed this process of revision, adaptation and refinement is part and parcel of model development. Once the model is handed over to users this kind of maintenance typically becomes their responsibility. It is, however, a responsibilty which users are not always equipped to carry. They may not have the necessary technical expertise for major reworkings and adaptations, although they may be capable of routine updating of data files or parameter estimates for a largely unchanged structure. Even in the latter case, however, where no major modifications are involved, the size of the task should not be underestimated. A quantified model is usually not simply the outcome of application of a certain estimation technique to a given set of data. The actual numerical values assigned to the various parameters are sometimes arrived at in a far less mechanical fashion. They may, for example, be modified subjectively to accommodate relevant extraneous information, or 'fine-tuned' to improve the tracking or forecasting performance of the model. Effective adjustment demands a high level of econometric expertise and must be based upon an intimate knowledge of the structure and causal ordering of the model in question, knowledge of which the model-builder would have the greatest command. If users do not have the necessary expertise to maintain models, then some kind of 'maintenance contract' with the builders will be required. The cost of this may, however, prove prohibitive from the user's point of view, while the commitment involved would probably be unattractive to model-builders. Model-builders are typically happy to let their involvement terminate with the completion of the commissioned model, since this marks the end of the 'creative' phase of modelling.

Costs and Benefits

The difficulties of defining the contribution of econometric modelling were noted in Chapter 1. Some kind of precise cost-benefit calculation for econometric modelling and advice is not really feasible. The costs of model construction and operation might be quantified relatively easily as the sum of resources used. While there can be little doubt as to the general contribution of econometric models to an improved understanding of how agricultural commodity markets function, quantifying the benefits of a model to decision-makers is problematic. Even if the welfare gains from improved decision-making could be quantified and valued, the proportion to be attributed to the econometric model would be difficult to assess. If it is assumed that more information is to be preferred to less as a basis for decision-making then there will always be some benefit to be derived from econometric models. Whether this is a *net* benefit, and whether investment in econometric research represents an optimum use of resources, however, cannot in general be ascertained. Just as more information is preferred to less as a basis for decision-making, so the type of quantitative information provided by econometric models, albeit subject to confidence limits, is widely considered more useful than qualitative generalisations. In any case the former implies and normally subsumes the latter.

In many real world situations econometric analysis may be the only way of accounting for highly complex, dynamic and non-linear relationships between the key economic variables concerned. Policy objectives and the effects of policy measures, for example, are rarely singular. A comprehensive econometric model can facilitate the identification of trade-offs between policy objectives and an appraisal of all the effects - direct and indirect - of proposed policy changes. More generally, econometric models can contribute to the improving of policy debate via the discipline they can impose upon the policy analyst and decision maker. With an econometric model, the assumptions on which a policy viewpoint is based and the methodology by which it is reached are explicit. Policy conclusions are therefore reproducible and verifiable, and hence more rigorous, consistent and informed discussion is promoted. The limitations of econometric models must, however, be kept in mind. Model-builders have a responsibility to highlight the weaknesses of their models as well as their technical strengths. At the same time, the naive optimism or alternatively the unfounded scepticism of some model-users - actual or potential - is not constructive in improving the effectiveness with which models are used.

Further Reading

The uses of econometric models are reviewed in greater detail in a companion volume, W.C. Labys and P.K. Pollak, *Commodity Models for Forecasting and Policy Analysis* (Croom Helm, London, 1984), Chs. 4 and 5.

Stability analysis and multiplier analysis are described in W.C. Labys, *Dynamic Commodity Models: Specification, Estimation and*

Simulation (D.C. Heath, Lexington, 1973), Chs. 7 and 8.

The practicalities of forecasting are described by L.R. Klein and R.M. Young, *An Introduction to Econometric Forecasting and Forecasting Models* (D.C. Heath, Lexington, 1980). Methodological considerations in forecasting are discussed in T.W. Hutchison, *Knowledge and Ignorance in Economics* (Blackwell, Oxford, 1977), Ch. 2.

E.O. Heady, 'Models for Agricultural Policy', *European Review of Agricultural Economics*, vol. 10, no. 1 (1983), pp. 1-14 provides a short review of the use of models in the formation of agricultural policy. A standard text on simulation methods and their applications is T.H. Naylor, *Computer Simulation Experiments with Models of Economic Systems* (Wiley, New York, 1971). G.C. Rausser and E. Hochman, *Dynamic Agricultural Systems: Economic Prediction and Control* (North Holland, New York, 1979) describes methods of control and gives some useful illustrative examples.

Finally, the collection of papers in G.C. Rausser (ed.), *New Directions in Econometric Modeling and Forecasting in US Agriculture* (North Holland, Amsterdam, 1982) presents a survey of the current or recent state of the art in econometric modelling of the agricultural sector. Almost all of the papers will be of interest, but those in the final part of the book deal with the uses of models.

Notes

1. For a detailed discussion see W.C. Labys and P.K. Pollak, *Commodity Models for Forecasting and Policy Analysis* (Croom Helm, London, 1984), Chs. 4 and 5.

2. Imperfect market models and disequilibrium models remain relatively uncommon, however. The former are considered in A.H. Sarris, 'Empirical Models of International Trade in Agricultural Commodities', in A.F. McAlla and T.E. Josling (eds.), *Imperfect Markets in Agricultural Trade* (Allanheld Osmum, Montclair, 1981), pp. 87-112.

3. See, for example, B. Traill, 'Risk Variables in Econometric Supply Response Models', *Journal of Agricultural Economics*, vol. 29, no. 1 (1978), pp. 53-62.

4. G.C. Rausser, E. Lichtenberg, and R. Lattimore, 'New Developments in the Theory and Empirical Applications of Endogenous Government Behaviour', in G.C. Rausser (ed.), *New Directions in Econometric Modeling and Forecasting in US Agriculture* (North Holland, Amsterdam, 1982), pp. 547-614.

5. For a comprehensive analysis of elasticities and flexibilities see J. Chavas, Z.A. Hassan and S.R. Johnson, 'Static and Dynamic Elasticities and Flexibilities in Systems of Simultaneous Equations', *Journal of Agricultural Economics*, vol. 32, no. 2 (1981), pp.177-187.

6. A general dynamic model can be written $\mathbf{Y}_t\mathbf{B} + \mathbf{Y}_{t-1}\mathbf{A}_1 + \mathbf{X}_t\mathbf{A}_2 = \mathbf{E}_t$, where $\mathbf{Y}_t$ and $\mathbf{Y}_{t-1}$ are nxg matrices of n observations on each of g current and lagged endogenous variables respectively, $\mathbf{X}_t$ is an nxk matrix of n observations on each of k exogenous variables, $\mathbf{B}$ is a gxg matrix of coefficients on the current endogenous variables, $\mathbf{A}_1$ is a gxg matrix of coefficients on the lagged endogenous variables, $\mathbf{A}_2$ is a kxg matrix of coefficients on the exogenous variables, and $\mathbf{E}_t$ is an nxg matrix of stochastic disturbances. The reduced from is $\mathbf{Y}_t = \mathbf{Y}_{t-1}\Pi_1 + \mathbf{X}_t\Pi_2 + \mathbf{V}_t$, where $\Pi_1 = -\mathbf{A}_1\mathbf{B}^{-1}$, $\Pi_2 = -\mathbf{A}_2\mathbf{B}^{-1}$ and $\mathbf{V}_t = \mathbf{E}_t\mathbf{B}^{-1}$. Each element of Π_2 is an impact multiplier showing the effect of a one unit change in an exogenous variable upon an endogenous variable within the current period. By substituting for $\mathbf{Y}_{t-1}$ the dynamic multipliers showing the effects of changes in exogenous variables after one period can be seen to be $\Pi_2\Pi_1 + \Pi_2$, after two periods $\Pi_2\Pi_1{}^2 + \Pi_2\Pi_1 + \Pi_2$, and after n periods $(\Pi_1{}^n + \ldots + \Pi_1{}^2 + \Pi_1 + \mathbf{I})\Pi_2$.

7. The condition for stability is that the characteristic roots of Π_1 are less than one or, if complex, have modulus less than one. Complex roots indicate oscillatory behaviour. See, for example, W.C. Labys, 'Dynamics of the International Lauric Oils Market', in W.C. Labys (ed.), *Quantitative Models of Commodity Markets* (Ballinger, Cambridge, Mass., 1975), pp. 213-232.

8. T.W. Hutchison, *Knowledge and Ignorance in Economics* (Blackwell, Oxford, 1977), Ch. 2.

9. See, for example: C.J. Gellatly, 'Forecasting NSW Beef Production: An Evaluation of Alternative Techniques', *Review of Marketing and Agricultural Economics*, vol. 47, no. 1 (1979), pp. 81-93; I.J. Bourke, 'Comparing the Box-Jenkins and Econometric Techniques for Forecasting Beef Prices', *Review of Marketing and Agricultural Economics*, vol. 47, no. 1 (1979), pp. 95-106; R.E. Just and G.C. Rausser, 'Commodity Price Forecasting With Large-Scale Econometric Models and the Futures Market', *American Journal of Agricultural Economics*, vol. 63, no. 2 (1981), pp. 197-208.

10. Just and Rausser, 'Commodity Price Forecasting With Large-Scale Econometric Models and the Futures Market'.

11. D.J. Smyth, 'The Effect of Public Price Forecasts on Market

Price Variation: A Stochastic Cobweb Example', *American Journal of Agricultural Economics*, vol. 55, no. 1 (1973), pp. 83-88.

12. Labys and Pollak, *Commodity Models for Forecasting and Policy Analysis*, p. 160. For such an example, see H.K. Kim, L.M. Goreux, and D.A. Kendrick, 'Feedback Control Rule for Cocoa Market Stabilisation' in Labys (ed.), *Quantitative Models of Commodity Markets*, pp. 233-263.

13. S. Harris, M. Salmon, and B. Smith, *Analysis of Commodity Markets for Policy Purposes*, Thames Essay no. 17 (Trade Policy Research Centre, London, 1978), pp. 75-77.

14. C.A. Sims, 'Policy Analysis With Econometric Models', *Brookings Papers on Economic Activity*, vol. 1, no. 1 (1982), pp. 107-164.

15. R.E.J. Lucas, 'Econometric Policy Evaluation: A Critique', in K. Brunner and A.M. Meltzer (eds.), *The Phillips Curve and Labour Markets* (North Holland, Amsterdam, 1976) pp. 19-46 .

16. Lucas, 'Econometric Policy Evaluation: A Critique', p. 20.

17. See, for example, Sims, 'Policy Analysis With Econometric Models'.

18. K.F. Wallis, 'Econometric Implications of the Rational Expectations Hypothesis, *Econometrica*, vol. 48, no. 1 (1980), pp. 49-72. Also see B.S. Fisher, 'Rational Expectations in Agricultural Economics Policy and Research, *American Journal of Agricultural Economics*, vol. 64, no. 2 (1982), pp. 260-265 for a simple illustrative example.

19. Sims, 'Policy Analysis With Econometric Models'.

20. T. Goodwin and S.M. Sheffrin, 'Testing the Rational Expectations Hypothesis in an Agricultural Market', *Review of Economics and Statistics*, vol. 64, no. 4 (1982), pp. 658-667.

21. B.S. Fisher and C. Tanner, 'The Formulation of Price Expectations: An Empirical Test of Theoretical Models', *American Journal of Agricultural Economics*, vol. 60, no. 2 (1978), pp. 245-248.

22. See, for example, T.H. Naylor, *Computer Simulation Experiments with Models of Economic Systems* (Wiley, New York, 1971), p. 5.

23. Naylor, *Computer Simulation Experiments with Models of Economic Systems*, p. 5.

24. R.C. Meier, W.T. Newell and H.L. Pazer, *Simulation in Business and Economics* (Prentice-Hall, Englewood Cliffs, 1969), p. 22.

25. E.O. Heady, 'Models for Agricultural Policy', *European Review of Agricultural Economics*, vol. 10, no. 1 (1983), pp. 1-14.

26. G.C. Rausser and R.E. Just, 'Principles of Policy Modeling in Agriculture', in G.C. Rausser (ed.), *New Directions in Econometric Modeling and Forecasting in U.S. Agriculture*, pp. 763-800.

Bibliography

Adams, F.G. 'Implementation of Commodity Market Theory in Empirical Econometric Models', in F.G. Adams and J.R. Behrman (eds.), *Econometric Modelling of World Commodity Policy* (D.C. Heath, Lexington, 1978), pp. 47-70.

---- and Behrman, J.R. *Econometric Models of World Agricultural Commodity Markets* (Balinger, Cambridge, Mass., 1976).

---- and Behrman, J.R. (eds.) *Econometric Modelling of World Commodity Policy* (D.C. Heath, Lexington, 1978).

Aigner, D.J. 'MSE Dominance of Least Squares with Errors of Observation', *Journal of Econometrics*, vol. 2, no. 3 (1974), pp. 365-372.

Almon, S. 'The Distributed Lag Between Capital Appropriations and Expenditures', *Econometrica*, vol. 33, no. 1 (1965), pp. 178-196.

Anderson, J., Blitzer, C., Cauchois, T. and Grilli, E. 'A Dynamic Simulation Model of the World Jute Economy' in World Bank, *World Bank Commodity Models*, vol. 1, World Bank Staff Commodity Working Paper No. 6 (World Bank, Washington, 1981).

Ash, J.C.K. and Smyth, D.J. *Forecasting the UK Economy* (Saxon House, Farnborough, 1973).

Askari, H. and Cummings, J.T. 'Estimating Agricultural Supply Response With the Nerlove Model: A Survey', *International Economic Review*, vol. 18, no. 2 (1977), pp. 257-292.

Beach, C.M. and MacKinnon, J.G. 'A Maximum Likelihood Procedure for Regression With Autocorrelated Errors', *Econometrica*, vol. 46, no. 1 (1978), pp. 51-58.

Behrman, J.R. *Development, the International Economic Order, and Commodity Agreements* (Addison-Wesley, Reading, Mass., 1978).

---- 'International Commodity Market Structures and the Theory Underlying International Commodity Market Models', in F.G. Adams and J.R. Behrman (eds.), *Econometric Modelling of World Commodity Policy* (D.C. Heath, Lexington, 1978), pp. 9-45.

Belsley, D.A., Kuh, E. and Welsch, R.E. *Regression Diagnostics: Identifying Influential Data and Sources of Collinearity* (Wiley, New York, 1980).

Berndt, E.R. and Savin, N.E. 'Conflict Among Criteria for Testing Hypotheses in the Multivariate Linear Regression Model', *Econometrica*, vol. 45, no. 5 (1977), pp. 1263-1277.

Bishop, R.V. 'The Construction and Use of Causality Tests', *Agricultural Economics Research*, vol. 31, no. 4 (1979), pp. 1-6.

Bond, M.E. 'Agricultural Supply Responses to Prices in Sub-Saharan African Countries', *IMF Staff Papers*, vol. 30, no. 4 (1983), pp. 703-726.

Bourke, I.J. 'Comparing the Box-Jenkins and Econometric Techniques for Forecasting Beef Prices', *Review of Marketing and Agricultural Economics*, vol. 47, no. 1 (1979), pp. 95-106.

Box, G.E.P and Jenkins, G.M. *Time Series Analysis* (Holden-Day, San Francisco, 1970).

Brennan, M.J. and Carroll, T.M. *Preface to Quantitative Economics and Econometrics*, 4th edn (South-Western Publishing Company, Cincinnati, 1987).

Breusch, T.S. and Pagan, A.R. 'A Simple Test for Heteroscedasticty and Random Coefficent Variation', *Econometrica*, vol. 47, no. 5 (1979), pp. 1287-1294.

Carter, R.L. 'Least Squares as an Exploratory Estimator', *Canadian Journal of Economics*, vol. 6, no. 1 (1973), pp. 108-114.

Challen, D.W. and Hagger, A.J. *Macroeconometric Systems* (Macmillan, London, 1983).

Chavas, J., Hassan, Z.A. and Johnson, S.R. 'Static and Dynamic Elasticities and Flexibilities in Systems of Simultaneous Equations', *Journal of Agricultural Economics*, vol. 32, no. 2 (1981), pp. 177-187.

Chen, D.T. 'The Wharton Agricultural Model: Structure, Specification and Some Simulation Results', *American Journal of Agricultural Economics*, vol. 59, no. 1 (1977), pp. 107-116.

Chow, G.C. 'Tests of Equality Between Sets of Coefficients in Two Linear Regressions', *Econometrica*, vol. 28, no. 3 (1960), pp. 591-605.

Chung, C. and Ukpong, G. 'The World Tea Economy: An Econometric Model of Its Structure, Performance and Prospects' in World Bank, *World Bank Commodity Models* (2 vols., World Bank, Washington, 1981), vol. 1, pp. V-1 - V-49.

Colman, D.R. and Young, T. *A Forecasting System for UK Grain and Oilseed Imports*, University of Manchester Department of Agricultural Economics Bulletin 179 (1981).

Cooley, T. and Prescott, E.C. 'Varying Parameter Regression: A Theory and Some Applications', *Annals of Economic and Social Measurement*, vol. 2, no. 4 (1973), pp. 463-473.

Cragg, J.G. 'On the Relative Small Sample Properties of Several Structural Equation Estimators', *Econometrica*, vol. 35, no. 1 (1967), pp. 89-109.

Davidson, R. and Mackinnon, J.G. 'Several Tests for Model Specification in the Presence of Alternative Hypotheses', *Econometrica*, vol. 49, no. 3 (1981), pp. 781-793.

Doran, H.E. and Griffiths, W.E. 'Inconsistency of the OLS Estimator of the Partial Adjustment - Adaptive Expectations Model', *Journal of Econometrics*, vol. 7, no. 1 (1978), pp. 133-146.

Durbin, J. 'Testing for Serial Correlation in Least Squares Regression When

Some of the Regressors Are Lagged Dependent Variables' *Econometrica*, vol. 38, no. 3 (1970), pp. 410-421.

Fair, R.C 'The Estimation of Simultaneous Equation Models With Lagged Endogenous Variables and First Order Serially Correlated Errors', *Econometrica*, vol. 38, no. 3 (1970), pp. 507-516.

---- and Jaffee, D.M. 'Methods of Estimation for Markets in Disequilibrium', *Econometrica*, vol. 40, no. 3 (1972), pp. 497-514.

---- 'A Comparison of Alternative Estimators of Macroeconomic Models', *International Economic Review*, vol. 14, no. 2 (1973), pp. 261-277.

FAO *Agriculture: Toward 2000* (FAO, Rome, 1979).

Fisher, B.S. 'Rational Expectations in Agricultural Economics Policy and Research', *American Journal of Agricultural Economics*, vol. 64, no. 2 (1982), pp. 260-265.

---- and Tanner, C. 'The Formulation of Price Expectations: An Empirical Test of Theoretical Models', *American Journal of Agricultural Economics*, vol. 60, no. 2 (1978), pp. 245-248.

Forrester, J.W. *Industrial Dynamics* (MIT Press, Cambridge, Mass., 1965).

Frisch, R. 'Editorial', *Econometrica*, vol. 1, no. 1 (1933), pp. 1-4.

Fromm, G. and Schink, G.R. 'Aggregation and Econometric Models', *International Economic Review*, vol. 14, no. 1 (1973), pp. 1-31.

Gellatly, C.J. 'Forecasting NSW Beef Production: An Evaluation of Alternative Techniques', *Review of Marketing and Agricultural Economics*, vol. 47, no. 1 (1979), pp. 81-93.

Glaister, S. *Mathematical Methods for Economists*, 3rd edn (Blackwell, Oxford, 1984).

Glejser, H. 'A New Test for Heteroscedasticity', *Journal of the American Statistical Association*, vol. 64, no. 325 (1969), pp. 316-323.

Goldfeld, S.M. and Quandt, R.E. 'Some Tests for Homoscedasticity', *Journal of the American Statistical Association*, vol. 60, no. 310 (1965), pp. 539-547.

Goodwin, T.H. and Sheffrin, S.M. 'Testing the Rational Expectations Hypothesis in an Agricultural Market', *Review of Economics and Statistics*, vol. 64, no. 4 (1982), pp. 658-667.

Goreux, L.M. 'Income and Food Consumption', *FAO Monthly Bulletin of Economics and Statistics*, vol. 9, no. 10 (1960), pp. 1-12.

Grennes, T., Johnson, P.R. and Thursby, M. *The Economics of World Grain Trade* (Praeger, New York, 1978).

Griliches, Z. and Rao, P. 'Small Sample Properties of Several Two-Stage Regression Methods in the Context of Autocorrelated Errors', *Journal of the American Statistical Association*, vol. 64, no. 325 (1969), pp. 253-272.

---- 'Economic Data Issues', in Z. Griliches and M.D. Intriligator (eds.), *Handbook of Econometrics* (3 vols., North Holland, Amsterdam, 1986).

Hallam, D. 'Producers' Response to Supported and Free Market Prices', *Journal of Agricultural Economics*, vol. 29, no. 2 (1978), pp. 119-131.

---- *Econometric Forecasting in the UK Egg Market* (Eggs Authority,

Tunbridge Wells, 1981).

---- *The Estimation of Dynamic Commodity Models*, University of Reading Department of Agricultural Economics Discussion Paper 83/3, 1983.

---- 'An Econometric Model of the UK Egg Market', *Oxford Agrarian Studies*, vol. 14 (1985), pp.170-191.

---- *The Neglect of Simultaneity in Agricultural Market Models*, University of Reading Department of Agricultural Economics Discussion Paper 86/1, 1986.

---- *The United Kingdom Market for Fresh Exotic Fruit* (Overseas Development Natural Resources Institute, London, 1988).

Harris, S., Salmon, M. and Smith, B. *Analysis of Commodity Markets for Policy Purposes*, Thames Essay No. 17 (Trade Policy Research Centre, London, 1978).

Harvey, A.C. *Econometric Analysis of Time Series* (Philip Allan, Oxford, 1981).

Heady, E.O. 'Models for Agricultural Policy', *European Review of Agricultural Economics*, vol. 10, no. 1 (1983), pp. 1-14.

Heien, D., Matthews, J. L. and Womack, A.W. 'A Methods Note on the Gauss-Seidel Algorithm for Solving Econometric Models', *Agricultural Economics Research*, vol. 25, no. 3 (1973), pp. 71-80.

Hendry, D.F. and Mizon, G.E. 'Serial Correlation As a Convenient Simplification, Not a Nuisance', *Economic Journal*, vol. 88, no. 351 (1978), pp. 549-563.

---- and Richard, J. 'On the Formulation of Empirical Models In Dynamic Econometrics', *Journal of Econometrics*, vol. 20, no. 1 (1982), pp. 3-33.

---- and Wallis, K.F. 'Editors' Introduction', in D.F. Hendry and K.F. Wallis (eds.), *Econometrics and Quantitative Economics* (Blackwell, Oxford, 1984), pp. 1-12.

Hey, J.D. *Data in Doubt* (Martin Robertson, Oxford, 1983).

Hildreth, C. and Houck, J. 'Some Estimators for a Linear Model With Random Coefficients', *Journal of the American Statistical Association*, vol. 63, no. 322 (1968), pp. 584-595.

Huntzinger, R.L. 'Market Analysis With Rational Expectations', *Journal of Econometrics*, vol. 10, no. 1 (1979), pp. 127-145.

Hutchison, T.W. *Knowledge and Ignorance in Economics* (Blackwell, Oxford, 1977).

Idaikkadar, I. D. *Agricultural Statistics* (Pergamon, Oxford, 1979).

Intriligator, M.D. *Econometric Models, Techniques and Applications* (North Holland, Amsterdam, 1978).

Johnson, G.L. 'Supply Functions - Some Facts and Notions' in E.O. Heady, H.G. Dresslin, H.R. Jensen, and G.L. Johnson (eds.), *Agricultural Adjustment Problems in a Growing Economy* (Iowa State University Press, Ames, 1958), pp. 74-93.

Johnson, M.A. and Pasour Jnr., E.C. 'An Opportunity Cost View of Fixed Asset Theory and the Overproduction Trap', *American Journal of*

Agricultural Economics, vol. 63, no. 1 (1981), pp. 1-7.
Johnson, S.R. 'Discussion', *American Journal of Agricultural Economics*, vol. 59, no. 1 (1977), pp. 133-136.
Johnston, J. *Econometric Methods*, 3rd. edn (McGraw-Hill, New York, 1984).
Judge, G.G. 'Estimation and Statistical Inference in Economics' in L.R. Martin (ed.), *A Survey of Agricultural Economics Literature* (3 vols., University of Minnesota Press, Minneapolis, 1977), vol. 2, pp. 3-49.
---- , Griffiths, W.E., Hill, R.C., Lütkepohl. H. and Lee, T. *The Theory and Practice of Econometrics*, 2nd edn (Wiley, New York, 1985).
---- , Hill, R.C., Griffiths, W.E., Lütkepohl. H. and Lee, T. *Introduction to the Theory and Practice of Econometrics*, 2nd edn (Wiley, New York, 1988).
Just, R.E. and Rausser, G.C. 'Commodity Price Forecasting With Large-Scale Econometric Models and the Futures Market', *American Journal of Agricultural Economics*, vol. 63, no. 2 (1981), pp. 197-208.
Kelejian, H.H. and Oates, W.E. *Introduction to Econometrics*, 2nd edn (Harper and Row, New York, 1981).
Kennedy, P. *Guide to Econometrics*, 2nd edn (Blackwell, Oxford, 1985).
Klein, L.R. 'Estimation of Interdependent Systems in Macroeconometrics', *Econometrica*, vol. 37, no. 1 (1969), pp. 171-192.
---- 'Economic Policy Formation Through the Medium of Econometric Models' in M.D. Intriligator (ed.) *Frontiers of Quantitative Economics* (3 vols., North Holland, Amsterdam, 1977), vol 3b, pp. 765-781.
---- and Young, R.M. *An Introduction to Econometric Forecasting and Forecasting Models* (D.C. Heath, Lexington, 1980).
---- *Lectures in Econometrics* (North Holland, Amsterdam, 1983).
Kmenta, J. *Elements of Econometrics* (Macmillan, New York, 1971).
Koyck, L.M. *Distributed Lags and Investment Analysis* (North Holland, Amsterdam, 1954).
Labys, W.C. *Dynamic Commodity Models: Specification, Estimation, and Simulation* (D.C. Heath, Lexington, 1973).
---- 'Dynamics of the International Lauric Oils Market', in W.C. Labys (ed.), *Quantitative Models of Commodity Markets* (Ballinger, Cambridge, Mass., 1975), pp. 213-232.
---- and Pollak, P.K. *Commodity Models for Forecasting and Policy Analysis* (Croom Helm, London, 1984).
Liu, T.C. 'Underidentification, Structural Estimation and Forecasting', *Econometrica*, vol. 28, no. 4 (1960), pp. 338-348.
Lucas, R.E.J. 'Econometric Policy Evaluation: A Critique' in K. Brunner and A. Meltzer (eds.) *The Phillips Curve and Labour Markets* (North Holland, Amsterdam, 1976), pp. 19-46.
Maddala, G.S. *Econometrics* (McGraw-Hill, New York, 1977).
Meier, R.C., Newell, W.T. and Pazer, H.L. *Simulation in Business and Economics* (Prentice-Hall, Englewood Cliffs, 1969).
Meilke, K.D. 'A Comparison of the Simulation Results from Six International Trade Models', University of Guelph Department of Agricultural

Economics and Business Working Paper WP87/3, 1987.

Merrill, W.C. and Fox, K.A. *Introduction to Economic Statistics* (Wiley, New York, 1970).

Miller, R.B. *Minitab Handbook for Business and Economics* (PWS-Kent, Boston, 1988).

Morgenstern, O. *On the Accuracy of Economic Observations*, 2nd. edn (Princeton University Press, Princeton, 1963).

Muth, J.F. 'Rational Expectations and the Theory of Price Movements', *Econometrica*, vol. 29, no. 3 (1961), pp. 315-335.

National Food Survey, *Household Food Consumption and Expenditure* (HMSO, London, annual).

Naylor, T.H. *Computer Simulation Experiments With Models of Economic Systems* (Wiley, New York, 1971).

Nerlove, M. *Dynamics of Supply* (John Hopkins, Baltimore, 1958).

Pindyck, R.S. and Rubinfeld, D.L. *Econometric Models and Economic Forecasts* (McGraw-Hill, New York, 1976).

Quantitative Micro Software, *MicroTSP*, Version 5.0 (Quantitative Micro Software, Irvine, 1988).

Rausser, G.C. 'New Conceptual Developments and Measurements for Modeling US Agriculture', in G.C. Rausser (ed.), *New Directions In Modeling and Forecasting in US Agriculture* (North Holland, Amsterdam, 1982), pp. 1-14.

---- and Just, R.E. 'Principles of Policy Modeling in Agriculture' in G.C. Rausser (ed.), *New Directions In Modeling and Forecasting in US Agriculture* (North Holland, Amsterdam, 1982), pp. 763-800.

---- , Lechtenberg, E. and Lattimore, R. 'New Developments in the Theory and Empirical Applications of Endogenous Government Behaviour' in G.C. Rausser (ed.), *New Directions In Modeling and Forecasting in US Agriculture* (North Holland, Amsterdam, 1982), pp. 547-614.

---- and Hochman, E. *Dynamic Agricultural Systems: Economic Prediction and Control* (North Holland, New York, 1979).

Reusse, E. 'Liberalisation and Agricultural Marketing', *Food Policy*, vol. 12, no. 4 (1987), pp. 299-317.

Rhodes, G.F. and Westbrook, M.D. 'A Study of Estimator Densities Under Misspecification', *Journal of Econometrics*, vol. 16, no. 2 (1981), pp. 311-337.

Roningen, V.O. *A Static World Policy Simulation (SWOPSIM) Modeling Framework*, ERS Staff Report AGES 860625 (USDA, Washington, 1986).

Rouhiainen, J. 'The Problem of Changing Parameters in Demand Analysis and Forecasting', *European Review of Agricultural Economics*, vol. 5, no. 3/4 (1978), pp. 349-359.

Salathe, L.E., Price, J.M. and Gadson, K.E. 'The Food and Agricultural Policy Simulator', *Agricultural Economics Research*, vol. 34, no. 1 (1982), pp. 1-15.

---- , Price J.M. and Gadson, K.E. 'The Food and Agricultural Policy

Simulator: The Poultry and Egg Submodel', *Agricultural Economics Research*, vol. 35, no. 1 (1983), pp. 23-34.

Salmon, M.H. and Eaton, J.R. 'Estimation Problems in Large Econometric Models: An Application of Various Estimation Techniques to the London Business School Model' in G.A. Renton (ed.), *Modelling the UK Economy* (Heinemann, London, 1975), pp. 323-348.

Saylor, R.G. 'Alternative Measures of Supply Elasticities: The Case of Sao Paulo Coffee', *American Journal of Agricultural Economics*, vol. 56, no. 1 (1974), pp. 98-106.

Sheffrin, S.M. *Rational Expectations* (Cambridge University Press, Cambridge, 1983).

Sims, C.A. 'Policy Analysis With Econometric Models', *Brookings Papers on Economic Activity*, vol. 1, no. 1 (1982), pp. 107-164.

Smyth, D.J. 'The Effect of Public Price Forecasts on Market Price Variation: A Stochastic Cobweb Example', *American Journal of Agricultural Economics*, vol. 55, no. 1 (1973), pp. 83-88.

Spanos, A. *Statistical Foundations of Econometric Modelling* (Cambridge University Press, Cambridge, 1986).

Stewart, I.M.T. *Reasoning and Method in Economics* (McGraw-Hill, London, 1979).

Stojkovic, G. 'Market Models for Agricultural Products' in H.O.A. Wold (ed.), *Econometric Model Building: Essays On the Causal Chain Approach* (North Holland, Amsterdam, 1964), pp. 386-419.

Strotz, R.H. and Wold, H.O.A. 'Recursive v. Non-recursive Systems: An Attempt at Synthesis', *Econometrica*, vol. 28, no. 2 (1960), pp. 417-427.

Tang, J.C.S. 'Estimating the Demand Functions for Fresh Citrus', *European Review of Agricultural Economics*, vol. 7, no. 3 (1980), pp. 341-346.

Theil, H. *Linear Aggregation of Economic Relations* (North Holland, Amsterdam, 1954).

---- *Applied Economic Forecasting* (North Holland, Amsterdam, 1966).

---- *Introduction to Econometrics* (Prentice-Hall, Englewood Cliffs, 1978).

Thomson, K.J. and Rayner, A.J. 'Quantitative Policy Modelling in Agriculture', *Journal of Agricultural Economics*, vol. 35, no. 2 (1984), pp. 161-176.

Thurow, L.C. *Dangerous Currents: The State of Economics* (Oxford University Press, Oxford, 1983).

Thursby, J.G. and Schmidt, P. 'Some Properties of Tests For Specification Error in a Linear Regression Model', *Journal of the American Statistical Association*, vol.72, no. 359 (1977), pp. 635-641.

Tintner, G. *Methodology of Mathematical Economics and Econometrics* (University of Chicago Press, Chicago, 1968).

Tobin, J. 'A Statistical Demand Function for Food in the USA, *Journal of the Royal Statistical Society*, Series. A, vol. 113, no. 2 (1950), pp. 113-141.

Traill, B. 'Risk Variables in Econometric Supply Response Models', *Journal of Agricultural Economics*, vol. 29, no. 1 (1978), pp. 53-62.

---- , Colman, D.R. and Young, T. 'Estimatimg Irreversible Supply Functions', *American Journal of Agricultural Economics*, vol. 60, no. 3 (1978), pp. 528-531.

TSP International,*TSP User's Manual*, Version 4.0B (TSP International. Stanford, 1983).

Tukey, J.W. *Exploratory Data Analysis* (Addison-Wesley, Reading, Mass., 1977).

Turnovsky, S.J. 'The Distribution of Welfare Gains from Price Stabilisation: A Survey of Some Theoretical Issues', in F.G. Adams and S.A. Klein (eds.), *Stabilising World Commodity Markets* (D.C. Heath, Lexington, 1978), pp. 119-148.

Wallace, T.D. 'Pretest Estimation in Regression: A Survey', *American Journal of Agricultural Economics*, vol. 59, no. 3 (1977), pp. 431-443.

Wallis, K.F. 'Econometric Implications of the Rational Expectations Hypothesis', *Econometrica*, vol. 48, no. 1 (1980), pp. 49-72.

Ward, R.W. 'Time Varying Demand for Oranges in the EEC', *Journal of Agricultural Economics*, vol. 33, no. 1 (1982), pp. 57-70.

Wickens, M.R. 'A Note on the Use of Proxy Variables', *Econometrica*, vol. 40, no. 4 (1972), pp. 759-761.

---- and Greenfield, J.N. 'The Econometrics of Agricultural Supply', *Review of Economics and Statistics*, vol. 55, no. 4 (1973), pp. 433-440.

Wolffram, R. 'Positivistic Measures of Aggregate Supply Elasticities: Some New Approaches - Some Critical Notes', *American Journal of Agricultural Economics*, vol. 53, no. 2 (1971), pp. 356-359.

Womack, A.W. and Matthews, J.L. 'Linear Approximations of Nonlinear Relationships by the Taylor's Series Expansion Revisited', *Agricultural Economics Research*, vol. 24, no. 4 (1972), pp. 93-101.

Wonnacott, R.J. and Wonnacott, T.H. *Econometrics*, 2nd edn (Wiley, New York, 1979).

World Bank, *World Bank Commodity Models* (2 vols., World Bank, Washington, 1981).

Young, T. *The Position of the UK Cereals Market Within the EEC*, University of Manchester Department of Agricultural Economics Bulletin 170, 1979.

---- 'Modelling Asymmetric Consumer Responses, With an Example', *Journal of Agricultural Economics*, vol. 31, no. 2 (1980), pp.175-186.

Zellner, A. 'An Efficient Method of Estimating Seemingly Unrelated Regressions and Tests of Aggregation Bias', *Journal of the American Statistical Association*, vol. 57, no. 298 (1962), pp. 348-368.

---- 'Statistical Analysis of Econometric Models, *Journal of the American Statistical Association*, vol. 74, no. 367 (1979), pp. 628-651.

---- *Basic Issues in Econometrics* (University of Chicago Press, Chicago, 1984).

Index